changing

CONVERSATIONS

changing
CONVERSATIONS

RELIGIOUS REFLECTION & CULTURAL ANALYSIS

edited by **Dwight N. Hopkins &**
Sheila Greeve Davaney

Routledge   New York and London

Published in 1996 by

Routledge
29 West 35 Street
New York, NY 10001

Published in Great Britain in 1996 by

Routledge
11 New Fetter Lane
London Ec4P 4EE

Copyright © 1996 by Routledge

Printed in the United States of America on acid free paper.

Library of Congress Cataloging-in-Publication Data available from the Library of Congress.

/CONTENTS/

INTRODUCTION

Dwight N. Hopkins

CHANGING CONVERSATIONS

This anthology of essays represents a decisive turn in the development of religious reflection informed by cultural analysis; specifically, the crucial role of cultural studies in the articulation and practice of religious studies. It indicates a changing of conversations in at least two respects. First, authors here engage in critical analytical investigation of religious reflection with a new attention to the disparate manifestations of the religious in culture. Second, these essays specifically turn to the inquiries from the social sciences, thus broadening the number of participants in theological discussion beyond the dominant traditional partners of philosophy and Biblical studies.

Across a number of intellectual fields of knowledge, there has been a major shift toward cultural studies during the last decade. History, literary studies, anthropology and the social sciences have all sought methodologies and analytical tools to map the interconnections between their subject matter and cultural formations and processes. Until recently, scholars engaged in the study of religions have not been significant participants in this intellectual movement. While some thinkers working in conjunction with the social sciences or particularly interested in liberation movements exhibited interest in these trends, most scholars in theology, philosophy of religion, historical inquiries and even comparative studies failed to focus upon these connections or to utilize the approaches taking shape in other disciplines. This is now changing as more scholars of religion begin to enter the interdisciplinary conversations and debates that have followed the turn to cultural studies. Various modes of cultural analysis are increasingly part of the study of religions as scholars seek to trace the interconnections of cultural realities and religious beliefs, practices, and functions.

This volume reflects the vanguard of this movement within religious studies. A collection of essays by noted younger scholars focusing primarily on Christian discourses, it represents new methodologies and approaches within religious reflection. As such, it contributes both to the study of religion, seeking to redefine disciplinary self-understanding, and to the broader arena of cultural studies, introducing religion as an important component of cultural analysis. By so doing, the authors hope to foster a broader conversation among scholars of religion and other academic disciplines.

In contrast to a claim that the academic study of religion or theology entails a metaphysical approach, with theology somehow sheltered from other bodies of knowledge, the contributors of this book argue for a specific method in which ways of thinking about and doing religious studies or theology are both embedded in local cultures and committed to voices most often shut out of the formal intellectual enterprise of religious reflection.

Our approach, therefore, contrasts the conservative view of religion as God, faith, or spirituality being a top-down, unchanging essence removed from society and the world, as well as the liberal paradigm, which asserts and seeks a universal and all-encompassing understanding of religion with the hope that Reason (or the Logos) employed will yield a recognizable Truth surpassing the power and particularities and positivity of diverse cultures. The conservative religious model posits theology or religious reflection in an antagonistic relation by often contrasting God, faith, and spirituality with transforming structural configurations between and among peoples. The liberal project, though attentive to affairs of society, nonetheless, explores human interactions without sufficient attention to race, gender, class, and sexual orientation. Hence, both the conservative and liberal approaches leave the status quo, broken humanity, in place—the conservative by placing religious reflection "above" systemic realities and the liberal by seeking theological implications (oftentimes unintentionally) from the perspective of society's structural status quo.

The essays in this collection, however, deploy a posture explicitly and consistently committed to the poor, the marginalized, and other disenfranchised experiences and communities in theology or religious reflection. The method and viewpoint of these chapters pursue the concerns of the oppressed. Contributors mark the local and specific as constitutive of cultural and religious investigation of those communities considered expendable who, most often, lack material resources to determine a new vision of society and, simultaneously, struggle to carve out space in which to identify more clearly their own idiom. We explore and explicate the cultural, political, and economic dimensions of religion and the religious dimensions of culture, politics, and economics. Moreover, our presupposition is that theology, or religious reflection, is a dynamic that is bounded by those realities. Therefore, since it is not separated from or above human activity, the theological process by definition necessitates a multidisciplinary and interdisciplinary move. Religious reflection has never been neutral; nor has its object of study and practice, whether that be God, spirituality, or any other ultimate concern. To amplify the voices and movements of marginalized communities, especially Christian discourses, we turn to the multidisciplinary, interpretive approaches provided by cultural analysis. Cultural studies allow questions to be posed and envision future conversations about the nature, definition, role, context, and direction of religious reflection that have heretofore been ignored.

Before entering an extended narrative of the thematic commonalities of this anthology's essays, it would be helpful to offer a genealogy of the text's two major conversational partners: cultural studies and progressive theology, both of which flow from the intellectual mood of the 1960s and 1970s.

CULTURAL STUDIES THEMES

The roots of cultural studies, as a contemporary moment in disparate disciplines, appeared in England during the 1940s and 1950s. For promoters of cultural studies, at stake was the cultural enlightenment of the English working class. To combat the two major sociological trends that emerged after World War II—the decline of Christianity and the influence of mass media, particularly television—advocates of cultural studies worked to establish a literary canon that would inculcate moral character and values among the working class. From the beginning, the proponents of the cultural studies movement sought to slow the proliferation of mass culture (that is, the commercialization of popular culture) by disseminating institutionalized high culture for specific class purposes. This sociological wing of contemporary cultural studies, which sought to explain how classes have produced and used cultural texts, broke with social scientific positivism. Cultural analysis became a committed enterprise concerned with political issues.

Though the antecedents of English cultural studies of the late 1940s and early 1950s self-consciously linked culture to politics, thus the contribution of locating culture, much of this negative cultural analysis advocated bourgeois politics or high culture over and against the "social anarchy" of a working class aesthetic or mass commercialized culture. It took a second wave of more self-identified English cultural studies workers, during the late 1950s and the 1960s, particularly by the originators of the Centre for Contemporary Cultural Studies (CCCS) in Birmingham, to move the debate to new horizons. The CCCS offered four intellectual contributions.

They argued, first, that the working class are producers of culture, rather than simply passive consumers of mass culture; second, that culture consists of the ordinary, everyday experiences of working class men and women; third, that this ordinary culture of the majority of society embodies value(s) worthy of study; and fourth, that culture can be better comprehended by freeing Marxist criticism from its mechanical base-superstructure catechism. This last move, inspired by a reaction to Stalin and the Soviet Union's 1956 invasions of other socialist countries, allowed cultural studies to open itself up to the constructions of non-economic realities, especially those of gender, age, race, aesthetics, and language.

English cultural studies, then, entailed the politics of culture linked to social movements, deployed reassessed working class and Marxist analyses of culture, and marked a decisive turn toward affirming the lived experiences of culture from below. The English wedded the total working class way of life with a more fluid, revised Marxism. Culture is ordinary and linked to other systems. With their conceptualization of culture as a total way of life, these cultural analysts saw both cultural production and the reading of cultural texts as circumscribed by all aspects of life.

During the early and mid-1970s, English cultural studies began to incorporate international intellectual currents, notably one form of French structuralism and the thought of the Italian communist Antonio Gramsci. In structuralism, ideology (the structures of dominant and pervasive sets of values, understanding, or common sense) constituted people. Ruling classes utilized ideology to curtail social transformation. Social configurations of exploitation and discrimination (all humanly created) were made to seem natural, universal and permanent. The dominant ideology, consequently, provided a false consciousness for the popular citizenry, who willingly perceived themselves in a positive light within this symbolic order of ideology.

Similarly, Gramsci grappled intellectually with how rightist segments of society could rule the popular masses not only with force but more decisively through building a cultural hegemony which subsumed and distorted the interests of the working class. And conversely, he asked how the working class could create and diffuse its own hegemony. For his answer, Gramsci understood culture as the realm in which forces spread ideologies; in other words, as the space in which social blocs and strata forge their hegemonies, which are manifest in national common sense. The organic intellectual employs the realm of culture to create a new hegemony (war of position)—or common sense—a new intellectual and moral hegemony at the service of ultimate social transformation. Though culture could entail economic and state social relations, Gramsci highlighted civic society (with its semi-autonomy from the economy and the state) as a key locus of struggle. Here intellectuals, organically linked to the working class, would construct their hegemony over other classes and strata. Within English cultural studies, Gramscian influence nuanced notions of human agency, and led to an emphasis on systemic limitations.

Propelled by the failure of the working class to seize power during the 1968 student uprising in France, and discontentment with existentialism, phenomenolgy, and Marxism, by the late 1970s French cultural studies developed in different directions from its counterpart in England. Though the English had opened their conversation beyond the economic base-epiphe-nomena-superstructure formula (thereby providing room for the impact of

non-economic and non-state actualities), the importance of ideological considerations connected to an agenda seeking proletarian hegemony pervaded
British cultural studies.

At this juncture one could argue that the British continued to theorize
primarily around one social agency—economics. The French, however,
posited multiple social fields which were, moreover, partially autonomous,
therefore reconfiguring even a revised base-superstructure paradigm. In contrast to the British meta-analysis of class cutting across all of life, the French
claimed that people reside in various institutions or fields which entail
power and hierarchy, as well as opportunities for self-government. Because
citizens inhabit multiple fields or discursive formations, no one structure determines how people actually live their lives. People's participation in daily
life is mediated by various interactions—with or in prisons, schools, insane
asylums, hospitals, aesthetics, sexuality, family, leisure, to name a few.

The French intellectual contribution to cultural studies was to problematize metanarratives, meaning and language, truth claims, and power
with arguments for particularity, polyphony, and instability of meaning.
Metanarrative examinations were holdovers from the Enlightenment project
which posited the rational, autonomous subject employing science and a scientific worldview to control the environment and progressing inevitably toward a future of self-initiated human emancipation. Concomitantly, history
entailed a linear movement from primitivism and irrationality to civilized
culture. The French debunked universal grand schemes of history, emphasizing instead disjunctures and incongruities in the human past. Notions of social evolution could no longer stand because no economic law of history,
divine providential plan, or philosophical power of reason was seen to be
coordinating and guiding human activities. Without such a dynamic, a tele-
ology toward a future utopia did not exist.

Perhaps the greatest metanarrative to fall, from the French perspective, was Marxism and various revisions of its base-superstructure model.
Though Marxism asserted an antagonistic posture toward bourgeois
philosophy and economics, it was nonetheless heir to the Enlightenment—
that is, a teleological argument for a utopia realized through scientific
thought and organization which envisioned the proletariat in an ultimate
dictatorship over all others. The proletariat remained the autonomous, self-
propelled vanguard marching progressively through history. Analytically,
even variations on the parameters of Marxist interrogation did not attend to
the multiplicity of asymmetrical social interactions. The totality of the
Marxist paradigm was in fact, in the French vein, a dictatorship of the
economic over non-economic social relations, historical incongruities, and
divergent philosophical views.

With the displacement of metanarrative, meaning and language came under sharp scrutiny. French cultural studies destabilized a foundational structure to language which, with its formulaic claims that meaning is derived through unlocked codes, served as a template to interpretation. The relation between words and the thoughts or things that they stood for is arbitrary, and not readily apparent. Instead of a fixity, interpretation and meaning lead to more meaning and interpretation. Meaning, therefore, is unstable. There exists no linguistic structure which reveals transparently the author's language and intentions. Interpretations proliferate. If anything, there is a multitude of language games.

Similarly, all truth claims are reduced to competing language games or discursive formations. No one claim has a normative foundation by which it privileges itself over another. Instead of being autonomous, rational self-directing subjects (of the Enlightenment), people are dispersed or decentered into a polyphony of fields or discourses. There remains no common ground for adjudicating conflict and diversity. Marxism and other Enlightenment projects stood for the truth of the sovereign subject with one history of truth—the truth that "man" is positively moving through history. On the contrary, the French argued that there are many truths to history and reality. In fact, instead of sure foundations with a unitary Truth, human beings experience a relativism waged in the marketplace of power persuasion.

For the French power was not confined to or circumscribed by macropolitics or economic structures. Power was diffused throughout human relations, knowledge systems, and behavioral patterns. Power did not reside in the province of a bourgeoisie; it was a site of contestation and asymmetrical relations, where the powerless contended against the powerful. Power was a network, extending everywhere. Many micro-power dynamics operated outside, below, and alongside the state apparatus. Power performed on the plane of daily life.

The fragmentation of metanarratives into micro-politics and local spheres of social interactions and thought, plus the growing openness of English cultural studies to feminist theory and black culture, enlarged the concept of culture to include the intellectual category of "difference." To this theoretical framework were attracted a variety of American voices seeking a hearing over and against a standardized narrative defined by wealth, gender, "whiteness," and heterosexuality. American intellectuals and activists who were minorities of color, women, lesbian, gay or working class began to incorporate aspects of cultural studies into their cultural analyses and practices of everyday life in the late 1970s and early 1980s. Because this moment in cultural studies evinced partiality and not totality and because many marginalized groups in the United States began to perceive their cul-

tures as distinct and local, cultural studies became even a more global movement. Culture studies broadened to include cultures of "difference" and of
the "Other."

FROM THE 1950s–PROGRESSIVE STREAMLETS

Contributors to this volume also draw on intellectual traditions and conversations from various progressive streamlets of thought originating in the
1960s and 1970s in the United States. During this period, the United States
witnessed many changes out of which arose new liberation theologies and
branches of reformist thought. The 1950s and early 1960s civil rights movement, the Black Power movement, and the defeat in Vietnam in the 1970s
caused the face of America to change radically. Amidst the uproar—assertions of civil rights based on race, gender, class, and sexual orientation, and
calls to end imperialism—some religious scholars and church members
began to question the relation between Christianity and social change. What
were churches doing and what was the Christian religion saying about the
many voices of "the people" that were erupting on the stage of history?
What intellectual guideposts could religious people turn to for clarity?
Furthermore, could one remain a Christian when so many religious institutions were entrenched against the "people"? What academic traditions
could be revamped, what tools of analysis could be reigned in, what philosophical worldviews could be harnessed to accommodate and offer insight
to the volatile alterations in American culture?

The religious analyses and theological views in this collection represent the trajectories of progressive philosophical lineages and Christian liberation theologies which surfaced out of and paralleled the particular
movements for justice during the 1960s and 1970s in the United States.

In July of 1966, an ad hoc committee of African American clergy published in the *New York Times* a full page advertisement supporting the secular call for Black Power as enunciated by African American community and
student activists a month earlier. This religious apologia was the first attempt by academics to link Christianity with the concerns of a positive affirmation of black culture. In March of 1969, James H. Cone (the originator of
a black theology of liberation) published *Black Theology and Black Power*,
the first scholarly and theological treatment of the same theme. Cone's book
was the first indigenous work in the United States to tie liberation of the
poor to Christianity as the central operative theme. It positioned religion
within culture, particularly the racial and power dynamics of culture, and
classified "white theology" (Christians with privilege who maintained the
status quo) as demonic and "black theology" (Christians whose central
issue was freedom for the least in society) as authentic religion. If the central

narrative of the Hebrew Scriptures (the Old Testament) was the deliverance of Hebrew slaves out of bondage, argued Cone, and if the Jesus of the Christian Scriptures (the New Testament) came as a poor person to liberate the poor of this world, then one would have to acknowledge where this freedom activity was occurring during the 1960s. Since Cone perceived the most oppressed, despised, and exploited segment of American society to be blacks, therefore, the contemporary Christian revelation was in the movement of those blacks (and others engaged in the movement) who struggled for liberation.

Cone's intellectual paradigm shifted theology from a history of great "men" with great ideas, and from a religious history of official church dogma to the tracing of, primarily, unlettered poor blacks. His methodology questioned established ways of distancing conceptual claims from the life and death happenings in any epoch. Religious silence on the race issue implicated one as a collaborator in racial hierarchical asymmetry. Furthermore, Cone asserted that racial concerns had always been the starting point for "white theology." Conservative white churches, in his view, had openly stated their religious segregationist views towards blacks; but in his opinion, white liberal Christians were equally accountable for racial discrimination because of either their silence or their token theological efforts. For Cone, Christianity was embodied from below, in poor African Americans waging efforts in the streets for radical social transformation. The role of religious reflection and the theologian was to be at the service of the Spirit of justice and right relationship revealed in the culture of oppressed people. A year later, in 1970, Cone published his second book, a comprehensive, systematic treatment of liberation theology—which entailed a detailed reworking of traditional Christian doctrines infused with the norm of liberation.

Mary Daly's 1968 text, *The Church and the Second Sex*, was a clarion call against patriarchy and misogyny in mainstream Christian churches and religious analysis or doctrines and thus marked the beginning of feminist theology. Daly, and others, critiqued male normativity in images of the divine, authority, leadership, language, definition-makers, symbol-creators, and general way of life in theological thought and cultural analyses. The cardinal characteristics of patriarchal Christianity were androcentrism and misogyny. The status of women in academic and ecclesial realms, conversely, was subordinate and auxiliary.

Rosemary Radford Ruether's *Sexism and God Talk* published in 1983 was the first systematic feminist theology. For a constructive feminist theology, the norm is woman's experience; in other words, all that liberates women will yield a holistic environment for all humanity because the lifting of restrictions against women will remove men's power to impose their domi-

nance in society. Intellectually, feminist theology offered several novel positions for religious reflection. To start, women's experiences (in the broader
American culture, the church, poetry, diaries, traditions, etc.) were made
genuine sites for religious reflection. Next, the philosophical and practical
worldview, in feminist theology, assumed an all encompassing posture
against the patriarchal style of privileging dualism or an either/or mentality.
No split existed between thought and action; religious reflection interroga-
tions were circumscribed by experience.

Third, feminist theologians argued that social context affects and im-
pacts theological investigations; intellectual ideas do not simply fall from the
sky, rather, social configurations assist in establishing normative queries. If
religious reflection arises from material culture, then such reflection must be
rooted in practice. Thinking and doing complement one another dynamically. The process of doing theology became key, and women's theological
voices arose in a process. Hence the language of religious reflection expresses itself more as poetry (in contrast to the false "scientific" texture of patriarchal discourses) with organic metaphors and life-giving substance.
Furthermore, one cannot sever language from the originating context of specific communities which speak it. Images, language, and naming are all important. The liberation of language and the power to name are the liberation
of women. Language and naming strike at patriarchy, hierarchy, dominance,
and competition. And finally, both the personal and the structural serve as
contested locations for religious reflection; the personal is always political.

Latin American liberation theology (LALT) also influenced sectors of
religious analysis in the 1970s and 1980s. It was rooted in the works of
church activists from the United States and academics involved in labor organizing and solidarity support for Latin America. The 1971 English translation of Gustavo Gutierrez's *A Theology of Liberation* introduced academically the new style of religious reflection within the culture of class
exploitation and resistance in Latin America. LALT began its dialogue with
the social sciences, emphasizing sociology and Marxist political economy in
order to break with European and North American liberal political theology, which grounded itself in philosophy. In any development of religious reflection, claimed the Latin Americans, the first step is commitment to
liberation. The theologian opts for the struggle of the poor and the oppressed as the new "theological locus" for reflection. Without active affirmation of the oppressed and a liberating consciousness, theology becomes
bourgeois. The second step is to understand religious reflection or theology
as a discipline. That is, critical thinking must emerge from the context of engaged militant action for freedom. Critical reflection on the Christian faith
is expressed both by the working class and by intellectuals in light of the

spirit of liberation working for a new humanity on earth. While engaging in the first step of social change, religious reflection is aided by Marxist analysis; for, from Latin American liberation theology's vantage, the preeminent sin is structural monopoly capitalism, and the prism of class informs both the diagnosis of sin and the prescription for a new reality.

Methodologically, LALT calls for a dialectical social analysis; epistemologically, a shift from given beliefs to reflection upon praxis. The content of religious reflection thus becomes political engagement anchored in the people's struggle for liberation, and the mark of faith is Christian obedience shown in revolutionary change.

Philosophically, Latin American liberation theology draws on three European lineages—Freud, Nietzsche, and Marx—with primary emphasis on Marxist political economy. These three "masters of suspicion" allowed a decisive break with European and North American liberal political religious reflection. The latter grouping responded to the first part of the European Enlightenment—the groundbreaking writings of Kant, Rousseau, and Hegel which exalted critical reason to clarify the superstitious dimension of religion for the non-believer. On the contrary, Latin Americans gravitated philosophically to the second response to the Enlightenment: Freud because he persuasively demonstrated that humanity is not autonomous and that people are not masters of their own psyches due to the impact of the unconscious; Nietzsche because he articulated that all philosophy is constructed by the will to power; and especially Marx because he demolished bourgeois historiography in asserting that all history reflects the history of the ruling class ideology.

Another important streamlet of conversation in which authors of this anthology locate themselves is womanist theology, which initially accepted the rubric of black feminist theology. Jacquelyn Grant penned the first article addressing the particular dynamic of African American women's religious and cultural sensibilities (Grant, 1979). Her 1979 text posited several broad outlines, parameters which became foundational for future debate and creativity for womanist theology. Grant offered the perceptive insight that African American women were invisible in the writings of black theology and in the leadership of the black church. Moreover, her core critique advanced the central paradox of black theology and feminist theology. For black theology, one discovered a fundamental flaw both in terms of its logic and its faith. Argumentatively, African American male scholars had posed trenchant assessments of the ways in which white religious analyses wrenched liberation from the essence of Christian claims. Agreeing with this conclusion, Grant then applied the same criterion of freedom to black male religious appraisals and found liberation wanting because African American women were both absent and oppressed in black theology and ecclesial formations. How can liberation serve as the normative gaze when African American women are subordinated in black male theology?

Similarly, feminist theology spoke in universal terms while interrogating traditional theology for generalizing male perspectives as representative of the female and thus oppressively hierarchializing one gender over another in the name of authentic religious scholarship. Reversing the same lens of critique on feminist theology, womanist theologians (black female religious intellectuals) named feminist theology as a signifier of white middle class religious scholars' experiences. The latter privileged white women while participating in racial discrimination of African American women. In the theoretical systems of feminist theology, woman meant "white"; in the theoretical systems of black theology, black meant "male." Therefore, black female religious scholars problematized the "feminist" in white women's culture and the "black" in African American men's culture.

Existentially and analytically, womanists found themselves at the overlapping crossroads of gender, race, and class. In brief, as women of color they experienced triple oppression and, accordingly, could draw positively from three sources for a comprehensive religious analysis. A tripartite reality comprised black women's culture. By the mid-1980s, a consensus coalesced around the term "womanist," which came from Alice Walker. Womanism brought the following in its religious reflection of black women's culture: Distinct from black male theology, womanist theology nonetheless saw itself as closely tied to black men, as well as to lesbians, the family, and community. Separation time from men was necessary for the African American woman's own health. They moreover stressed a strong intergenerational tie to grandmothers, mothers, and daughters. Energized by the Spirit, black female religious scholars perceived themselves as one moment in the liberation theology process. A constructive religious analysis, from the womanist voice, would draw on traditional religious sources as well as folklore, slave narratives, poetry, fiction, personal family memories, and black women's history. Finally, womanist theology advocated a holistic religious reflection—a norm of freedom for all heretofore locked voices, both in humanity and nature. Because African American women occupy multiple sites of identity formation (with attendant problems and possibilities) and because, philosophically and theologically, they include all of humanity and the creation and not simply one slice, womanist theology by definition is a dynamic, complementary and open-ended religious reflection of the Spirit in culture.

The culture of black gay men developed as a location for religious reflection much more recently. However, the nurturing of such a voice has precedents from the 1950s and 1960s. At that time, Bayard Rustin, James Baldwin, and Little Richard were symbolic national images for a much larger closeted African American gay community. Rustin, a Quaker civil and labor rights organizer, may be best known as the chief organizer for the 1963 March On Washington, where Reverend Martin Luther King, Jr. delivered his "I Have A Dream" speech. Rustin, in his rhetoric and life, combined the gay struggle with civil rights, class consciousness, and a theology of nonviolence. James Baldwin, an internationally acclaimed author, made black gays part of history for the first time by consistently interspersing such characters throughout his work. Baldwin made African American gays recognizable as human beings with real positive and negative dimensions like any other communities and people.

Little Richard, singer and performer, presented a more ostentatious and flamboyant lifestyle to the public. As a gay who was "out," he crossed over in the entertainment industry in spite of popular mores against his sexual orientation and his up front, in your face bold proclamations. Against the tide of rejection coming from black churches and heterosexual communities, Rustin, Baldwin, and Richard advanced a spirituality in which love became a political strategy during the 1950s and 1960s.

Throughout the 1970s, the manifestation of a black gay spirituality springing from African American gay culture surfaced in a rise of related journals, magazines, and newsletters, particularly in the genre of poetry. Poetry enabled the free and spontaneous venting of the intellectual, cultural and political issues of the black gay community. Indeed, poetic discourse has been a medium of black gay spirituality, even when that conversation entered academic space. At least three changes took place in the 1970s: the articulation of black gays' right of separation from African American heterosexuals as well as from white gays who perceived black gays as sexual objects; the transformation of liberating love between black men, initiated by Rustin and Baldwin, into a broad movement; and the development of strong organizational ties between African American gays and African American lesbians. This decade further crafted a spirituality which nurtured a dialectical relation between love and risk.

The 1980s traumatized the black gay community with the plague of AIDS, the "Virus." The Virus became the touchstone for how one handled, intellectually and poetically, issues of love, life, death and other considerations unique to African American gays. Recognizing that help could come only from their community, black gays became more involved in political and civic life across the country with increased material and spiritual solidarity provided by a rise of support groups. A significant development was the creation of the first black gay church in Los Angeles. The 1980s, with the Virus, defined spirituality as the interplay between love and death. What powers were at work when the very act of love could mean death? Stigmatized by same-sex preference and the AIDS plague, black gay religious scholars reached deeper into the depths of their street wisdom to identify for themselves a Spirit of love living with death.

RELIGIOUS TALK IN CULTURAL CONTEXT

The contributors to this anthology engage religious reflection and cultural analysis from diverse intellectual and social positions. Still, the central question pursued entails the discovery of the divine or ultimate concern in specific cultural locations. Though culture and religious reflection act as hinges in these conversations, not all the contributors agree on one definition of culture or of religious reflection. All, however, do operate from Christian contexts; yet they glean implications for non-Christian discourses. All concur on the vital dimension of religion in human relations, with most approaching religion from a theological perspective though with influence from the history of religions. Furthermore, at least three major demarcations underscore the arrangement of these essays. Some deploy theory as a tool to negotiate insights on religion and culture; others utilize method; and still others bring their own positions to the surface through application—scrutinizing literary texts or case studies.

Sheila Greeve Davaney's entry provides an overview of the current map of the theological scene in the United States. For her, the two cognate genres are postliberalism and revisionist theologies. Her choice of these two cornerstones flows from her grounding her own religious reflection in what she terms a radical "pragmatic historicism." In a word, historicism is the benchmark of religious reflection because religion is radically implanted in culture, which also is constituted by the same historicism. In her mapping of a theological guide, she adeptly sifts through the theoretical nuances of the "sense of the historicity of human existence that has come to pervade our era." Drawing insights from cultural studies, she underlines the radical locatedness and particularity of humanity. What she adds is attention to how today's realities are deeply contextualized by their emergence from complex historical processes. While acknowledging the contributions of the postliberal and revisionist models of contemporary theology, she takes on the two major representatives of both discourses—George Lindbeck and David Tracy, respectively. Then, having cleared the way, she develops her notion of a pragmatic historicism as it relates to religious reflection and cultural analysis.

She first decenters the subject, wrenching it from the modernistic framework of a unitary reality. For Davaney, human beings reside within complex fabrics of interwoven realities. Hence historical traditions are neither static nor homogenous; they are, in fact, internally multiple. Religious traditions have no unchanging essences. Similarly, cultural and religious traditions do not maintain impenetrable boundaries, but are porous with accumulation of new information and experiences. Diverse traditions with their symbols too are not free floating (a form of Platonism), but ensconced in the material practices of wider cultural systems and webs of power. The theoretical turn of situating both religious reflection and cultural analysis within a radical historicism unveils a democratizing process, because one no longer focuses on formalized doctrines of a tradition.

Mary McClintock Fulkerson, in her essay, poses the query: how does a Christian engage in social criticism? She concludes that a faithful Christian social criticism resists and transforms corrupted social practices of race, gender, and class—forms of brokenness—from the vantage of a just and loving realm of God. By putting into conversation culture theory and liberation theology's view of social criticism, she evolves, in her words, a materialist theory of culture. She unravels the conceptual underpinnings of the conservative Christian right for its defining Christian identity over against a corrupting secular culture. Similar to Davaney, she dismisses theoretically the postliberal theological paradigm which takes culture seriously but which then argues that a Christian culture with its core biblical narrative should absorb the secular world, warding off theological doctrines deriving from secular culture.

Raymond Williams informs Fulkerson's position, especially her conclusions that culture is ordinary (non-elite), a whole way of life, and linked to economics and politics. She ties culture to material production, in contrast to postliberal and Christian right assertions of an autonomous culture with a split between the ideal and the material. After interweaving the highlights of Williams' theory of material culture, Fulkerson calls for a quest for new forms of resistance or the "emergent" which, for her, can be found in a transformative feminist woman-church liturgy and practice.

Like Fulkerson, David Batstone proposes material culture as the parameter for "transcendence." But instead of Raymond Williams, Batstone deploys theoretical insights from Hegel, Feuerbach, and Marx to put religious reflection and culture into conversation. Hegel and Feuerbach, from Batstone's reading, were both idealists, projecting transcendence from the human consciousness. It took Marx to ground both theoreticians and their concern for Spirit in material culture, that is, political economy and the mode of production. Batstone brings together philosophy and economics to illustrate how Hegel, Feuerbach, and Marx traced the development of the Spirit construct through feudalism and modernity. Batstone then analyzes contemporary culture as an economy of information where only the image is real and the real is only an image. Such an information-based economy or culture allows for diversification of consumer targeting with increased images and desires. Thus transcendence in a postmodernist context reflects heterogeneity, difference, pluralities of meanings and eclecticism. Religious reflection, the analytic of postmodern transcendence, and cultural analysis, the polyphonous and polymorphous effects of postmodern economy, revolve around material culture.

The theoretical addition to this changing conversation offered by James A. Noel comes with the employment of a conceptual paradigm mediated by a historical tact. Like Batstone, Noel begins with the interstices of European modernity. While Europe congratulated itself for its Enlightenment and modernity, argues Noel, Africans and African Americans (as New World slaves) suffered the dark side. That is, the culture of the Enlightenment and its modern moment were fundamentally expressive symbols, imaginative forms, rituals, and capitalist formations anchored in rationalism or a bureaucratism of life. The dark side was the suffering by Africans and those of their descent, revealing a postmodern condition beneath Europe's move to modernity. The freedom of Europe entailed slavery, colonialism, the loss of meaning, dread, the lack of a meta-view, and fear— all important constituents of what European and Euro-American intellectuals characterize as the postmodern condition today. The simultaneity of the arrival of modernity (for Europeans and their New World descendants) and postmodernity (for Africans and their New World descendants) corrspondingly impacted religious reflection. Prior to the European Enlightenment, only Christianity existed. But with the encounter with the "other," in particular Africans, Europe contrived the notion of "religion" as an opposition to the perceived primitives of the dark side. Thus one discovers a parallel between European culture (the manifestations of bureaucraticism in modernity) versus the decentered subject of the African (the manifestations of a postmodern condition), on the one hand, and European noetic religion versus the African's irrational primitivism, on the other.

In response, continues Noel, African Americans crafted a culture saturated with religion; in this sense, postmodern religious texts (evidencing liberation spiritual striving) resulted from postmodern culture (displaying multiple self-identity formations). Noel, furthermore, offers shadows of Derrida, Foucault, and Ricoeur in his play of the silent term in historical difference, in his genealogy of unorthodox disjuncture, and in his literary critical practice of hermeneutics.

The final theoretical essay, that of Kathryn Tanner, complements Noel's treatment of the underside; but with Tanner, the specificity becomes "ordinary people." She changes conversation from religious reflection and philosophy to religious reflection and social science in order to wed theology and culture at the site of ordinary people. She perceives instances of theologies of the people as illustrations of popular culture, informed by theories of popular culture within cultural studies, and asks what implications this perception might augur for traditional theology.

Drawing on the theoretical conceptualizations of Stuart Hall, she appropriates the definition of the "people" as a loose and fluid classification in contrast to the elites in the "power-bloc." The religious reflection and practice of the people (popular theology) combines at least three dimensions: a practicality serving the everyday needs of people; a syncretistic incorporation of diverse religions; and a flexible, open-ended way of life. Furthermore, synthesizing Hall's and Michel de Certeau's thinking, Tanner sees popular culture as a creative dynamic between agency of the people and tension-filled encounters with elite culture, which in fact provides the materials for popular culture to ingenuously appropriate. Hence popular culture, given a lack of control over elite cultural production, is a process of productive resistance rather than of passive objectification, a process that transforms elite cultural forms through novel and unanticipated routes.

A parallel dynamic unfolds relative to elite culture and thereby traditional theology. Just as popular culture is not passive to cultural production not its own, so too elite culture and traditional theology constitute themselves by incorporating and reusing aspects from popular cultural productions as well as from the wider cultural spheres of society. Elite theological productions take elements from the wider culture just as popular theology takes from traditional theology. Theories of popular cultural paradigms model for all theological production (elite and popular) in this manner: all draw on tradition, present theological productions, and the wider culture.

A second cluster of contributors, though attentive to theory, brings theological method into the conversation between religious reflection and cultural analysis. Religious reflection constitutes, for Mark McClain Taylor, how one goes about tracking the notion of spirit within culture, and particularly how one discerns spirit within popular culture. McClain Taylor centers his methodology on spiritual presence outside of established religious traditions by selecting popular artistic expressions. He understands culture as a whole way of life, including attitudes, ideas, languages, practices, institutions and structures of power. Culture is negotiated within and between definite populations. Moreover, he works with cultural practices as a broad range of domains or spheres. To further embellish and clarify his method of tracking spirit, he uses Bruce Springsteen, Arrested Development and Derrida to signify aspects of popular culture's revelations of spirit.

Offering a novel and creative approach for sighting spirit, McClain-

Taylor concludes that critical and transformative spirituality surfaces when three "family-resemblances" arise—liminality (between spatial and temporal locations), integrative relations (seeking holistic vision), and emancipative concerns (a drive toward liberation). With the merging of these three foci, cultural critics discover spirit in culture. The task of theology is to track these prominent interactive family resemblances, with an accent on liberation. Theological discourse as cultural critique as it participates in spirit in culture embodies, for McClain-Taylor, the formulating of literary and cognitive arguments. But most importantly, theology qua theological critique has to itself participate in the critical spirit at work in cultural practices. This is both how one locates spirit in culture and how theology and theologians involve themselves in transformative genres and practices.

Karen Baker-Fletcher engages method like McClain-Taylor. But instead of popular culture delimiting her mode of God-talk, she lifts up the cutting edge discourse of "womanist theology," exploring the means by which one constructs womanist theology. Religious reflection centers in black women's culture. Hence the primary sources in her theological method are what she calls "narratives"—African American women's texts such as scriptural readings, songs, poems, intellectual essays, autobiographies, fiction, and oral-aural traditions. These sources bring to light and preserve black women's moral wisdom and symbolizations of the divine.

In addition to the sources, Baker-Fletcher proffers a norm in her theological methodology, a norm which vivifies and gives substance to the sources. For her, the norm enables the generation of positive, life-affirming black women's cultures which aid in survival and liberation. For womanist theology this norm is revealed as a creative spark, God's creative power within African American women, a spark filled with empowering wisdom and creativity, mediated and passed along by black mothers and grandmothers.

Cultural codes must be deciphered to fully develop womanist theology; such codes, facilitating effective communication, again draw on mother-daughter paradigms, as mothers bequeath to their female children wisdom. The code of female care integral to the survival and transformation of the entire black community and the code of skin color tensions reveal that those unfamiliar with black culture bypass the more profound depths of these codes. The point, for Baker-Fletcher's method, is that one must decode codes to appreciate the sacred in culture, including the self and community.

Womanist theological method advocates and applies a contextual approach, a deductive epistemology and practice, commencing with a critical and theological analysis of social-historical and religio-cultural realities. And, perhaps more consistently than the multiplicity of other religious reflections of culture, womanist theology steadfastly holds in creative tension a proliferation of overlapping realities, that is, racism, sexism, classism, heterosexism, and environmental racism. The presupposition here is that dominant Euro-American norms secure such systemic injustices.

In my own contribution, I likewise aim at crafting a theological method in conversation with cultural studies by focusing on African American slave religious experiences. I modify Raymond Williams' definition of culture as a total way of life thus broadening culture to constitute religious culture. Similar to Baker-Fletcher, my religious reflection (attempt at theological method) draws on the idea of diverse sources; in this instance, the primary illustration being slave religious experiences. Moreover, this method entails dynamic interpenetrating couplets or guidelines; in other words, a worldview of "both-and" as opposed to "either-or." Again like Baker-Fletcher's womanist approach, I situate holistic liberation as my theological norm. Within the sources, with their guidelines and norms, I perceive persistent and recurring theological patterns (such as, God or ultimate concern, intermediaries or Jesus Christ, and human purpose or "to get over"). Finally, I call for a theoretical dimension for methodology with revisionist insights from political economy (Marx), micro-powers (Foucault), language (Ricoeur and Eco), and identity-formation (Malcolm X). My use of theoretical methodology materializes out of foundational religious reflections and cultural analyses originally forged and envisioned by James H. Cone's black theology of liberation.

The final selection of chapters exhibit the performance or application of cultural analysis and religious reflection on and to specific case studies: literature, gay identity, and theologies in Africa. Religious reflection and cultural analysis converse, but the latter's constructs are more subtle and, at times, oblique. James H. Evans, Jr. handles Toni Morrison's seminal novel, *Song of Solomon*, and argues for its inherent moral vision. Concentrating on the African American predicament and prospects—that is, cultural uprooting and cultural grounding—Evans heralds a redemption defined as reclaiming the original religious spiritual resources of black culture. Such a successful reclamation derives only from a profound recovery of sacred myth.

His usage of irony and paradox suggests the discipline of literary criticism and his powerful references to pregnant metaphors and symbolic images and coded signs hint at interpolations of Ricoeur's thought and of structuralism, but with an African American conceptual difference. Furthermore, culture for Evans consists in large measure, as seen in Morrison's text, of song and music, following the pioneering work of W. E. B. Du Bois. And though bringing to bear his own Christian sensibilities, he reflects on both Christian and non-Christian discourses with a commitment to the intermingling of aesthetic and religious quests. On a larger scale, this essay confronts the dilemma of a culture of alienation and return to primal ultimate concerns by way of literary hermeneutics.

Bill Smith situates his construction of the black gay self within a unique definition of religious reflection and cultural analysis. For him religious reflection takes place as "liberating love" and cultural analysis as "critical street wisdom." The knowledge and application of this dynamic are lodged methodologically in both risk taking and conversation. Religious reflection and cultural analysis employ conversation between the street (using its non-traditional tongue) and the academy (confronting its normative presuppositions) to fashion a common language, but one that is stretched and expanded. This process helps unfamiliar interlocutors to become acquainted. Method, for Smith, is both personal (offering memory as personal archaeology and intimate archetype—thus his usage of critical autobiography and seemingly stream of consciousness diaries) and academic (assisting the reader with timely intellectual analyses). Smith argues that a very large dimension of conversation is location, the location of both speakers and listeners. Because he encounters his sacred space within, Smith's liberation journey is a personal archaeology. Smith grafts strands of Foucault's archaeological and genealogical method and notion of power as distributive field into his own emancipatory love-wisdom synthesis. The power of Smith's essay, moreover, is undergirded by the question: what sacred space is there to connect with resources of culture when one is dying of AIDS? In a culture of extreme repression, at the innermost zone of sexual intimacy, liberation of the self mediated by love and street wisdom entails radical risks: fighting for one's life while under attack by family and church, exposing oneself in academic conversation, coming out of invisibility and silence, participating with the stranger in forbidden places, and cohabiting in one body with the plague of AIDS.

Finally, the essay by Edward P. Antonio applies an insightful treatment of culture and politics to the debate in Africa, principally South Africa, between African theological and black theological assertions. Essentially, for Antonio, culture is a contestable idea shot through with power politics and struggle over multiple sites of hegemonic conflict and control (akin to Gramsci). There exists no culture without politics. Culture is contentious but inherently hegemonic, its symbols and meanings anchoring in control systems of discursive formations (akin to Foucault). Drawing on Foucauldian conclusions of the episteme or discursive formations to enhance Gramscian hegemony notions, Antonio elaborates hegemony as a "group of statements" which dominate both symbolic and material dynamics, determining what is knowledge and what is falsehood. Systems of discursive control center Antonio's concepts of symbols and meanings, hidden rules within these systems regulate culture's content and hegemonic establishment. These rules are socially constructed and, in turn, form the lives of the people who construct them.

Applying this theoretical framework to the debate between African and black theologies, Antonio concludes that both suffer from a bankrupt interrogation of the social formations of religious reflection and culture due to a severe case of essentialism. One, African theology, incorrectly cordons off culture from the contestation of hegemony and power. The other, black theology, privileges politics to the exclusion of that region of human experience shaping the form and content of human life. In sum, exclusionary dualism, pitting one theology against the other, thrives on a naive essentialism, an ahistorical methodology of unchanging givens. Antonio casts anathemas against both forms of theologies, decentering the essential "African" and "black" subjects by way of a fluid cross fertilization and enmeshing of politics and culture. He offers his contribution of "a multivocal hermeneutic of the social," winged with both different cultural and political aspects. And, for religious reflection and cultural analysis in general, Antonio, adopting Bourdieu's phraseology, ends by characterizing both as engaged enterprises in conversation, conversing from postures of "position takings" saturated in power.

The diversity of discourses in this anthology around the dynamic of religious reflection and cultural analysis indicates that there exists no meta-narrative or static foundation in theology's changing conversations. Fluid characteristics and flexible indications are associated with all writers including theologians and other scholars of religion. The conversation between religious reflection and cultural analysis draws on all bodies of knowledge (whether inter- or multi-disciplinary) germane to achieving specific projects or contextualized movements. Religious reflection and cultural studies are syncretic endeavors, synthesizing disparate aspects of a host of theoretical paradigms and conceptual frameworks. Both are committed dynamics and processes, taking positions in the genealogies of subjugated knowledges—presenting the intellectual's hermeneutic toward marginalized communities. A total way of life determines religion and culture; high culture and elite religion are not the exclusive locales of human experiences. A style of living is constituted and demarcated by a contested terrain of practices, forces of habit, beliefs, ideas, institutions, common sense, presentations, and representations, that are spiritual, material, affective, physical, intellectual, and sensual. Furthermore, in this anthology, religious reflection and cultural analysis engage in a dance as partners in a new conversation, one in which religion and theology open themselves to culture's conceptual interrogation over the fundamental presuppositions of those who study and live out their faith commitments. And likewise, theology and, more broadly, the study of religions challenge cultural analysis to take seriously the adage that philosophers have interpreted the world, and we must keep the analytic project going, drawing upon the silent spaces of history and the disjunctures of present day struggles as the telos of a possible new imaginative horizon.

REFERENCES

Beam, Joseph, ed. 1986. *In the Life*. Boston: Alyson Publications.

Cone, James H. 1969. *Black Theology and Black Power*. New York: Seabury Press.

Daly, Mary. 1968. *The Church and the Second Sex*. New York: Harper and Row.

Grant, Jacquelyn. 1979. "Black Theology and the Black Woman." In Black Theology: A Documentary *History, 1966-1979*, ed. Gayraud S. Wilmore and James H. Cone. Maryknoll, N.Y.: Orbis Books.

Gutierrez, Gustavo. 1973. *A Theology of Liberation*. Maryknoll, N.Y.: Orbis Books.

Hemphill, Essex, ed. 1991. *Brother to Brother: New Writings by Black Gay Men*. Boston: Alyson Publications.

Ruether, Rosemary Radford. 1983. *Sexism and God-talk*. Boston: Beacon Press.

Smith, Bill. 1993. "Locating My Theology in Sacred Space." In *New Visions for the Americas*, ed. David Batstone. Minneapolis, Minn.: Fortress Press.

Walker, Alice. 1983. *In Search of Our Mothers' Garden*. New York: Harcourt, Brace, Jovanovich.

one

THEORY

MAPPING THEOLOGIES:

AN HISTORICIST GUIDE TO CONTEMPORARY THEOLOGY

SHEILA GREEVE DAVANEY

Map makers are always faced with the recognition that while they seek to be faithful to a particular landscape or territory, their renderings are selective, carried out for particular purposes and highly dependent upon the interplay of imagination and material. Maps highlight different landmarks, tell you how to get to different places and utilize varying identification schemas. In short, different maps suggest different ways of construing material reality.

This diversity of purpose and result also characterize the maps or interpretive pictures we compose of our intellectual landscapes. The depictions we draw of who we are today and how we got this way are never self-evident or incontrovertible; they too are always acts of imaginative interpretation carried out for particular reasons that are infused with values and goals and issue forth in different effects. Depending on the intellectual maps we utilize, different questions emerge as important; some positions seem central and others peripheral and indeed, depending upon the boundaries we draw, certain options are included in the landscape while others fade into uncharted wilderness beyond recognized borders.

This process of mapping also goes on in theology, offering us various ways to orient ourselves amongst a plethora of confusing options. Perhaps the major theological map in use today, what historian Peter Novick would call a "regulative fiction," is one that identifies the two major possibilities on the current scene as postliberal and revisionist theologies (Novick 1988, 16). A perusal of current theological journals and publishers' back lists will give ample evidence that these two theological trajectories are centering the discussion. While other theological approaches appear on the scene, they tend to be either interpreted as variants of post-liberal or revisionist thought or relegated to the margins of viable theological reflection, as interesting sidelights but off the beaten path. Moreover, the major horizon against which the contrast of these two positions is played out is the distinction between Enlightenment and liberal modernity on the one hand and contemporary postmodernism on the other.

When this map is utilized certain features or issues dominate the theological discussions. Hence there is an enormous emphasis upon the question of how contemporary theology should be related to the founding, assumed to be normative, elements of Christianity. Or there is debate about who is more postmodern and who embodies tendencies toward either premodern fideistic nostalgia or modern uncritical universalism. This map and the concerns that organize it are important; they have guided us well for many purposes. But they have also focussed our attention so thoroughly on certain topics and ways of construing the theological typography that, most often, other theological paths that might be taken are left unexplored.

This essay is an exercise in imaginative cartography. It presents a map of the current theological scene that, while indebted to ones presently on this scene, seeks to redraw some of the boundaries, add a few new landmarks and thus suggest some new ways of looking at our theological landscape. It will resemble mainstream cartography in many respects, but it will also seek to take us off these well-worn paths in the hope that as our vistas change so will our sense of what is important and what is peripheral, what is at the center and what resides at the perimeter.

The horizon against which I want to delineate my theological map is the profound sense of the historicity of human existence that has come to pervade our era. Turning to historicity is not a repudiation of the convictions that are expressed in the notion of postmodernism. Indeed, for many postmodernists historicism is central to the break from the modern period. However, by focussing upon historicism I hope to sidestep, for the moment, the endless debates between modernism and postmodernism, debates that are most often predicated on rather ahistorical and univocal readings of each period. My approach will be to set forth a brief and general statement of current historicist assumptions and then elaborate upon those assumptions through the exploration of present theological options.

It has become common in the late twentieth century to acknowledge that humans reside neither everywhere nor nowhere but are situated within particular locales demarcated by distinctive languages, political and economic structures, worldviews, everyday practices and rituals, forms of embodiment and streams of feeling. This acknowledgement, moreover, has usually included the recognition that our current context is the product of complex historical processes that preceded our era, as well as of our responses to them. Thus human beings always reside in particular contexts and those contexts have emerged out of and in relation to other prior sites of human life.

The conviction that human beings are historical has found expression in several interconnected assumptions. Epistemologically, historicism has presupposed that all knowledge is localized, relative to its time and place, shaped by its history, infused by interests and interpretive in character, and part of a historical strand of other interpretations. Humans have no unmediated access to the world nor any way to compare an uninterpreted reality with our various accounts of it and thereby ascertain whose version of reality is the true one. Hence, for historicists, attempts to achieve sure and certain knowledge, applicable for all times and places, and predicated upon unquestionable foundations appear misguided and illusory.

Ontologically, contemporary historicism has increasingly portrayed the larger reality within which humanity is situated and with which humans continually interact as both fluid and forceful, altered by human action and presence but determining human prospects as well. Moreover, both the efficacy and receptivity of each, humans and our encompassing reality, occur in and through a rich spectrum ranging from the rational, logical and mechanical to the murkier realms of the intuitive, the affective, and the aesthetic. Humans are not simply cognitive agents manipulating a passive material reality; we are also bodies, and our environments are also affective. The interaction, thus, between humans and these environments, throughout the full range of efficacies and meanings, is dynamic and constantly affecting both us and our world.

Precisely because it is malleable, fluid and dynamic, reality is not of a piece, it is not the same everywhere. Neither, for the same reasons, are humans. Thus has emerged the notion of the historicized subject. According to historicism, human existence is embedded in the matrix of specific, concrete histories; humans emerge from our particular pasts and contribute to the formation of our particular presents and futures. As historical, human life is also social and interconnected. Moreover, its interconnections occur not only at the natural and biological levels but also in the interactions of economic, political, and psychological processes and across the full range of the intellectual, affective, and material vectors of human life. To affirm the fully social character of the human, however, is not to detract from the diversity of historicized existence. It is instead to insist that our varied forms of human life influence and are influenced by each other and by the larger environment, and it is that through and by virtue of these interactions that particularity emerges.

Permeating these anthropological, ontological and epistemological shifts toward historicism is the general recognition that humans are preeminently linguistic and cultural beings dependent upon language as a primary, though certainly not exclusive, means of engaging and interpreting the world. Historicism does not deny the enormous power of the non-cognitive in the lives of creatures such as ourselves who have bodies and quite literally feel our way through life; indeed, much that historicism has to offer discussions today follows from its increased recognition of the embodiedness and material embeddedness of historicized existence. But it remains the case that language is one of the most prominent and powerful dimensions of existence through which we form and are formed by the world, both human and non-human, around us. Our language, like all other dimensions of human existence, is neither universal, static nor neutral. Language, too, is the product of particular historical processes and carries the particularities of time and place. The linguistic worlds we inhabit are not impartial and transparent; they are the bearers of the powers, ideological commitments, and specific values that operate, consciously and unconsciously, in human life. To acknowledge the centrality of our linguistic formations is not to reduce life to language; it is to affirm the distinctive role that language plays in our varied worlds of feeling, thinking and acting.

These historicist sensibilities have raised questions for numerous disciplines concerning the character of knowledge, claims to validity and the norms by which competing claims might be adjudicated. And theology, perhaps more than most disciplines, has been compelled to reconsider its nature, the status of its proposals and its function both within the academy and in relation to religious communities. In this essay, I shall discuss several theological movements that reflect these historicist sensibilities, turning first to the theological perspectives known as postliberalism and revisionist theology. I will explore each in terms of the historicist assumptions set forth thus far, analyzing their interpretation of the historicist turn and its implications for theology and critically evaluating these options. Then I will outline an emerging theological trajectory, what I term pragmatic historicism, as an alternative historicist rendering of theology, one that suggests a different way of mapping the theological terrain, its questions and proposals.

The theological perspective known as postliberalism articulates an orientation that reflects many of the historicist assumptions set forth above. Associated prominently with the Divinity Schools of Yale and Duke, postliberalism has been influenced by social-scientific, especially anthropological, approaches that argue for the centrality of language and culture in human life, and by theological and philosophical perspectives that emphasize the "traditioned" or historical character of all human experience and knowledge. The combination of these insights has led proponents of postliberalism to develop not only a view of the human as socially, historically and linguistically constituted, but of religion as a this-worldly phenomenon that functions in, contributes to, and reflects the constraints of the historical process.

The tenets of postliberalism have been most fully developed by George A. Lindbeck. In *The Nature of Doctrine: Religion and Theology in a Postliberal Age*, Lindbeck repudiates both the older, pre-modern cognitivist view that religious assertions were primarily propositional claims about reality and the modern liberal, Schleiermachian-inspired view that religious claims are expressions of more fundamental, pre-linguistic, immediate experiences (Lindbeck 1984, 17). In relation to the first, Lindbeck disavows the assumption that objective, universally valid knowledge is possible, as well as the correspondence theory of truth that has often attended that assumption. Lindbeck also eschews the liberal view—which he calls experiential-expressivism—that human beings have fundamentally unmediated experiences, universal in scope and common in character, that then find secondary articulation in historically particular and culturally specific forms (Lindbeck 1984, 33, 39-41).

Over against these positions, Lindbeck argues that human beings are thoroughly linguistically and culturally constituted creatures who depend upon social and historical context for the resources that make experience possible at all. We exist in very particularized strands of social reality and all that we experience and know is filtered through, indeed determined, by these specific locales (Lindbeck 1984, 36).

Such cultural contexts are, moreover, according to Lindbeck, historical in nature. They have developed over long periods of time and embody and continue particular historical lineages that are not reducible to one another. Thus, to be human is not only to be constituted by culture and all that entails but also to be traditioned; human beings are the bearers of history, who live out of and carry on the past (Lindbeck 1984, 116).

This emphasis upon the traditioned character of life is central to Lindbeck's interpretation of religion. For Lindbeckian post-liberalism, religions are the most encompassing and overarching interpretative schemas within which humans reside, think, act and experience. They are comprehensive worldviews that express our deepest convictions about reality and about how humans should relate to such a cosmic context. These over-arching frameworks are thoroughly historical. Far from fundamentally trafficking in the suprahistorical, religions offer historically-derived and tradition-specific portrayals of life and its significance. Thus to be religious is not to hold some indubitable belief guaranteed by an ahistorical reason or revelation. Nor is it to have a certain immediate experience. Rather it is to live out of an interpretive story and to become a practitioner of a specific tradition's way of life.

The view of Lindbeck and his cohorts is distinguished from those of other historicists by the definitive and normative status it bestows on the past. For Lindbeck, the historicized subject receives identity through the appropriation of a particular past, its convictions, values and commitments. To live outside of a specific tradition is to deny one's humanity, indeed it is to cease to exist as human at all.

Moreover, and very importantly, Lindbeck and his followers do not view traditions as simply temporally-linked events. A tradition is a historical line of development that embodies in an ongoing fashion a set of essential tenets. Likening such tenets to the grammatical rules that structure a language, Lindbeck asserts that these fundamental beliefs can be instantiated in diverse and creative ways, but they must be present and continually appropriated for a tradition to continue. Furthermore, these structuring beliefs can be traced, according to Lindbeck, to the origins of the tradition. Thus to be human is to stand within a particular encompassing interpretive tradition whose centering convictions emerged at its origin, and to live religiously is to live within and in faithfulness to a particular religious history (Lindbeck 1984, 33, 113f).

Given this view of tradition-funded existence, theology is no longer the pursuit of certain and unassailable truths or the expression of a universal religious essence; theology becomes primarily a descriptive endeavor that seeks to delineate and make clear the normative foundations of a specific tradition. As such it is, for the most part, an intrasystematic affair whose central criterion consists in faithfulness to the originating tenets of the tradition and whose reference is almost exclusively to the particular community and its history. Appeals to universal or cross-traditioned criteria are deemed inappropriate, indeed impossible, and conversation with those outside the perspective takes place in an ad hoc and unsystematic fashion. Thus, postliberal theology redirects its adherents back to primary communities and to the task of interiorizing particular historical modes of being. By so doing, postliberalism offers an historicism focussed on the conserving and conditioned character of human existence.

This version of historicism, in my judgment, is too one-sided and univocal. It fails to account for the complexity of concrete historical life in several important ways. First, while it rightly insists on the traditioned character of existence, it fails to acknowledge that humans, especially in the late twentieth century, are in fact multi-traditioned, shaped by more than one strand of history. To embrace an historicist perspective means that we must also take account of this multiplicity and find a means by which to relate its various, often tension-filled components. While postliberals insist that we do or should so reside within primary communities, in fact, many people today cannot easily find such a primary, encompassing perspective and are compelled to fashion, creatively and critically, the diverse traditions that impact them into some new, more adequate whole. A second, related problem is that the postliberal perspective, for all of its denials, appears very isolationist in relation to other traditions. A number of postliberals are responding to this charge by calling for an ad hoc apologetics—unsystematic and occasional conversations with other perspectives around specific shared concerns. Yet postliberals have no basis within their approach for entering these conversations or, once there, for making them much more than show and tell. Postliberals, in the end, fail to demonstrate why communities today should or how they could genuinely interact with other communities. The postliberals offer an account for how the present relates to the past, but are singularly unhelpful regarding relationships between contemporaries.

A third issue concerns how postliberals understand traditions. Lindbeck presents, finally, a very undynamic interpretation of cultural-linguistic traditions. While he allows that the central doctrines or "regulative principles" of a tradition may be instantiated over time in various, often tension-filled ways, the basic tenets themselves do not change. Thus, at the center of his program he introduces a thoroughly static, essentialist component that renders suspect all of his other claims to historical consciousness. For the notion that a belief, while instantiated variously, remains nonetheless essentially the same is, from the perspective of a fuller historicism, a reversion to an untenable Platonism. Moreover, it is a difficult claim to sustain in an analysis of any particular religious tradition. Real traditions seem not to exhibit the kind of continuity that Lindbeck posits for them.

Fourth, while postliberals have explored the relation of past and present, they have most often failed to include in that analysis a rigorous examination of the political, economic, social or broader cultural location of religious beliefs and practices, or the implications of these beliefs and practices for such settings. Instead, the grammar of faith and its surrounding narrative appear strangely disembodied, suspended in history but untouched by the multiple factors that shape and are shaped by interpretive traditions. Thus postliberals primarily ask how a later belief or practice is faithful to an earlier one, not how both are embedded in the concrete processes of history.

Finally, postliberals arbitrarily endow the past, in the form of a tradition's founding beliefs, with unquestioned authority. Our world, they claim, should allow itself to be absorbed by the world of our tradition, and where contemporary values or commitments or beliefs conflict with those of these regulative tenets, it is the present that must yield. But that certain aspects of the past possess such uncritical normativity is simply assumed, deriving from the questionable premise that traditions have an unchanging core that emerged at their origins and remains unchanged throughout history. Thus, with these misconstruals of the actual character of traditions goes a postliberal view of the authority of the past that wrongly releases us from our obligation to evaluate that past critically and to take responsibility ourselves for the creative construction of our present and future.

Postliberalism, in the end, appears to offer only a partial or fainthearted historicism. While drawing contemporary theology's attention to the past in a forceful and compelling manner, it nonetheless construes that past and our relationship to it in an ahistorical fashion. The result is a static view of tradition which fails to acknowledge or account for the continually innovative and inventive dynamics of historical traditions in which nothing, in principle, is immune to alteration. Accompanying this is an authoritarianism that begets an uncritical stance toward the past. In the name of historicism, postliberalism gives voice to an untenable essentialism and a stultifying conservativism.

Revisionist theology offers another historicist perspective. It is more difficult to draw the parameters of this perspective because revisionism has come to be something of a catch-all term, often used to group together a wide variety of persons who do not always agree with one another on central issues. Lindbeckians have tended to see revisionists as liberals of the experiential-expressivist type, while others have designated them as the left-wing, so to speak, of a general narrativist school, for which postliberals comprise the conservative wing. Further, the beginnings of revisionist theology predate the current postmodern shifts; it grew out of earlier methodological concerns, especially those arising from the recognition of the marginalization of theology in public life and the acknowledgement of the interpretive character of all human experience. And the concern with the interpretive nature of human existence arose not from a blanket repudiation of modern theological liberalism, but from an extension of hermeneutical discussions which originated in the nineteenth century. This pre-postmodern point of departure, together with revisionism's concern with the public status and role of theology and tendency, especially in earlier forms, to be universalistic in tone have led many to see revisionist theology as a continuation of the liberal project.

There are good reasons for such a view, as the work of David Tracy demonstrates. Tracy, the undisputed master of revisionist theology, early on offered a detailed vision of theology as deeply influenced by hermeneutical theory, with its driving desire to conceive of a creative relation between present and past (Tracy 1975, 1981). Hence, he set forth a correlational view of theology in which, in any historical period, human beings articulate fundamental questions about the nature and meaning of human life and correlate them with the answers their particular traditions have developed and expressed in their religious and cultural classics (Tracy, 1975, 1981). Moreover, Tracy contended, in a quite modern way, for the public character of theological criteria, asserting that it was both possible and necessary to delineate norms that persons, across religious and cultural traditions, could agree on and utilize to assess competing positions (Tracy, 1981). In his more recent work, Tracy has continued many of the interests that shaped his previous efforts but has sought to articulate a deepened sense of historicity (Tracy, 1987). He remains concerned with the relation of the classics of a tradition to contemporary society, but he now recognizes the ambiguous character of any tradition, including its classic symbols and beliefs. The past shapes the present for Tracy but it no longer does so in a wholly innocent or positive manner (Tracy 1987, chap 4). Thus our engagement with the past must be far more critical in a revisionist perspective than it is for postliberals. Moreover, while Tracy continues to appeal to the classics of a tradition these classics seem less and less to have a fixed content as Tracy begins to move away from essentialist notions of historical traditions. His revisionism always points back to the classics, but what might count as a classic is not determined for all time (Tracy 1988, chap 5). And finally, while not giving up all reference to public criteria, Tracy has greatly historicized his interpretation of such criteria. They no longer have an absolute or universal tone, but are conceived in terms of a relative adequacy that is historically derived and open to ongoing revision. Thus Tracy's version of revisionist theology still views theology primarily as a dialogue between the present and the past but this conversation is increasingly seen to entail critical consciousness.

In many ways Tracy and his revisionist companions can be said to have incorporated the strengths of postliberalism while avoiding its failures. Revisionist theology espouses the importance of tradition and the past while, increasingly, maintaining a critical stance toward both. Revisionist theology also acknowledges the problematic character of modernity, jettisoning the ahistorical elements of that project and incorporating within its model the critical dimensions of historicism, without abandoning the public sphere and the possibility of real encounters with the other.

Despite these accomplishments, there remain questions concerning the depth and adequacy of historicism in Tracy's revisionist mode. Two central and connected issues come to the fore. The first is Tracy's continued emphasis upon the classics of a tradition. While he now sees these as fraught with ambiguity, classics nonetheless remain center stage in this revisionist approach. Hence, while we dialogue critically with the past we still do so with a fairly narrow, albeit changing, section of the historical heritage—one privileged by processes of power that left out much more than they included. This continued prioritizing of the classics suggests a lingering essentialism in Tracy's position that belies his historicism; it implies that there is a true core of the tradition and that the classics represent this core because they carry a freight—indeed perhaps an ontological freight—that separates them from the other events and processes of any particular history. A more full-fledged historicism would need not only to see the classics as ambiguous but would also need to de-prioritize them and acknowledge their ontological equality with other historical events, texts, symbols and persons. A fuller historicism would resist all essentialist interpretations of traditions and instead insist that the historical traditions with which contemporary theology must contend are thoroughly pluralistic and devoid of abiding essences that are stable over time.

A related issue is the fact that Tracy continues to view theology as primarily a hermeneutical enterprise, in which the central task of the theologian is to correlate classics of the past with present concerns and proposals. While a fully historicist perspective will readily agree with Tracy that the past contributes to the present and must therefore engage it, it is unclear that such encounters should be for the purpose of correlating the claims of the past with the contemporary situation. The more pertinent theological task would appear to be a constructive one that engages its particular historical tradition, along with those of other traditions, in order to create identities and visions of reality that are viable for today. When the past is shorn of its privileged status, the hermeneutical moment becomes just one intermediate moment in the theological process, not its end and goal. Thus an historicist orientation suggests a move beyond the hermeneutics of revisionism toward a more constructive historicism.

The implication of the analysis presented thus far is that while postliberalism and revisionist theology both embody historicist sensibilities, they do so in an incomplete manner that significantly undermines their historicist commitments. Thus at this juncture I will identify what I take to be an emerging trajectory in theology that seeks to embody historicist insights more fully than either postliberalism or revisionist thought. I am particularly concerned with the implications of historicism for the adjudication of theological claims, and have therefore come to call this perspective pragmatic historicism. My colleague Delwin Brown, who has focussed on an historicist analysis of the formation of theological claims, labels this trajectory constructive historicism (Brown 1994, 112). Theologians whom I associate with this form of historicism include Gordon Kaufman, William Dean, Linell Cady, Brown, myself and, increasingly, Sallie McFague. There are others whose work clearly resonates with the position proposed in this essay, including South African theologian Simon Maimela, and Chinese theologian Kwok Pui-lan as well as philosopher of religion Cornel West. I will be presenting my own version of this view, one that parallels and is indebted to these thinkers but does not simply duplicate any of their positions and, indeed, differs from them in some important respects.

The perspective I call pragmatic historicism grounds itself in the assumption that human beings, as biological and cultural creatures, reside within the complex fabrics of interwoven realities, realities that depend upon both each other and the fabric as a whole to exist, survive and flourish. While sharing with all other entities participation in and contribution to the physical matrices of life, humans are also specifically cultural entities whose lives are shaped through the cultural organizations, practices and continual innovations that have emerged within human historical existence. Such cultural forms, embodied in language, institutions, ritual actions, and feelings, cannot be divorced from their physical setting and in turn have enormous impact on that context. Nonetheless, they give human existence its distinctive character and delimit the particular form of its evolutionary development.

A central repercussion of the historical character of human existence is that humans always exist within and receive direction from humanly devised interpretations of life, meaning and value. As Gordon Kaufman has emphasized, humans cannot survive outside the historically developed traditions of interpretation that have emerged over the vast span of human history (Kaufman 1981, chap 1; 1993, chap 8). These interpretive schemes name reality and humanity's place within it, and articulate what is valuable in life, what projects should be pursued and what loyalties should be followed. On these basic historicist assumptions pragmatic historicists firmly agree with postliberals and revisionists. But the way in which pragmatic historicism develops these basic ideas sets it apart from both of these positions.

According to pragmatic historicists these streams of interpretation have emerged in different places and out of unique circumstances and have developed over time in very different ways. Thus they represent real alternatives to one another; their differences are not superficial, hiding a common human experience or perception of human life, but substantial, resulting in distinctively different ways of being human. Moreover, these traditions of meaning and value always develop and take shape in localized and specific ways in response to particular pressures and events, and hence are internally pluralistic. Every tradition is in reality many traditions, conglomerations of distinctive and even heterogenous interpretations, sets of meanings and practices that cannot be assimilated or reduced to any universally present factor. Even when symbols, beliefs or ritualized actions recur they always do so in concrete forms that render themselves distinctive, making them unique construals of reality, not variations on a common theme. Historical traditions, including religious ones, have no stable and clearly identifiable essences that remain unchanging over time. What makes the multiple mini-traditions, so to speak, part of one tradition rather than another is that they emerge out of a particular historical lineage, a particular historical interaction, not that all of them exhibit some stability of meaning or unity of value. This historicist perspective wants to maintain, therefore, that, broadly speaking, different traditions can generally be distinguished from each other, but internal to each tradition are various, often conflictual, elements that in fact resist reduction to one another.

Moreover, if this historicist perspective is pushed to its limit, it must be acknowledged that throughout history, traditions have encountered each other and been reshaped by those encounters. Traditions, while relatively distinctive, are also porous, as Delwin Brown argues, with boundaries that are moveable, negotiable, and never finally set (Brown 1994, 83-92). Distinctions among traditions are real, but relative and ever changing.

These notions clearly indicate that traditions are loosely bound historical streams that change over time. If so, the return of much contemporary theology to some form of traditional commonality, albeit presented in historicist guise, represents a lingering essentialism that distorts the richly varied and dynamic character of our actual religious traditions.

But something else follows from these insights as well, something that has great import for how theology is to be conceived and conducted. It is not enough to acknowledge that traditions develop and accumulate new content as they go along and that, therefore, they are internally plural. Nor is it sufficient to admit that traditions interact along their boundaries, so to speak, and are altered. All this might still allow us to suppose that humans reside within clear, if ever changing perimeters, receiving orientation in life predominately from individual traditions. That may have been the case in earlier times, when cultures, civilizations and religions existed in relative isolation from one other. But that is not the situation today; whether in the great urban centers of the world or in isolated rural settings, humans are shaped by many conversations, by plural traditions that not only affect each other but co-mingle in historically specific ways. Humans listen and contribute to numbers of conversations simultaneously, and who they are as individuals and communities results from the interaction of these voices. Or to use another metaphor, they do not just stand on one side of their tradition's fence talking to those on the other side; they wander across boundaries and frontiers creating new configurations of landscape and identity. This is not to deny that humans are traditioned; it is rather to insist that they are multi-traditioned. At any given moment, an interpretive framework emerges not just out of a backward-looking engagement with one historical tradition, however pluralistic and porous, but as the product of the constructive intermingling of varied influences, historical and contemporary, from different strands of interpretation. A truly historicist perspective, therefore, must forgo not only essentialism but also the abiding desire for purity, a purity that those keepers of the gate, who benefit most from its illusion and who are ever vigilant against its loss in syncretism, guard fiercely, failing to note that it has long since disappeared.

Pragmatic historicism's version of the multi-traditioned and contextualized character of human existence is further specified by the recognition that interpretive traditions and their symbol systems are not disconnected from the material practices of those traditions, and that neither can be adequately understood apart from wider cultural and societal institutions, discourses and networks of power. To imagine that the human is reducible to the linguistic, or our diverse human worlds to human languages, or that language can be understood internally apart from its interaction with the non-linguistic dimensions of human reality is to commit the fallacy of linguisticism. A full-bodied historicism must recognize that symbol systems and beliefs are not just abstract linguistic configurations to be interpreted primarily in relation to other linguistic expressions. They are thoroughly embedded within, reflective of and have impact upon the material processes of life including biological, political, economic and psychological processes. Only by such recognition do we avoid a thin anemic form of historicism that is no more than an abstract and truncated linguisticism.

What emerges here is a picture of humans as multi-traditioned beings residing at the crossroads of dynamic, plural, incremental, porous and thoroughly concrete traditions. Such traditions are continually interacting with each other and their host cultures and thereby create in new historical moments novel understandings of reality that are connected to what has gone before but cannot be reduced to it. This picture also suggests that what we call particular traditions are really heuristic fictions that we should utilize but hold lightly, lest we mistake our abstractions for a vastly more complicated concrete reality and in the process empty history of its material content. This portrayal pushes in the direction of a very particular way of understanding theology in an historicist mode.

The perspective taking shape here understands the task of theology as the identification, critical assessment and reconstruction of historical interpretations of the nature of reality and of humanity's role within the cosmos in order that humans might more fruitfully and responsibly live life within our complex and interdependent universe. It affirms that theologians cannot carry out this task without the full engagement of historical traditions but simultaneously resists all tendencies toward essentialism and the desire for purity. Moreover, it rejects the reduction of such historical inheritance to texts, doctrinal formulations or symbol systems. Rather, to engage a tradition is to respond to its multiple concrete particularities, to contend with the messiness of its history.

Moreover, the drift of the present argument suggests that it is no longer adequate for us as theologians to understand ourselves as engaging one, predominant tradition from within whose clearly defined boundaries we converse with those outside. Instead we must recognize ourselves to be multi-traditioned; we must learn to decipher the multiple and contending assumptions, practices, forces and values that shape us and the concrete settings within which we reside. This suggests that theologians need to contend with vastly more materials than that of, say, the plural Christian tradition; we must also engage the material realities and traditions of nation, ideology, gender, race and class, as well as other religions and cultures with their concrete particularities.

This historicist orientation and its attendant view of tradition carry with them a number of other implications for theology. First, as was affirmed earlier, language remains an important focus of theology, but that focus now takes on a new cast. Pragmatic historicists will certainly continue to be interested in belief and symbol systems; theology, especially in its academic mode, can, as Delwin Brown has claimed, be interpreted as the "ethnography of belief" (Brown lecture). But as Brown has implied and this essay has asserted, such belief systems cannot be separated from their material locations and conditions. Hence an adequate ethnography of belief must trace the connection among these and other institutions, discursive formations and non-discursive practices.

If pragmatic historicism seeks a modified, more materialist view of language it also suggests that our views of culture require revision along these same lines. As this essay has posited, historicists generally have emphasized, along with the importance of language, the significance of culture as the arena within which human meaning is constructed and conveyed. Pragmatic historicism maintains the importance of culture but insists that it must not be interpreted as a separate sphere of symbols and ideas linked primarily to one another. It, like language, is part and parcel of other processes.

Moreover, pragmatic historicism suggests that while language should be viewed as part of culture, culture is not just linguistic in nature. This point is significant because often, in the contemporary context, language and especially texts have been invoked as the models for interpreting all human practices. When this is the case, exegesis and textual hermeneutics become the preferred method for approaching not only beliefs and symbols but nondiscursive practices as well. This model has certainly yielded many insights, especially in contexts such as the so-called "book-based" traditions and cultures of Christianity, Judaism and Islam. But this approach has also limited our investigations. Historian of religion Lawrence Sullivan, in a 1990 challenge to the "primacy of the text" as a model for cultural investigations, argues that the fixation on textual metaphors and methods misses the reality that "the religious conditions of humanity lie largely beyond the sacrality of scripture" (Sullivan 1990, 45). The proposal under consideration here takes such insight seriously, contending not only that the dialectic between linguistic expressions and non-discursive practices must be traced but also that our view of tradition pushes us beyond the merely textual and linguistic to explore other modalities of human meaning, intelligibility and intentionality, including those expressed in ritual and art.

Also implied in these assertions that beliefs, symbols and texts are embedded in broader social and cultural institutions, including political and economic networks, and that traditions are not exhausted by their textual and linguistic productions, is what might be termed the democratization of tradition and culture. In this view it is no longer adequate to focus only on the formalized doctrines of a tradition, its prevailing symbols, its recognized classics or even its dominant rituals and practices. Instead our theological reach must extend to consideration of and engagement with the worldviews, beliefs, symbols and practices of ordinary persons who, far from being passive recipients of the construction of value and meaning by those more powerful, are significant contributors to and conveyers of the traditions within which they reside. But if pragmatic historicism argues for the rehabilitation of the ordinary, resisting the long standing theological tendency to attend to and valorize the views and practices of the powerful, it also urges that we avoid the temptation to romanticize popular culture and religion as inherently oppositional and self-evidently more liberatory and valuable. In this view, the value and significance of all human efforts can only be judged in concrete contexts and cannot claim an automatic status applicable either in all contexts or apart from every historical milieu. As has been argued throughout this essay, human beliefs and practices lack essences that characterize them in all times and places; they are historical realities that can only be understood and evaluated concretely in their particular situations. Such specificity applies to popular movements, rituals, convictions and beliefs no less than to those of elites.

This historicist insistence that human efforts can only be evaluated concretely and "on site" entails for theology in this mode the conviction that it is, in the end, pragmatic norms developed in every present, localized setting that determine the viability and adequacy of theological practices and construals of reality. There can be no appeal to some ahistorical source of truth, for there are none; nor to a historical artifact arbitrarily elevated. Neither can a clear, ever present norm be discerned in the welter of our historical inheritance, but only a multiplicity of options awaiting our evaluation. Hence this form of theology pushes us to the present as the site of our normative decisions, as we appropriate our heritages and reconstruct them for today. However, the move to the present as the locale of normative decision-making only begins the discussion of what norms, in what contexts, should be invoked. This historicization of norms raises the specter of Balkanized communities, groups and individuals, each asserting the validity of their particular claims with little way to adjudicate among those claims except the rule of power. A fully elaborated pragmatic historicism requires sustained attention to these questions and to whether any pragmatic norms can be articulated that apply generally to human communities or whether our norms are always so context specific that nothing can be said apart from a particular setting.

And finally, it must be stated that the historicist proposal developed in this essay, with its orientation toward the concrete particularities of diverse traditions, strongly suggests that the traditional conversational partners of at least Christian theology—philosophy and biblical studies—are no longer adequate. Neither gives us material access to or conceptual tools for accessing the vast mosaic of the Christian tradition in its full historical messiness, and neither prepares us to trace the intricacies of other traditions that shape us or the complex contemporary contexts within which we reside. The mode of theology under consideration here increasingly appears as a form of cultural analysis, critique and reconstruction, and as such it seeks conversation with those disciplines and methodologies that will better equip theologians to enter the world of lived beliefs and practices. To that end, pragmatic historicists advocate that theologians attend to the developments in social and cultural theory, the shifting theories of the physical sciences, and developments in history of religions as we forego the quest for timeless truth or an assumed to be adequate past but rather immerse ourselves in the concrete specificities of historical existence. For pragmatic historicists, this is the direction theology must pursue if it is to be a viable voice on the current cultural scene.

REFERENCES

Brown, Delwin. 1994. *Boundaries of Our Habitations: Tradition and Theological Construction*. Albany: State University of New York Press.

————. Lecture, University of Colorado, May 1995. "Refashioning Self and Other: Theology, Academy, and the New Ethnography."

Kaufman, Gordon D. 1993. *The Theological Imagination: Constructing the Concept of God*. Philadelphia: The Westminster Press.

————. 1993. *In Face of Mystery: A Constructive Theology*. Cambridge, MA: Harvard University Press.

Lindbeck, George A. 1984. *The Nature of Doctrine: Religion and Theology in a Postliberal Age*. Philadelphia: The Westminster Press.

Novick, Peter. 1988. *That Noble Dream: The 'Objectivity Question' and the American Historical Profession*. Cambridge MA: Harvard University Press.

Sullivan, Lawrence. 1990. "'Seeking an End to the Primary Text' or 'Putting an End to the Text as Primary'." In *Beyond the Classics*, ed. Frank E. Reynolds and Sheryl L. Burkhalter. Atlanta, GA: Scholars Press.

Tracy, David. 1975. *Blessed Rage for Order: The New Pluralism in Theology*. Minneapolis: The Winston-Seabury Press.

————. 1988. *The Analogical Imagination: Christian Theology and the Culture of Pluralism*. New York: Crossroad Publishing Co.

————. 1987. *Plurality and Ambiguity: Hermeneutics, Religion, Hope*. San Franciso: Harper.

TOWARD A MATERIALIST CHRISTIAN SOCIAL CRITICISM:

ACCOMMODATION AND CULTURE RECONSIDERED

Mary McClintock Fulkerson

What does it mean to engage in social criticism as a Christian? Does it look like the aggressive anti-culture posture of the Christian right, which sees a corrupting culture of "secular humanism" as the enemy of a tightly defined Christian identity? Or does social criticism mean venturing radical critiques of the militarism, heterosexism, and patriarchal and racialized class system in the social formation of post-industrial capitalism? In the first view, the problem is "outside" Christian identity. In the second, characteristic of feminist, womanist and other North American varieties of liberation theology, the problematic "isms" are part of oppressive cultures found in Christian and secular social space alike. A third view has it that social criticism requires the claim of a distinctive Christian culture, of a Christian identity that clarifies itself against other secular distorting cultures. This postliberal theological position is more moderate than the first and open to insights of the second.

In a time when the deep fractures of race, gender and class still permeate the social whole and reproduce interpersonal forms of brokenness, my *own* position is that faithful Christian social criticism resists and transforms these corrupted social relations out of commitment to a vision of God's realm as just and agapic.[1] Thus, I reject outright the right's approach with its inability to think about salvation as social liberation and opt for a liberation approach. The more moderate view of social criticism implied by postliberalism, however, has yet to be assessed with care with regard to the crucial question of culture in Christian social criticism. I assume that the way a position understands culture is at least as important as how it envisions God's end for the Christian life. In this paper I will illustrate the import of culture theory by assessing versions of these positions in light of a liberationist account of theological social criticism and argue for a materialist theory of culture.

SETTING THE TERMS OF THE PROBLEM

It is not immediately obvious that culture is a key concept in theological thinking about social criticism in part because it is a remarkably slippery notion in contemporary writing. When it is not simply taken for granted, culture can refer to "society," civilization, or the so-called "fine arts" and literature as it does in the thinking of Paul Tillich or Nathan Scott, to name a few. Theologians less interested in the "elite" sense of culture are likely to reflect H. Richard Niebuhr's definition, where it is the worldview, beliefs, and practices of a society—"that total process of human activity and that total result of such activity," sometimes called "civilization" (Niebuhr 1951, 32). Not only is culture frequently undefined, but the most common definitions lack the capacity for making critical distinctions between beliefs and practices necessary to theological social criticism. Liberation theologies are incompatible with a definition of culture as the elite products of society, because they focus on the practices of the marginalized and thus must attend to folk culture.[2] The definition of culture as worldview is no better for liberation thinking, for its focus on the oppressed would translate simply into valorization of the worldview of the marginalized.

Emerging as they do from the "experience" of marginalized persons, liberation theologies further complicate the question of culture because they are coded in the discourse of ordinary life, not the official discourse of theology. This means that an account of Christian identity, the other common term commonly linked with culture in framing of social criticism, will be inextricable from the discourses most call "culture." To make distinctions more difficult, liberationists judge that oppression resides in Christian and "secular" discourses alike. Consequently a critical vantage against oppression can be located neither inside nor outside Christian community.

I interpret these difficulties to suggest that a proper frame for liberation criticism cannot simply pose culture and Christian identity as oppositional terms. Neither can be treated as formally immune to alterations of meaning that occur with time and place. To move toward an account that can, we must clarify what is meant by "culture" so that it is possible both to be "in" culture and "against" it and take seriously the enormity of the sinful patriarchal, racial and class hegemonies in contemporary North America— that is, to practice critical transformative faith. For this we need a more complex frame than that offered by the terms "culture" and "Christian identity."

In addition to exposing the problems of this frame as they occur in theologies illustrative of prominent frames for criticism, in this essay I will sketch the outlines of a more complex frame. I offer this as a contribution to liberation thinking about culture and criticism by commending the insights of Raymond Williams, British activist and proponent of a materialist theory of culture.

CULTURE: CORRUPT OUTSIDE OR REDEEMED INSIDE?

I begin with a look at two examples of theological social criticism which are framed in terms of Christian faith in relation to culture. The discourse of faith and culture is a way of thinking about Christian social postures that was popularized in this century by theologian H. Richard Niebuhr in his classic typology *Christ and Culture*. In this discourse "culture" is used by Christians to create a discourse about themselves in relation to the "outside" world and to criticize that outside. The normative referent for such discourse is Christian "identity," for the forging of a notion of the "outside" is always done in some relation to an account of who "we" are as Christians. In Niebuhr's terms the ideal Christian identity (signified by "Christ") is thus positioned relative to "culture" in a variety of ways: "against," "of" (or accommodated to), "above," "in paradox," or "transforming."

Two recent theological critiques have responded to the ills of the late twentieth century with a renewed emphasis on Christian identity, insisting that the strongest response to contemporary sin is a clarification of identity that will create an over-against posture. Framing social criticism in language about culture and Christian identity, these positions are not interesting for the different Niebuhrian types they represent, as I shall argue, but for what they share. Criticism of the "outside" emerges for these views around feminist issues, and I will take them up at this point to suggest how other liberation theologies might proceed.

The anti-feminist theologies that construe Christian faith and culture as distinguishable things interpret feminism as the incursion of a corrupting secular culture—an "outside"—that distorts the truth of faith. For these thinkers culture is corrosive and anti-Christian. It has a distorting effect on theology because it substitutes the "interests and values" and the "agendas" of the secular world for the interests of the gospel. Such thinking follows the terms of criticism offered by a Barthian reading of nineteenth-century liberalism. There the discourse of faith and culture (the church and culture, or Christ and culture) brings together two antithetical terms that need to be related. Culture is the dangerous term in the twosome, threatening to distort faith by imposing the agendas of a secular society that override the theological authorities of Christian faith. To be properly critical is to avoid being accommodated to culture, to resist succumbing to culture-Protestantism. Niebuhr calls this view, "Christ *of*" or *accommodated* to culture.

A recent critic of feminist theology, Leslie Zeigler, frames social criticism in this manner. He begins with Peter Berger's judgment that American

Protestant Christianity has "become a cultural religion" that basically serves to legitimate "the American way of life (Zeigler 1992, 315)." Zeigler then extends this diagnosis to feminist theologies: such a secularized Protestantism is the perfect setting for the agendas of feminists, to "legitimat[e] the interests and values of its culture," as he puts it (Zeigler 1992, 315-17). For those who find feminism antithetical to Christianity, this is the worst version of cultural accommodation. Feminist theology represents cultural religion of such a bad sort that it forces the choice of his title, "Christianity *or* Feminism?" (Zeigler 1992)

"Culture" on this first view is the signifier for the world as blinded and corrupt. The feminist renamings of God, found in alterations of the trinitarian formula "Father, Son and Holy Ghost" to more "inclusive" gendered forms—"Creator, Redeemer, Sustainer," or Mother-God—are denials of the particularities of the biblical revelation. As Elizabeth Achtemeier says, "the Bible's language for God is masculine, a unique revelation of God in the world" (Achtemeier 1992, 8). The feminization of deity is thus interpreted by Achtemeier and others as an example of cultural collapses of the divine and creation, collapses which underwrite the meaninglessness of life.

A second theological use of "culture" maintains a critical theological posture, but "culture" becomes the favored term. Postliberal theology uses culture to refer to what is distinctive about Christian faith to correct increasingly implausible propositional accounts of Christian doctrinal truth. In the place of a fixed view of biblical or doctrinal statements, postliberal theology solidifies Christian identity by defining it with grammar–like rules that form a cultural-linguistic community. Christianity itself is a distinctive culture, or cultural-linguistic system. For postliberal George Lindbeck the concept of culture serves to underwrite the holism of faith. The cultural rules function intrasystemically and thereby protect the particularity of Christian faith from distortion by other "languages." "One can in this outlook no more be religious in general than one can speak language in general" (Lindbeck 1984, 23).

Indebted to Weber, Durkheim, and Mead, Lindbeck's definition of religion as a cultural linguistic phenomenon is aligned with Clifford Geertz's focus on "an analysis of the system of meanings embodied in the symbols which make up the religion proper." The point is to determine the internal meanings of Christian faith before taking up the task of "relating these systems to social-structural and psychological processes," in Geertz' terms (Lindbeck 1984, 27-28). Lindbeck's preference is for a "cultural-linguistic" approach over strictly cultural approaches because of its focus on the "internal logic or grammar of religions."

Influenced by Wittgenstein, Lindbeck maintains that the life-form of Christian faith provides interiorized skills. This means that practices are the

best indicators of the most grammatical "speakers" of the faith. The possibility of judging distortion or "accommodation," however, is based upon a
core biblical narrative. Developed out of dissatisfaction with the frag-
menting effects of historical criticism, the "intratextual" now functions in
postliberal theological work to prioritize (typically) a core grammar or biblical narrative as the "plain sense" of the text. Shaped by this narrative a
Christian form of life should then "absorb" the secular world. Conversely,
the proper order is transgressed and the Christian form of life is accommodated when religion is redescribed or translated into "extrascriptural frameworks," or "popular categories," as opposed to its "intrinsic sense"
(Lindbeck 1984, 124).

On this logic feminist complaints are refusals to accept the cultural
specificity of the core Christian narrative and grammar, the "paradigmatic
biblical narrative" through which God "has disclosed himself." Thus,
postliberal Garrett Green argues that not only do feminist sympathizers use
a deeply flawed "view of human language and imagination" (Green 1992,
44), they also fail to see that "father" and other vestiges of patriarchal society are not the point. The narrative of the savior Jesus is the point. "Just as
words have definitions but no meaning until they are used by people speaking in sentences, so the specifics of culture—the Jewish man Jesus, or the
Roman practice of capital punishment by crucifixion—have no meaning
apart from the narrative of which they are constituents." That Judea was a
patriarchal society is "a cultural-historical fact." Once put back in this narrative, its male-valorizing effects (presumably) disappear (Green 1992, 63).[3]

Accommodation happens for a postliberal when theology learns its
doctrine of God from "the mores of secular culture-[or] from egalitarian lib-
eral-democratic culture." The error of feminist thinking is "to assume that
the cultural language of the story rather than the narrative depiction of the
protagonist is the theologically normative content." In other words, a logic
or syntax is the most important point of the gospel, and feminists have
missed this by focusing on the details (Green 1992, 56, 58-60).

On the basis of a liberation view, I can easily dispense with my first example of theological criticism where culture is the bad "outside," because
this view is unable to acknowledge that discourses are impacted by time and
place. Christian identity is guaranteed because in such views as Zeigler's and
Achtemeier's its meaning never changes: the signifiers of biblical and doctrinal texts are fixed to their signifieds and referents. We might say that on this
account Christian meaning is autonomous. On its terms of criticism, the
emergence of liberation thinking in the form of ordinary discourse—like
that of a feminist Christian—brings with it views that are "outside," and
threaten distortion. My second example of social criticism, theological

postliberalism, is more complex. Its insistence that cultural linguistic practice is the form identity takes is an improvement over the notion that identity is propositional—a fixed term from which to deploy criticism. For postliberals, there is an "unfixing" of the signifiers of faith's identity, which will link up with different signifieds or "worldviews." A life-form and its ordering syntax is always implicated in the discourses of its age, thus cannot be completely autonomous. What matters is "equivalent consequences," as Lindbeck puts it (Lindbeck 1984, 82-83, 93). Although the desire for "equivalent" is problematic, this at least suggests that location might register on "inside" and "outside" alike. Green's point is well taken: it is how a cultural particular is used in the story that is most important (Green 1992, 63).

Despite what appear to be variant uses of "culture," however, these cases have more in common than not. Culture, whether bad "outside" or distinctive "inside," is a worldview in both of these theological frames. It can be normatively defined prior to consideration of the socio-cultural and economic situation. One assumes that a Christian worldview in the Middle Ages or a late-twentieth-century Western worldview would operate in parallel isolation from the power arrangements of their respective social formations, unaffected by feudal arrangements or democratic capitalism. That is, in these models religious belief and judgment occur apart from politics or the economy, and their impact on the culture or "worldview."[4] It follows that an account of Christian identity is itself an autonomous sphere of practice or discourse, unrelated to economic and political process. To see why such a view is problematic we must turn to an account of the social whole as social formation in the tradition of Raymond Williams' cultural materialism.

CULTURE IS ORDINARY—AND POLITICAL AND ECONOMIC, TOO

The work of British activist-intellectual Raymond Williams has been groundbreaking for cultural studies.[5] He was one of the first figures to theorize the effects of twentieth-century capitalism and democracy on Western culture and counter the tradition of Matthew Arnold that defined culture as "the great literature" and art of a society—so-called "high culture." His claim that "culture is ordinary" influenced a move to popular culture (Williams 1989, 3-18). Focusing on the British working class, Williams inspired investigations of working class, feminist and black culture. This fact alone makes him important for liberation theology. The term "culture" has undergone important changes as a result of modernity, Williams tells us. Prior to the eighteenth century it referred to a *process*—one cultured something, such as animals or crops. The term only comes to mean some *thing* that can be defined by values, beliefs, arts, or literatures with the emergence of Western modernity. In some ways, the modern notion of "culture" refers to the development of "civil society" or that part of a social formation that gives social life some reality apart from the political.[6] Its modern valence emerged with a search for ways to speak of developed states of social organization, progress in contrast to barbarism, the development of values, and resulting institutional products. Thus culture has a complex (sometimes confused) relation to the nouns "civilization" and "society." Contrasted with nature by Romanticism, the notion of culture was also expanded to include folk-cultures. Most importantly, it became a critical term in the protest against the perceived inhumanity of industrialism, gradually taking on the sense of the very best products of a society in the work of British thinker Matthew Arnold. In these developments we see different dimensions of what Williams calls the "basic element" of the modern notion of culture, "its effort at total qualitative assessment" (Williams 1983, 295).

By the nineteenth century, Williams shows us, the modern Western project of assessment is found in three broad definitions of culture. Culture is an abstract noun that refers to "a general process of intellectual, spiritual and aesthetic development," the influence of eighteenth-century usage; a whole "way of life," be it a specific community, a historical period, or a universal way of being—a view characteristic of modern social sciences; the products of a society that display intellectual and aesthetic values—music, theater, film, literature, the plastic arts. All together these definitions combine the facilities of communities for certain kinds of processes with the actual products of those processes (Williams 1977, 11-20).[7] The notion of culture thus becomes a tool for historical description and offers an angle from which normative judgments can be made.

While Williams respects the function of culture as critique, he makes two crucial changes in the definition, arguing that culture theory has to start from the recognition that culture and its normative function are ordinary. His commitment to the value of his own working class background led to his insistence that culture represents a "whole way of life, material, intellectual and spiritual" that refuses any diminished sense of culture as "elite" creation. (Williams 1989) Williams also alters the modern view by insisting that culture is material, that is, inherently connected to the social relations and to the forces of production and politics that constitute those relations. His groundbreaking proposal for "cultural materialism" results in "a theory of culture as a (social and material) productive process and of specific practices, of 'arts,' as social uses of material means of production (from language as material 'practical consciousness' to the specific technologies of writing and forms of writing, through to mechanical and electronic communications systems)" (Williams 1980, 243, 233-251.) The modern concept of culture as a "way of life" is thus corrected to register essential elements of human sociality, human labor and its social arrangements, elements that have changed dramatically with the shift to modern industrial capitalism.

Theorists of modernity typically say that one of its defining features is the differentiation of reality into separate, autonomous spheres (such as the aesthetic, moral, and theoretical) that operate as self-legislating realities. Williams' materialism criticizes such differentiation and autonomy by insisting that there is a relation between a notion of culture and the radical changes in the organization of human labor. Thus capitalism has altered human relations and the way in which values are constituted. The accompanying dichotomization of material and intellectual/spiritual is found in orthodox Marxist as well as modernist accounts (Williams 1977, 18-19).[8] A more accurate perception of how deeply capitalism has penetrated into twentieth-century social experience suggests that a theory that reproduces such splits between material and ideal is not simply inaccurate but dangerous. Modern notions that culture is the highest ideas, artifacts or worldview of a society that can be abstracted from material relations are just such a dangerous development.

Williams' alternative materialist theory of culture corrects the ideal/material dichotomy along with theories of autonomous spheres. Rather than a fixed entity comprised of separate realms, he understands the social as a *formation* consisting of a process of intersecting forces—the political (or the state), the economic (the mode of production), and culture (or civil society, the ways or ordering lived experience through activities such as education, religion, art and literature). Because the social is a living formation—a totality—no one "piece" has a unilateral force on this whole, but each operates in mutual relations with other forces, exerting pressures and creating constraints and conditions.[9] The notion that the economy directs or determines the rest of the social formation is as false to that living whole as is the notion that ideas control it. Although each may be treated in isolation for analytical purposes, the cultural is the economic which is also the political, in Williams' account. Culture, then, may function as a source of criticism, but it is material, that is, constrained by the social relations that result from late-twentieth-century capitalism and liberal democracy.

CULTURE CRITICISM REVISITED

Williams' cultural materialism helps us think about how the Christian identity-world or "Christ-culture" relation frames theological social criticism. For a Williams-inspired account of the position of the Christian in the world, I propose that we analyze the material nature of culture in terms of our participation in the "imagined community of the nation" (and global neighborhood). This analysis demonstrates that the Christian is herself produced by modern processes in ways that the theological critics have not begun to address. It also reveals the crucial role of desire and its production by social processes. Let me explain.

On Williams' view, the "political" is not simply what pertains to the nation-state and its capacities for legislation and force. It is that, of course, but must be seen also as a culturally produced imaginary world in which the "we" that is the U.S. affectively participate. The "we" is, more precisely, a culturally produced entity that emerges with the modern capitalist era. That "we" is, as Benedict Anderson says, an "imagined community" in the sense that the kinship with the largely anonymous group of people that comprises it is created and sustained not by face-to-face relations but by a consciousness made possible with modernity (Anderson 1991).[10] This sense of "we" came into being with the development of "a new print-mediated public space," as Charles Taylor puts it, that first emerged with the daily newspaper (Taylor 1990, 110).[11] This "we" is a cultural space, but it requires the conditions of capitalist modes of production and dissemination to exist. Thus as *culture* it cannot be understood without consideration of its *political-economic* constitutive elements.

This example of the mutual determination of economics, politics, and culture is suggestive for thinking about the peculiar situatedness of twentieth-century Christian communities. The "imagined community" of the nation conditions contemporary subjects almost prior to their acts of choice or refusal of values. Christians in the United States can hardly avoid being produced as members of "the nation" because even to read the newspaper is to participate in this imagined community. Through these everyday acts we come to exist in a "sociological organism"—the nation—with its own time/space. We are induced into "modern" time/space, moreover. Culturally produced time is empty and calendrical, punctuated by homogenous events which have no connection. They have no connection because the very nature of modern events is to be simultaneous, nonintersecting and without connection to ultimacy or meaning (Anderson 1983, 26). Modern space is desacralized as well; both time and space are only given value through the production of nationalism's memory and place.

Our imagined worlds are populated as well as being spatial and temporal. National "kin" and loyalties are produced by the "deep, horizontal comradeship" that is evoked by being an "American"—although no longer restricted legally to its original population of white, propertied males, this fellowship is much less horizontal-egalitarian than its founding imagery admits. Our imagined community is populated by who counts as "not-kin" or "outsiders"—the "strangers, others, aliens and foreigners"—that make up the different "ethnoscapes" in our imagined worlds.[12] We may wish to value a genocide differently than a Hollywood scandal, but the forces of our cultural production may give these equal news-space (or visual media-space, or cyber-space). We may repudiate xenophobia, but the force of our cultural production subtly reproduces its local forms. As newspaper readers we are induced to imagine against the grain of sacred teleological space/time and kin, and to do so every morning.

To treat culture as material is to recognize that not only the content, but the mode of reproduction of "ideas" is crucial to critical analysis, along with the associated questions of access to production and power. If the delivery of "culture" by capitalism is pervasive and subtle, as the forces of print capitalism suggest, then the over-against posture of theological criticism is misdirected. From the vantage of Williams' materialist account of culture, the theological proposals considered earlier—Christian identity versus culture, and Christian identity *as* culture—actually employ one of the modern notions of culture. To identify culture as the outside and alien agenda of secularism, or "the American way of life," as one theologian did, is to employ the broad definition Williams offers when he says culture is "a whole way of life." (Zeigler 1992, 315). Eschewing the narrowing of culture to the fine arts, those who locate culture outside the church say they are against the whole way of life, material, intellectual and spiritual that is secularism.

Criticism and resistance, on these terms then, take the form of denunciation and repudiation of such ideas as the secular, or the absolute good of the nation, or capitalist greed, or whatever the secular culture offers up. In the case of the first critical model theology marshals all its convictions to resist such false values and loyalties. With regard to feminist theology which it casts as a pernicious "outside," the Christian community refuses the alien ideas and way of life that come with feminism. Commitment to traditional trinitarian language is considered protection from the false gods intimated by female images. The more positive postliberal view of culture as a distinctive Christian way of life makes assumptions about culture that are only slightly improved. A corrective Christian culture works to instill "dispositions" that dissuade one from the distortions of secularism, not simply ideas. Thus the whole self, not simply the cognitive self, is engaged in the resistance. However, both positions assume that Christian discourse and practice can be discussed apart from the social formations of the state, civil society and economy, and its intersection by global capitalism and its cultural formations. Or they assume that Christians can efface or transform the effects of these social forces with their ideas. Either way they fail to take secular culture seriously by treating it as easily defeated ideas/values that function *without the determinations of advanced global capitalism or the political.* As a consequence they *fail to link the channeling of desire (and dispositions) by these omnipresent processes.*[13]

If Williams is correct, the very employment of these modern concepts of culture implicates these theologies in the modern error—a denial of material relations. In contrast, we must frame the unavoidable immersion of Christians in the social formation in terms that recognize this reality. A liberation theology of culture must take seriously the fact that culture is a dynamic and circulating reality in late-twentieth-century global capitalism; it is the production of everyday realities that cannot be escaped. Out of its specificities persons carve out identities and projects. They do not do this as a neutral making of choices, but through a priori cultural meanings that produce desire and pleasure; culture creates the things that matter for subjects—"mattering maps," as Lawrence Grossberg calls them (Grossberg 1992, 82).[14] Such culture is "ordinary," and it is, thanks to the media of late-twentieth-century technologies, everywhere disseminated in ways that confound the boundaries of church, neighborhood and nation. There is no personal identity or commodity that does not have attached to it associations that provoke and channel desire.

To replace the dualities of Christian identity versus culture and Christian culture versus secular culture I propose that theological social criticism think of Christian participation in the imagined worlds that produce subjects in various locations. That way culture's determination by the economic and political can be marked. For the prophetic impulse to criticize—to be "overagainst"—I propose that theology think in terms of the nurture of oppositional structures of feeling, assessed in relation to the dominant cultural formation, my final topic.

IMAGINED COMMUNITIES AND RESISTANCE

I close with a brief consideration of this alternative frame for social criticism. Williams shows us that culture is material and that ours is distinctive to advanced capitalism. From that I have surmised that it is inaccurate to conceptualize the intersection of Christian communities with the social formation in terms of the relation of monolithic block-like realities. Rather, they intersect through the production and reproduction of secular distinctions which channel desire, pleasure and yearning at the level of the everyday. I locate these intersections analytically in the imagined communities in which we are inscribed and the imagined worlds that accompany them.

The effects of late global capitalism have penetrated so completely into the daily practices of life that only an alternative cultural formation can resist, in Williams' view. The ecclesial community that would refuse this racialized, gendered, classist and non-sacred "imagined community" that is our nation can learn from his account. It must conceive resistance to the dominant order by the nurturing of emergent or new forms of life.

To conceptualize that resistance Williams offers a category that corresponds to the lived and living reality of the social formation (and shifts away from the traditional Marxist focus on the state as the autonomous vehicle for social change). "Structures of feeling," the "affective elements of consciousness," are the malleable realities of social experience that locate the opening for alternatives. They lie somewhere between the fixed (and past) social and the "subjective" and, therefore, ephemeral (and present) social. Neither ideology or worldview, on the one hand, nor mere emotional feeling, on the other, this category is "thought as felt and feeling as thought: practical consciousness of a present kind." A structure of feeling locates the desires and lived realities of a social phenomenon. It is something that "might be" in a social formation—a "cultural hypothesis," in Williams' terms (Williams 1977, 132, 128-135).

These "social experiences in solution" indicate the shifting and uneven character of social processes and the non-monolithic character of any dominant order. They also mark the places where new relations may be forged. In order to create long-term effects, structures of feeling must be inscribed and developed in cultural forms. For example, for the new sensibilities of British poets about the relation of poverty to human failings to impact nineteenth-century society, the rigid moral thinking previously connected to poverty had to be broken up by this new structure of feeling and expressed institutionally. In this process, judgments about the relationships of these structures to the wider social formation are determined by their links with the dominant cultural form—capitalism (and its patriarchal, racialized structures as well) (Williams 1977, 134).

Of three possible links to the dominant, Williams says, the least transformative is the *residual*. These are practices which get carried along in a social formation from the past, such as the persistence of rural formations in the capitalist order. They frequently have no effect other than that of supporting the status quo. Linkages for resistance occur when new forms of experience emerge. When a structure of feeling becomes solidified into a new form of social life it is an *emergent*—a new way of linking poverty and urban life with religion, for example, such as the Catholic Worker movement, a new way of envisioning women's capacities with a reinvention of the (previously androcentric) *imago Dei* (Williams 1980). While the relation of a structure of feeling to the dominant can be truly resistant, it can also be deflected. The power of late capitalism to *incorporate* social experiences to its own ends is inordinate.

EMERGENT ECCLESIASTICAL POSSIBILITIES

What will ecclesial resistance look like? Clearly I think it would be an emergent that avoids incorporation as it embodies alternative forms of life. In Williams' terms, we might say that women's longing to be named, to be visible, is a contemporary structure of feeling, a possibility for something transformative. It is determined by links to the dominant gender ideologies and the forces of late capitalism as well, but not necessarily captive to them. Like any other structure of feeling, that longing for the *imago Dei* of women can become accommodated, for example, into the incorporated emergent of "equality for women"—an ideal that assumes that the political is free of the economic. When this happens the ecclesial possibility in the structure of feeling that is women's longing is occluded by its blindness to the racialized and class structures that the global capitalist formation continues to reproduce. Because this ecclesial possibility must appropriate the Christian tradition, which we might think of as a residual, its peculiar challenge is not only to avoid incorporation, but to appropriate the past in ways that confute the status quo, nurturing an emergent residual that can take on solid social forms.

Williams' materialism is suggestive of important clues about Christian social resistance. Postliberals are right that ecclesial criticism happens as communities get dispositions shaped distinctively by Christian stories. However, this is so only insofar as we find syntaxes for solidarity that can work in different imagined worlds. Thus postliberals are wrong to think the directional force is from some fixed narrative out to the world. (The language for solidarity—for "being in the same boat"—will differ for women-church groups and Baptist coalminers, but the syntax must address both.) What cannot be determined in advance if we take cultural materialism seriously is the critical force of a biblical narrative, for imagined communities are already formed by an ethnoscape of Others and corresponding social relations. Theologians inhabit imagined communities, too. Their accounts of the grammar happen *in*, *not outside of*, their cultural production. Theology is culture—determined by and determining of the larger world. As such it can also enable the discernment of real possibilities for more gracious socialities.

Guided by a Jesus narrative with a syntax of solidarity with the Other rather than a postliberal commitment to the "residual" of masculine images in biblical texts about Jesus, Christian social engagement on Williams' model must look for structures of feeling that portend alternatives to the oppressive effects of the imagined community of the nation. That "community" is a false liberal community of "equals" that obscures radical disparities, a homogenized space/time that turns Christian life into subjective "values" and reproduces subtle racial and class loyalties. In relation to it, feminist woman-church liturgy is one such emergent that resists women's "un-marked," denigrated status in the "brotherhood" of the imagined communi-ty of the nation, and not an "accommodation" to secular values. Its regularized worship displays the sacred, telelogical nature of God's time/space and thus resists the secularized commodified time/space of the community of the nation as well.

A materialist theological criticism can nurture this cultural possibility into social forms that resist the reproduction of loyalty to the imagined com-munity of the nation and its gender, class and race blindness. As such, it will confound accommodation by its faithfulness.

REFERENCES

Achtemeier, Elizabeth. 1992. "Exchanging God for 'No Gods': A Discussion of Female Language for God." in *Speaking the Christian God: The Holy Trinity and the Challenge of Feminism*, ed. Alvin F. Kimel, Jr. Grand Rapids, Minn.: William B. Eerdmans Publishers.

Anderson, Benedict. 1991. *Imagined Communities: A Reflection on the Origin and Spread of Nationalism*. London: Verso.

Appadurai, Arjun. 1990. "Disjuncture and Difference in the Global Economy." *Public Culture* 2:1-24.

Asad, Talal. 1993. *Genealogies of Religion: Discipline and Relations of Power in Christianity and Islam*. Baltimore and London: Johns Hopkins University Press.

Candaleria, Michael R. 1990. *Popular Religion and Liberation: The Dilemma of Liberation Theology*. Albany: State University of New York Press.

Chatterjee, Partha. 1990. "A Response to Taylor's 'Modes of Civil Society.'" In *Public Culture* 3:119-132.

Green, Garrett. 1992. "The Gender of God and the Theology of Metaphor." In *Speaking the Christian God: The Holy Trinity and the Challenge of Feminism*, ed. Alvin F. Kimel, Jr. Grand Rapids, Mich.: William B. Eerdmans Publishers.

Grossberg, Lawrence. 1992. *We Gotta Get Out of This Place: Popular Conservatism and Postmodern Culture*. New York: Routledge.

Hoyles, Martin, ed. 1977. *The Politics of Literacy*. London: Writers and Readers Pub. Cooperative Society, Ltd.

Lindbeck, George A. 1984. *The Nature of Doctrine: Religion and Theology in a Postliberal Age*. Philadelphia: Westminster/John Knox Press.

Niebuhr, H. Richard, 1951. *Christ and Culture*. New York: Harper & Row.

Taylor, Charles. 1990. "Modes of Civil Society." *Public Culture* 3:95-118.

Williams, Raymond. 1977. *Marxism and Literature*. Edited by Steven Lukes. Oxford: Oxford University Press.

———. 1980. *Problems in Materialism and Culture: Selected Essays*. London: Verso.

———. 1982. *Sociology of Culture*. New York: Schocken Books.

———. 1983a. *Culture and Society: 1780-1950*. With a new introduction by the author. New York: Columbia University Press. (c. 1958)

———. *Keywords: A Vocabulary of Culture and Society*, revised ed. New York: Oxford University Press. (Originally published London: Fontana Paperbooks, 1976.)

———. 1989. *Resources of Hope: Culture, Democracy, Socialism*. Edited by Robin Gable with an intro-duction by Robin Blackburn. London and New York: Verso.

Ziegler, Leslie. 1992. "Christianity or Feminist?" In *Speaking the Christian God: The Holy Trinity and the Challenge of Feminism*: 313-334. Edited by Alvin F. Kimel, Jr. Grand Rapids, MI: William B. Eerdmans Publishers.

NOTES

1. My own vision is greatly indebted to the work of Fred Herzog, who is one of the first North American liberation theologians, and also an incomparable example of faithfulness, a friend, and my favorite "next-door neighbor." I dedicate this essay to his memory.

2. For a discussion of popular culture and its various effects, see *Popular Religion and Liberation: The dilemma of Liberation Theology* (Albany: State University of New York Press, 1990) Candeleria 1990. The shift to explicit popular culture is occurring in liberation theologies in the United States, particularly in African-American writing.

3. According to Green the meaning emerges from "the use to which the cultural particular is put in the narrative."

4. For a critique of Geertz along these lines see Talal Asad (Asad 1993, 27-54).

5. Williams was the most important twentieth century British theorist of culture. He influenced Edward Said, Stuart Hall, Terry Eagleton, and the Centre for Contemporary Cultural Studies at the Univesity of Birmingham. Influenced by Marx, Lukacs, Gramsci and Goldmann, he expanded Marxist cultural theory and the work of the British left.

6. For a helpful overview of the concept of "civil society" see Charles Taylor, "Modes of Civil Society," *Public Culture* 3:1 (Fall, 1990), 95-118. For the addition of "the story of capital" see Partha Chatterjee, "A Response to Taylor's 'Modes of Civil Society.'" In *Public Culture* 3:1 (Fall, 1990), 119-132.

7. See also Williams' *Culture and Society: 1780-1950* (New York: Columbia University Press, 1958, 1983), where he makes the connection between the emergence of modern notions of culture in Britain and the Industrial Revolution. His 1983 updated version of these definitions: culture is "a general state or habit of the mind,. . .' 'the general state of intellectual development in a society as a whole,' 'the general body of the arts,' and 'a whole way of life, material, intellectual and spiritual'" *(Culture and Society,* xvi).

8. Williams would say that the reduction of culture in history and cultural studies to signifying or symbolic systems often results in the concealment of the constitutive relation between material and symbolic.

9. For some of Williams' thoughts about models of causality see his entry on "determination" in *Marxism and Literature,* (Williams 1977, 83-97).

10. This is a Williams-inspired analysis that draws upon Anderson's account of the nation as a culturally produced "imagined community" dependent upon the emergence of capitalism.

11. Also see Martin Hoyles, *The Politics of Literacy* (London: Writers and Readers Pub. Cooperative Society, Ltd., 1977).

12. Arjun Appadurai extends Anderson's "imagined communities" to "imagined worlds." He uses ethnoscapes as one of several categories that further specify the landscapes of imagined worlds (Appadurai 1990). See his "Disjuncture and Difference in the Global Cultural Economy," *Public Culture* 2:2 (Spring, 1990):1-24.

13. As Asad says, "the insistence that religion has an autonomous essence—not to be confused with the essence of science, or of politics, or of common sense—invites us to define religion (like any essence) as a transhistorical and transcultural phenomenon..." 28) Using Geertz, he "examine(s) the ways in which the theoretical search for an essence of religion invites us to separate it conceptually from the domain of power." (Asad 28, 29, 32-3).

14. Indebted to Williams, Grossberg is also a critic. He is superb on the role of affect.

TRANSCENDENCE AND MATERIAL CULTURE

David Batstone

> *Sometimes you have to imagine things before they can become real.*
> — Jade Batstone, 4 years old, to her critical materialist father

The resurgence of public interest in spirituality within the post-industrialized society has come as a great surprise to many. Enlightened rationality had delivered its final rites long ago, confident that the spirit had been laid to rest. Secular society was maturing in its self-understanding and self-determination, quite fine absent the superstitions and phantasms of primitive culture.

Not that the spiritualities which are emerging in popular culture are resurrections from sealed tombs. The traditional purveyors of western religion are still mostly dying cults of distant gods and waxen saints. The journalistic penchant to name post-industrial spiritual sensibilities "religious" is commonly met with fervent protest by its practitioners. In the judicious judgment of *Esquire* magazine, "Spirituality is in, religion is out."

That distinction reflects more than a commodification of religious teaching and practice, although it is an unmistakable element of the process. More significantly, it indicates a transformation of the conditions which shaped the formation of cultural identity within an industrial political economy. These emerging social conditions are producing an epistemological watershed in understanding and perception, a revolution of consciousness perhaps as dramatic as that effected by the advent of capitalism itself within the feudal order.

For the last few centuries, what marked religious discourse and practice in Euro-American culture were its contestations over authority and tradition, as well as the separation of the private from the public realm. In a large measure these ideological conflicts were driven by the demand for broader (bourgeois) access to resources and goods. They signified in consciousness what was occurring in dominant culture—the gradual demise of the formal (institutional) center of religious inquiry.

Religion had served to integrate pluralistic social institutions in feudal society; now religion itself became subject to pluralization. In fact, for the emerging mercantile class, cultural identity was at least partially shaped through an economic and political struggle against systems that had been sanctioned by religious institutions. It was in their material interests for the principle of exchange to regulate social relationships, codified in the structures of the modern nation-state. All other subject valuations were best left to the private, individual sphere. With characteristic polemic, Marx described this link in the bourgeois consciousness of economic theory and religious self-understanding:

> *Engels was therefore right to call Adam Smith the Luther of the Political Economy. Just as Luther recognized religion . . . as the substance of the external world and in consequence stood opposed to Catholic paganism—just as he superseded external religiosity by making religiosity the inner substance of man— just as he negated the priests outside the layman because he transplanted the priest into the laymen's heart, just so with wealth. (1970, vol. 3.290)*

It is perhaps this movement toward interiority that was most fundamental to religious consciousness in the dominant sectors of the industrialized society. In its idealized form it freed the subject from the hierarchical externalities of the feudal religious order, setting in motion an inevitable— albeit incomplete—retreat of religion from the public realm. That shift was accompanied by the internalization of moral conscience within the self-identity of the citizen-consumer.

What modernist religious consciousness did not do, by and large, was sever its conceptual relationship to a transcendence 'from beyond.' In many respects, its orientation was framed by many of the same concerns that characterized the quest for transcendence in pre-industrial cultures: (1) In response to the frightening inevitability of death, how is it possible to arrive at a self-understanding and life orientation that reaches beyond this world; (2) In response to the frightening potential of social disorder (not to mention the interest of the temple to control human behavior), where can be found an existential grounding for moral practice?; (3) In response to human vulnerability before the forces of nature, how is it possible to influence or control, befriend or domesticate, co-exist with or coordinate the natural world?; (4) In response to the regenerative production (if not reproductive generation) of centers of dominance, how does one practice effective strategies of resistance and survival?

Religion has been a ready dealer of hope as well, but only as a function of its capacity to provide satisfactory resolutions to the above dilemmas. "Perfect hope casts out fear," promised an early Christian writer, perhaps thereby identifying the primordial ground of the religious experience.

The attempt to signify transcendence with images and figures of language—the project of theology—has lived in a state of perpetual crisis in the industrialized world. Most religious practitioners have had great difficulty sustaining a subjectivity of transcendence whilst their material culture was undergoing perpetual objectification. Once the advancement in the modes of production—both social organization and the tools of technology —made it increasingly untenable to sustain a cosmology of a world beyond, the search for transcendence turned to a depth of meaning in the surfaces of material culture. "God" became the supernatural in the ordinary, the meaning 'under-the-standing,' the critical in the conceptual. That shift in consciousness is reflected in the musings of German theologian Dietrich Bonhoeffer, writing from prison in the middle of the twentieth century: "I should not like to speak of God on the boundaries but at the center, not in weakness but in strength; not at the boundaries or beyond in the midst of life, but in the middle of the village" (1981: 325-6).

It became the task of modernist theology then—with the virtual disappearance of a reality from above and beyond—to find the kernel in the husk, the depth of transcendence in the superficiality of cultural forms. But what happens once the depth flattens, if all that remains are the surfaces?[1] At the dawn of the post-industrial age, there is a heightening suspicion that a superficiality of perception and understanding may be inescapable. Identity increasingly is fashioned in the throes of fragmentary contributions to production, rapidly changing simulations and commodifications of the self, and unending relations of difference.[2]

These changes in the modes of production have had a considerable impact on our social practices and self-understanding. The intent of this essay is to focus particularly on the changing constructs of transcendence within dominant forms of Euro-American consciousness during the development of a capitalist economy. My points of reference for interpreting material culture is the dialectical hermeneutics which has its roots in Hegel, particularly as elaborated by Ludwig Feuerbach and Karl Marx. Perhaps more accurately, I refashion their respective constructs of transcendence as a response to social worlds that were being radically transformed by forces of capital accumulation. In many ways their critiques of existing discourses of transcendence mirrored the broader erosion of ideologies in support of "Old World Europe." For that reason they provide a useful starting point for appreciating the possible impact of current, more technologically advanced modes of production within the North Atlantic economies (and only indirectly the global economy). When the discussion moves at the end of the essay toward emerging constructs of transcendence, it then should be all the more evident why critical materialist readings of consciousness are giving way to diacritical ones that are embedded in complex relationality.

This essay, then, is a beginning attempt to reconstruct a language of transcendence by sketching a cartography of its historical relationship to the dynamic modes of production in modern Euro-American society. A descriptive treatment of the multiplicity of spiritualities that are finding expression in recent times, and of the diversity of their practice, is beyond the scope of this essay. All the same, I will argue that it is the quality of their plurality and difference which indicates the uniqueness of the milieu within which they are presently taking form.

TRACING THE SPIRIT INTO MODERNITY

Feuerbach's work in the middle of the nineteenth century marked an important turn in speculative metaphysics. He laid the foundation for a hermeneutics of suspicion, particularly suspicious that rational religion is inescapably a signification of material culture. Feuerbach was at one and the same time a disciple and a critic of Hegel. He admired Hegel's efforts to reconcile spirit and nature, philosophy and history, rationality and religion. But he found it untenable that human consciousness might arrive at an objective understanding of the divine Spirit (Geist) by deducing its progressive self-realization within culture.

The Christian concept of incarnation was central to Hegel's ontology, of course. The Spirit/Idea undergoes externalization and alienation—that is, incarnation—in material culture so that it may return eventually to full self-consciousness. For Hegel, everything that exists is a dialectical moment in the unfolding of divine consciousness.

The Idea is essentially a process, because its identity is the absolute and free identity of the notion, only in so far as it is absolute negativity and for that reason dialectical. It is the round of movement, in which the notion, in the capacity of universality which is individuality, gives itself the character of objectivity and of the antithesis thereto; and this externality which has the notion for its substance finds its way back to subjectivity through its immanent dialectic (Hegel 1975, 278).

Hegel argued that religion is ever reflective of this movement, though in the form of representation. On the one hand, its rituals, teachings and doctrines are an evolving expression of "the Divine Being as It empties Itself and is made flesh" (1974, 776). These forms of religious expression remain alien to their practioners, on the other hand, until their existence is understood rationally as a momentary stage in the progression of Spirit. All the same, Hegel viewed every stage of religious development as a "necessary" moment in human consciousness of this transcendent movement.

The Spirit was for Hegel no flight of fancy; to the contrary, the Idea is already embodied in space and time. "What is reasonable is actual, what is actual is reasonable" (1975, 9, n.4). By this he did not intend to suggest that all forms and constructs of the Spirit are of equal maturity, but that rational discernment yields those aspects which embody immanent reason—that is, the manifestation of the Idea at a particular stage—and those which contradict it. God is present in the world, in the actual, recognizing Self through human subjectivity, until "[God] surrenders again His immediate existence, and returns to His essential Being" (1974, 776).

Hegel signified transcendence, then, in the unfolding of human activity. It must not be overlooked that he was living in Central Europe during a time of transition from a feudal social order to one mediated by a craft economy. It is therefore significant that he located creative consciousness—which he understood as participation in transcendence—in the self-understanding of a producer who is embedded in material culture. The producer then no longer merely finds glory in fulfilling the obligations to the lord/Lord of the earth, but becomes subjectively aware of his or her own creative power. The subject becomes as the subject acts.

It is Hegel's genius that he intuitively recognized the potential objectification of human subjectivity once a "spiritual" relationship to its embodiment was lost (a dynamic worked out more explicitly by Marx, of course). He feared that the rationalist construct of enlightenment discourse—which in his opinion practically divorced culture from spirit—would result inevitably in the alienation of the subject itself. For that reason, he inextricably linked event to process, identity to difference, substance to relation, praxis to theory, and subject to transcendence.

Feuerbach sought to turn Hegel's system on its head, though it was Marx who claimed to have finished the task. In place of interpreting the movement of culture as the incarnation of Spirit, Feuerbach relocated the dialectic within human consciousness itself. His hermeneutic was laid out most comprehensively in his seminal work, *The Essence of Christianity*: "Man—this is the mystery of religion—projects his being into objectivity, and then again makes himself an object of this projected image of himself, thus converted into a subject" (1957, 29-30).

What Hegel devised as theology, Feuerbach converted into anthropology. He argued that the Mind (Geist) out of which flows all Hegelian existence is itself a product of the mind (geist) of human imagination. Embodiment is not generated by thought, but thought from embodiment.

In Feuerbach's anthropology, what distinguishes the human species is its capacity to think of itself as "at once I and thou," that is, as what it is and what it might become (1957, 2). Human imagination is capable of idealizing the possibilities of understanding and action well beyond its present capacities and limitations. In the process of coming to self-consciousness, then, the human subject objectifies its "thou" as a means of expressing and measuring its own knowledge of itself.

Feuerbach interpreted the religious enterprise as the unfolding of transcendence in material culture, that is, as an intuitive sense of the actual which passes beyond the limits of one's own rationality. While it is often assumed that the ultimate concern of religion is the being or non-being of God, Feuerbach reoriented it toward the being or non-being of the human species (1846, xiv-v).[3]

His critique was in many respects an effort to wrestle the identity of consciousness away from the aristocratic control of its codification. The feudal society relied on fixed concentrations of resources and labor, supported by institutions whose authority to regulate social behavior was grounded in their mediation of the transcendent. Time and space remained static in that social world because that world was sacred; to violate that order, and the sanctity of its tradition, was nothing short of profanity. In this context, Feuerbach's location of transcendence *within* consciousness is quite radical, for it implies a desacralizing of sacred space and a delegitimizing of the cosmic foundations for social organization. Within the organic ontology of Hegel's system, on the other hand, everything is reconcilable. State and religious institutions are understood not merely as contingent, historical entities, but as intrinsic expressions of the reconciled Idea. Hence, in his "philosophy of right" Hegel did not "attempt to construct a state as it ought to be. . . . It can only show how the state, the ethical universe, is to be understood" (1967, 11, n.9). For that reason, however much he hoped to present the movement of culture as "the progress of the consciousness of Freedom" (1900, 19, n.7), his constructs often lend a conserving ethos to existing social relations.

Feuerbach internalized the dialectic, thereby diminishing the external (institutional) mediation of meaning and moral order; so religion turns into an illusion whenever the Spirit takes on an objectivity external to human consciousness. Once that occurs, human longings, ideals and desires are personified in a divine Subject, which, once reified, acts back on its creators to control and govern their lives. The will of God even becomes disassociated from humanity's own interests. The object becomes Subject, while the actual subject becomes an object. The human self, thus estranged from itself, loses a sense of its own value and significance.[4]

Regaining a unity of consciousness—an act to which he applies the religious term redemption—means recuperating those ideals which have been projected as divine attributes. Feuerbach the Christian thus finds idealized in the cross of Christ the highest realization of the possibilities of human love.

> God suffers—suffering is the predicate—but for men, for others, not for himself. What does this mean in plain speech? Nothing else than this: to suffer for others is divine, he who suffers for others, who lays down his life for them, acts divinely, is a God to man (1957, 60, n.6).

True religious sentiment, free from illusion, is for Feuerbach nothing more than faith invested in those ideals—such as love, wisdom, justice—which have reached sedimentation in the collective mind (geist) of human culture. The essence of religion (Christianity) is not an error, but a reversal. It is in the worship of its ideals that believers unconsciously seek to declare their ultimate value. The enduring and essential truth of those aims are best known "in the sense of reason, in the sense of the universal, the only true love" (1957, 64). Transcendence emerges in the coming-to-itself of human consciousness.

At first, it seems ironic that Feuerbach ends up just about where Hegel left off: "What is reasonable is actual, what is actual is reasonable." On further reflection, however, it is not all that surprising since Feuerbach's projection is not a reversal in the production of consciousness per se, but is merely a reversal within the Hegelian system itself. It is still consciousness that generates material culture (and its activities), not material culture (and its activities) which generates consciousness.

Though Feuerbach claimed to "found [his] ideas on materials which can be appropriated only through the activity of the senses,"[5] there is every indication that his appreciation for cultural production nonetheless rests distinctively in the idealist tradition.[6] In fact, in the outworking of his method he rarely explored the dynamic flow of social organization and cultural reproduction as a means of interpreting "the life of the human species."

To be fair to Feuerbach, on occasion he did suggest that divine attributes might correspond to particular cultural exigencies. For example, "physical strength is an attribute of the Homeric gods: Zeus is the strongest of the gods. Why? Because physical strength, in and by itself, was regarded as something glorious, divine. To the ancient Germans, the highest virtues were those of the warrior; therefore their supreme god was the god of war, Odin. . . . Not the attributes of the divinity, but the divineness of the deity of the attributes is the first true Divine Being" (1957, 21, n.1).

But from such a specific case he deduces the projection of the will-to-power in religion *sui generis*, virtually ignoring the particular ways that these images simulate their own cultural space. It would seem consistent with his hermeneutic to ask whom the primary weavers of these myths were and how they were disseminated among the populace, as well as to explore the presence of alternative and/or conflicting images within the culture and the site of their production.

It is both the promise and disappointment of Feuerbach's work that, in while he recognizes the signifying that takes in religious imagery, he places it an autonomous relationship to material culture. Marx was soon to name that estrangement: "As far as Feuerbach is a materialist he does not deal with history, and as far as he considers history he is not a materialist" (1970, vol. 5:41). All the same, he was to utilize Feuerbach's hermeneutic as a launching point from which to interpret not only religion, but all cultural production.

MARX, TRANSCENDENCE, AND FETISHISM

While the projection of the self was for Feuerbach a gateway to the mystery of transcendence, for Marx it was the primary source of false consciousness:

> Man, who looked for a superhuman being in the fantastic reality of heaven and found nothing there but the reflection of himself, will no longer be disposed to find but the semblance of himself, only an inhuman being, where he seeks and must seek his true reality (1970, vol. 3:175).[7]

In Marx's early writings, however, the extent of his break from Feuerbach is not apparent. To the contrary, he hailed Feuerbach's reversal of subject and predicate as a masterful key to interpret the illusion of consciousness, whether in religion or the political economy. "Just as it is not religion which creates man but man who creates religion, so it is not the constitution which creates the people but the people who create the constitution" (1970, vol. 3:29).

Marx found embedded in consciousness a host of objectifications which, once projected, gain an autonomous existence, returning to make objects of those whom it now governs. In the instance of the state, its constitution exercises powers of eminent domain over its citizens irrespective of the degree of justice which it achieves. The value and rights of the citizen then are determined by the application of constitution/law, not by the citizen's inherent status as a member in the community and the justice one is thereby due (1970, vol. 3:77).

Marx identified this reversal—which he later named "fetishism"[8]—in the division of labor as well, and once again he drew a parallel to the false consciousness that emanates from religion:

> *It is clear that the more the worker spends himself, the more*
> *powerful becomes the alien world of objects which he creates*
> *over against himself, the poorer he himself—his inner world—*
> *becomes, the less belongs to him as his own. It is the same in re-*
> *ligion. The more man puts into God, the less he retains in*
> *himself (1970, vol. 3:72).*

Marx argued that within the capitalist system workers have the fruit of their labor taken from them as soon as it becomes a commodity, or more specifically, when their use value becomes subordinate to their abstract equivalence. Productivity is in real terms transformed into the private property of another, yet this expropriation is ideologically validated as the natural law of the market. As a result, for the majority of people the most fundamental exercise of human creativity—labor—turns into little more than a means to satisfy basic needs:

> *Just as in religion the spontaneous activity of human imagi-*
> *nation, of the human brain and the human heart, operates on*
> *the individual independently of him—that is, it operates as an*
> *alien, divine, or diabolical activity—so is the worker's activity*
> *not his spontaneous activity. It belongs to another; it is his loss*
> *of self. (1970, vol. 3: 274)*

Marx is well-known for his criticism of religion, though often his reasons are misrepresented. He was primarily interested in exposing the cultural forms that function to commodify and take ownership of the "spontaneous activity" of other human subjects. That is why he found Feuerbach's hermeneutic so useful, since it demonstrated how extensively religious ideas, concepts, and images had been manipulated to represent a false consciousness of human experience so as to reinforce and justify the separation between creativity and creator.

It was also the reason Marx eventually found Feuerbach's hermeneutic inadequate. Though Feuerbach aimed to sustain the Hegelian immanence of spirit within material culture, he did so through the abstraction and autonomy of consciousness. Marx argued that autonomy so conceived was yet another illusion, for the sole reason that it did not reflect the actual nature of human activity: "The essence of man is no abstraction inherent in each single individual. In its reality it is the ensemble of social relations" (1970, vol. 5:4).

Marx was convinced that the truth of reality did not exist independently, accessible to pure reason. He contended that it only arose from critical reflection on actual human activities and the socio-economic structures which condition their relations. In brief, productive forces produce certain social relations, in the context of which ideas arise.[9]

In his own time he witnessed the rapid industrialization of the craft economy, a movement that meant a radical shift in the modes of production, particularly labor. Products and tasks became increasingly more standardized so that workers as well as mechanical parts could become interchangeable pieces in factory production. This movement toward mass production was reflected in the abstraction and "de-particularization" (even if coded as "universalization") of social location and consciousness. As Marx realized, at a relatively early stage in industrial development, its economy relied extensively on "a continual movement of growth in productive forces, of destruction in social relations, of formation in ideas; the only immutable thing is the abstraction of movement" (1970, vol. 6:166).[10]

It is remarkable to note the extent to which this "abstraction of movement" has progressed at the present time. I recently led a series of workshops for sixty graduate students from Stanford University, and the University of California at San Francisco and at Berkeley. The students, all practicing Christians, were interested in exploring the place of religion in culture.

The majority of them spoke of their disillusionment with the institutional church and confessed that they no longer considered it a relevant place to explore spirituality. Those who did attend a weekly religious meeting were attracted to groups with informal membership boundaries and a non-dogmatic approach to belief. By and large, historic traditions within the Christian family—e.g., Baptist, Lutheran, Roman Catholic—held little significance for them.

In the first workshop we identified their social location. Nearly all came from white, middle-class families. Now aged in their late twenties to late thirties, only a handful had grown up in Northern California; the rest had relocated to study at the various universities. Few anticipated returning to their hometowns after graduation; they "would go wherever the jobs are." Most of the students were pursuing a graduate degree in computer technology, biochemistry or a variety of medical fields. A good number already were working in the private sector within their areas of expertise. Typically, their employment was secured by two to three year contracts. They explained that the fast-moving pace of technology and capital requires the development of intellectual projects with specified goals and time constraints. Quite a few of the computer engineers who worked in Silicon Valley had already changed companies several times, making a transition at the end of each contract period. They reported that it was very unusual to meet somebody at their companies who had stayed at one place for more than seven years.

I brought the conversation back to their alienation from the church. I asked whether it was any wonder that few of them wanted anything to do with an institution bound by historic traditions, conserving structures and, oft-times, set obligations. Given the fluidity of the market and their relationship to it, it seemed unlikely that they would establish long-term relationships with any cultural institution. In order to meet their needs, the institution would have to be as fluid as their lifestyles.

The group's response was fascinating. There was a broad consensus that mobility, though stressful, set a positive condition for spiritual growth. "Since we no longer have as many people whom we depend upon, it means we have to rely more on God."

One woman was troubled by this notion that close relationships with other people were perceived as a "crutch." She demonstrated her point, appropriately enough, with a reference to mobility: "Several times when I've had to move apartments, I needed help lifting furniture and boxes. Let me tell you, it wasn't God who lifted up the other end of the sofa!" A man sitting nearby protested, "Maybe not, but when we trust in God alone, He will bring people to our aid. That is real faith!"

One of the leaders of the group then provided a scriptural rationale for so understanding God. "The Old Testament tells us that God punished the children of Israel whenever they put their trust in their own community rather than relying on God to meet their needs. The law and the prophets established a covenant between God and each member of the tribe; but they repeatedly rebelled against God and relied on their own resources."

It would be difficult to imagine a theology more suited to the managerial class in a highly developed capitalist economy. Not only are tradition and authority experienced as obstacles for personal freedom, but community itself signifies one more form of idolatry that competes with their loyalty to God.[11] It is a hyper-abstraction of transcendence.

Marx realized that the "dis-location" (abstracted from space and time) of consciousness was driven to a great extent by market forces demanding the mobilization of the means of production. It also became a necessary condition for the emergence of the mass consumer, a homogenization informed by the mercantile interest to manufacture desire for standardized products. The production of images of what is "real" became an essential element in shaping patterns of consumption. That partially explains why industrial capitalism moves cultural consciousness toward spaces of non-differentiation. Its ideal is utopia, literally "no place," a signification of cultural space where the elements of life are not implicated by their other(s). Michel Foucault so presented modernist constructs of utopia as a reversal of the cultural system, an inverted analogy of itself: "I see myself there where I am not, in an unreal, virtual space that opens up behind the surface . . . a sort of shadow that gives my own visibility to myself, that enables me to see myself there where I am absent" (1986, 24).

It is this objectification and reification of aesthetic presence, which transformed producers and their labor into commodities, that Marx identified as the root of human alienation. Dominant forces of production circumscribe and co-opt the ecstasy of lived experience from its subjects. They are forced to exist outside of themselves, in subservience to gods made by human hands.

Marx did not thereby deny the possibility of transcendence. In fact, he conceded that even "religion is from the outset consciousness of the transcendental arising from actually existing forces" (1970, vol. 6:93). Yet he never equivocated on the fundamental assumption of his anthropology: "As individuals express their life, so they are . . . , [and] what they are . . . coincides with their production, both with what they produce and how they produce" (1970, vol. 6:31-2).

POST-INDUSTRIAL SOCIETY AND TRANSCENDENCE

The term "information-based economy" is thrown around a great deal at the moment, often with little appreciation for its implications; most importantly, it is rarely stated how and why information has become such a valuable commodity. Its development can be traced to changing technologies and evolving patterns of consumption. In its most obvious form, the exploding network of telecommunications facilitates the global exploitation of potential resources for investment capital and enables extensions to new markets where previously distribution would have been cost prohibitive. In a world of diminishing natural resources, it also opens new frontiers wherein non-material commodities may be bought and sold. It all represents a complex relationship of continuity in the development of capitalism:

> *Accelerations in turnover times, in production, exchange and consumption . . . [as well as the] rapidity with which currency markets fluctuate across the world's spaces, the extraordinary power of money capital flow in what is now a global stock and financial market, and the votality of what the purchasing power of money might represent, define . . . a high point of that highly problematic intersection of money, time and space as interlock-*

ing elements of social power in the political economy of post-modernity. (Harvey 1989, 281, 289)

What is more subtle, yet equally significant, is how the sophistication of information systems reconfigures the relation between producer and consumer. While an industrial economy thrived on the standardization of consumer desire, the production of knowledge in an information-based economy allows for a diversification of consumer targeting that more readily responds to local market interests.[12] In this environment, production becomes less dependent upon the mass manufacturing of needs—though the rapidity of technological advances now creates needs through near instant product obsolesence—since it gears itself toward the perceived needs of the consumer. As a result, the producer and the consumer enter into a dynamic interchange of images and desires. Products multiply and diversify as the impulse toward standardization gives way to heterogeneity.

The organization of the modes of production are constantly restructured in order efficiently to keep pace with these evolving patterns of consumption. New technologies and products are rushed into production to meet consumer demands, while consumer demands, in turn, are shaped by new technologies and products. The lightening speed of this regeneration means that participants in the manufacturing process can no longer remain static. The skills and knowledge it takes to contribute to the productive process today quite likely will be obsolete tomorrow; of course, in most cases it is not possible for producers to learn new skills so rapidly. The organization of the production adapts by resorting to contract labor, whereby specific skills may be procured for the period of their productive relevance; fifty years and a gold watch is a relic of a by-gone era.

In sum, commodification of the self progresses to a degree beyond Marx's most apocalyptic visions. In the economy of information it is only the image that is real, and the real is "only" an image, be it within the discourse of the value of currency (money) or the currency of values (transcendence). As Mark C. Taylor points out, their respective discourses share the same (cyber)space in virtual reality:

> *Throughout human history, gold is not so much sign as the transcendental signified that is supposed to ground the meaning and value of other signs. . . . God functions in a semiotic system in the same way that gold functions in the economic system. The go(l)d standard is the base upon which everything rests. When this foundation crumbles or becomes inaccessible, signs are left to float freely on a sea that has no shores. (1994, 607)*

Where there is no foundation, value becomes relative, ever in flux. In a profound sense, these conditions introduce perpetual transition into cultural consciousness, for transience becomes an economic necessity. It very well may be that the fluidity and speed by which information (and other capital) is exchanged eclipses the conceptual space that had mediated meaning and act in modernist critical consciousness. If so, then it reflects the fact that all production in the post-industrial society becomes transitory and fragmentary, including the act of interpretation.

Initially it may seem tragic that "truth" has lost a secure mooring, swept away by an insipid wave of cultural relativism. After all, if all of our representations of reality are "only" images, how is it possible to have a meaningful conversation about truth? The possibility that we are consigned to superficial conversations—where understanding emerges from an ongoing interchange of multiple representations of reality absent an analytical standard—is a source of considerable anxiety in many quarters of post-industrialized society. What is assumed, of course, is that previous perceptions of reality were in fact something other than (more than) images.

It was one of Feuerbach's primary contentions that self-understanding and its connection to a meaningful cosmos is an act of the imagination. Marx refined the hermeneutic, arguing that the actual grist for the mill was based in the social organization of production. They were both in their own way attempting to reconstruct a Hegelian model of subjectivity that had an integral awareness of the objectifications of itself. Regardless of whether they succeeded in their respective projects, they did at least expose how existing representations (images) of the self and the social world were illusions that served the interests of centers of dominance. The eventual erosion of both feudalist and modernist representations of 'ultimate' reality—which in their own day had presented themselves as immutable—confirmed the temporality of their material interests. Perhaps the only difference in representations of reality and meaning at the present moment is the rapid pace of cultural transition.

The implications for the ways transcendence is being constructed within post-industrial consciousness are tremendous, beginning with pluralization. Since heterogeneity and difference are driving forces of consciousness that are useful in both consumption and production, pluralistic representations of reality and meaning seem unavoidable. It is reflected in the unraveling of the grand narratives of redemption; what we now have instead are bits and pieces of 'trans-figure-ation.'

In an extensive, recent study of "emerging spiritualities" I carried out in the San Francisco Bay Area, eclecticism was the overriding impression.[13]

While it was clear that there is a remarkably high interest in spiritual rituals and meditations, typically their forms were an amalgamation of various ancient wisdoms. For most people I interviewed this spiritual renaissance in their lives had little to do with a belief system; what counts is experience.

It was not uncommon for practitioners to have self-made altars in their homes, adorned with personal momentos from significant events in their lives. One popular renewal center placed at the front of its meditation room small statues of Ramakrishna, Sarada Devi (Ramakrishna's wife), Jesus, and Buddha. Above this 'altar' was a sign: "[We] do not care for dogmas or sects, churches or temples; they count for little compared with the essence of existence in each of us."[14] Even within more traditional centers of religious reflection in the Bay Area, I observed a prolific manufacturing of theologies and images.

In this milieu it becomes almost anachronistic to look for a kernel in the husk. Perhaps a more adequate image is an onion. Peel away the many layers and what you end up with are layers. But the fact that it has no center does not mean that the onion does not exist, only that it owes its existence to the relationship of the skins. So is transcendence in the post-industrial society the relation between skins.

Then again, maybe an even more relevant image is a musical key, for instance C-major. It is not possible to fix its existence in reality. The C-major key only has meaning in relation to other tones. And even the relations of the tones are perceptible only in relation to a constructed harmony that is itself a product of imagination. All the same, when I hear the C-major key in a piece written by Mozart, then again today in a song by U2, despite the vast differences in their representations, I experience resonance. It may be that the discourse of transcendence will turn to resonance in a post-industrial age; the identification of similar tones in the exchange of representations. But added to this is a further permutation; the arrangement of keys is constantly in transition.[15]

One of the more important epistemological turns in this emerging consciousness is the diminishing role of the individual as the primary interlocutor of meaning or, for that matter, the sole agent of action. Descartes' standard dictum for self-knowledge—which had a certain staying power in defining modernist conceptuality—was predicated on the capacity of consciousness to see itself as an object with qualities of consistency and value that were particular to itself, and which justified a sense of its autonomy. It has already been suggested that Hegel's concern, to the contrary, was to relate self-knowledge to a transcendent, collective consciousness, or Mind. In many respects, the new technologies of knowledge increasingly make his vision of associative consciousness a (virtual) reality.

Featured recently in *Wired* magazine—arguably the most influential forum for discussion about and promotion of new electronic media—was an extensive article on the spiritual dimensions of "net-based consciousness" (Kreisberg 1995, 108-13). The article relies extensively on the work of Jesuit priest-paleontologist Teilhard de Chardin, whose work was quite influential in the sixties, curiously fell into relative obscurity for the next two decades, and only now is being rediscovered.

Nearly sixty years ago, Teilhard foresaw the evolving of a complex network of consciousness that he believed would envelope the ecosystem:

> *Is this not like some great body which is being born—with its limbs, its nervous system, its perceptive organs, its memory—the body in fact of that great living Thing which had to come to fulfill the ambitions aroused in the reflective being by the newly acquired consciousness. (Teilhard 1959, 246)*

Teilhard's conceptuality is itself too complex for me to do justice to it here, but it rests in the notion that an evolutionary process of consciousness is leading the material culture to conditions more highly conscious of life forces. In his observations of society and nature he saw two fundamental sources of energy, "radial" and "tangential"(1959, 68-74). Radial energy, or the energy "without," is characterized by necessity. It is the energy of Newtonian physics, obeying mechanistic laws of cause and effect in the world of nature, structures of determination in the social world. But in tangential energy, or energy "within," the forces of life operate within a consciousness of relationality, brought by chance and choice. The primary channel for tangential energy in living organisms is the nervous system, because it extends the points of connection to other sources of its power, thus leading toward a greater consciousness (1959, 237-53).

"With cyberspace, we are, in effect, hard-wiring the collective consciousness," claims virtual reality guru John Perry Barlow. He is not alone in identifying in the 'world wide web' of image production a transcendence of consciousness that Teilhard observed breaking out of a mechanical world. Barlow suggests that its force is seen more visibly in the patterns between information, rather than in the analytical significance of its content. "Cyberspace helps us see these forms by taking us past the mechanical barrier" (Kreisberg 1995, 113).

It seems rather ironic that the advanced development of technology, fueled by a mechanical world that had little room for the transcendent, has given birth to an appreciation of mystical altered states of reality that connect us to a global life-force. The limitations of spatiality lose their binding force on the imagination, even while the imagination becomes a primary tool of productivity.

For instance, "interactive technology" is a popular buzz phrase these days, but its application goes far beyond the world of computer games. "Interactive" actually implies the condition of being unfinished, where the functional identity of objects are the product of our interaction with them. It is anachronistic to even speak of identity here, of course, for the nature of an object/subject is never static, but depends on where and when one finds it, not to mention for what purpose one plans to make use of it. So it is likely that our consciousness of cultural production, and hence our own identities, will move within a web of interactions.[16]

Has critical materialism thereby given way to diacritical immaterialism, that is, where all understanding is a product of imaginations in dialogue?[17] It remains to be seen, for it is quite possible that this optimism of a global consciousness is just a new fashion of clothing worn by an intellectual class who stand the most to benefit from a global economy. Where Hegel saw a fresh embodiment of the Spirit, Marx saw a new illusion.

REFERENCES

Batstone, David. 1991. *From Conquest to Struggle: Jesus of Nazareth in Latin America*. Albany: State University of New York Press.

Baudrillard, Jean. 1975. *The Mirror of Production*. St. Louis: Telos.

———. 1988 *America*. London: Verso.

———. 1990. *Cool Memories*. London: Verso.

Bonhoeffer, Dietrich. 1981. *Letters and Papers from Prison*. London: SCM Press.

Feuerbach, Ludwig. 1846. *Sämmtliche Werke*, vol 1. Leipzig: Wigand.

———. 1957. *The Essence of Christianity*. New York: Harper & Row.

Foucault, Michel. 1986. "Of Other Spaces." *Diacritics* 16:1.

Giddens, Anthony. 1985. *Central Problems in Sociological Theory*. London: Macmillan.

Hall, Stuart. 1980. "Cultural Studies and the Centre: Some Problematics and Problems." In *Culture, Media, Language*, ed. S. Hall, D. Hobson, A. Lowe, and P. Willis. London: Hutchinson.

Harvey, David. 1989. *The Condition of Postmodernity*. London: Blackwell.

Hegel, G. W. F. 1900. *The Philosophy of History*. New York: Wiley.

———. 1967. *Hegel's Philosophy of Right*. London: Oxford University Press.

———. 1974. *The Phenomenology of the Mind*. New York: Harper.

———. 1975. *Hegel's Logic*. Oxford: Clarendon Press.

Jameson, Frederic. 1991. *Postmodernism or The Cultural Logic of Late Capitalism*. London: Verso.

Kreisberg, Jennifer Cobb. 1995. "A Globe Clothing Itself with a Brain." *Wired*, 3:6.

Laclau, Ernesto. 1990. *New Reflections on the Revolution of Our Time*. London: Verso.

Lyotard, Jean-François. 1986. *The Postmodern Condition: A Report on Knowledge*. Manchester: Manchester University Press.

————. 1989. "Complexity and the Sublime." In *Postmodernism*, ed. L. Appiganesi, ICA Documents: London: Free Association Books.

Marx, Karl. 1976. *Capital*, Volume 1. London: Penguin Books.

Marx, Karl and Friedrich Engels. 1970. *Collected Works*. London: Lawrence & Wishart.

Poster, M. 1990. *The Mode of Information: Poststructuralism and Social Context*. Cambridge: Polity Press.

Sawicki, J. 1988. "Feminism and the Power of Foucaldian Discourse." In *After Foucault: Humanistic Knowledge, Postmodern Challenges*, ed. J. Arac. New York: Rutgers University Press.

Sayer, D. 1991. *Capitalism and Modernity: An Excursus on Marx and Weber*. London: Routledge.

Smart, Barry. 1992. *Modern Conditions, Postmodern Controversies*. London: Routledge.

Soja, Edward. 1989. *Postmodern Geographies: The Reassertion of Space in Critical Social Theory*. London: Verso.

Strauss, D. F. 1973. *The Life of Jesus Critically Examined*. London: SCM Press.

Taylor, Mark C. 1994. "Discrediting God." *Journal of the American Academy of Religion*, 62:2.

Teilhard de Chardin, Pierre. 1959. *The Phenomenon of Man*. London: Wm. Collins and Sons.

NOTES

1. The collapse of the real and its referent perhaps may best be traced to Saussure's theory of signification, with its stress upon the arbitrary dualism of signifier and signified. See the discussion in Stuart Hall (1980) and Anthony Giddens (1985).

2. Cf. Jean Baudrillard (1975; 1988; 1990); Barry Smart (1992); M. Poster (1990); and J. Sawicki (1988).

3. He was not the only of Hegel's disciples to arrive at this point. David Friedrich Strauss, while discussing the image of the God-human in the early christologies of the church, likewise identified in collective human consciousness the realization of the divine Mind: "Is not the idea of the unity of the divine and human natures a real one in a far higher sense, when I regard the whole race of mankind as its realization, than when I single out one man as such a realization? Is not an incarnation of God from eternity, a truer one than an incarnation limited to a particular point in time?" (1973, 757). Feuerbach took the criticism of Hegel much further, however, arguing that whatever is attributed to Spirit is in actuality a projection of the human species.

4. "Religion is man's earliest and also indirect form of self-knowledge. Hence religion everywhere proceeds philosophy, as in the history of the race, so also in that of the individual" (Feuerbach 1957, 13).

5. Feuerbach added this statement in the Preface to second edition (1957, ix).

6. Cf. Thesis One of Marx's critique of Feuerbach: "The chief defect of all previous materialism (that of Feuerbach included), is that things, reality, sensuousness, are conceived only in the form of the object of contemplation, but not as sensuous human activity, practice, not subjectively" (1970, vol. 5:3). The Eleven Theses were first published by Engels in 1888 along with an essay entitled, "Ludwig Feuerbach and the End of Classical German Philosophy." Engels found them in one of the notebooks Marx had used in preparation for the writing of *The German Ideology*, a work which contains an extensive criticism of Feuerbach.

7. Citations from Volume 3 of the *Collected Works* (1970) were published originally in "Critique of Hegel's Philosophy of Law: Introduction," *Manuscripts of 1844*.

8. Hegel had used "fetish" in his discussion of African religion, in reference to any material object which was regarded as having supernatural powers, with the consequence that once invested with this power, the object had tremendous control over the tribe (1900, 94, n.19). For Marx's appropriation of the term, see (1976, 165, n.5).

9. There has been, of course, a wealth of ink spilt over the implications of Marx's understanding of the production of consciousness, particularly his constructions of the base and the superstructure. Although I believe it does matter whether we read the relationships deterministically or, alternatively,

conceive them in terms of "hegemony" and "counterhegemony," or "discursive" and "non-discursive," I have in this essay, in pursuit of my major thesis, opted for a "naive" reading of the production of consciousness. I leave it to the reader to decide whether it is to the detriment of my argument.

10. Citations from volume 6 of *Collected Works* (1970) were published originally in *The German Ideology*.

11. An aside that has some relevance: when it came time to pass around a contact sheet at the end of the retreat, en lieu of a phone number or home addresses, most people gave their e-mail address, saying they now could best keep in touch through cyberspace.

12. Cf. David Harvey (1989) and Edward Soja (1989).

13. The study was commissioned by *SOMA* magazine. An anecdotal account was published by in *SOMA* (May-June, 1996).

14. Many religious systems, particularly emanating from Asia, identify a unity of consciousness which underlies the apparent contradictions of material culture; the Hegelian overtones are fascinating.

15. My representation here indicates a change in my own thinking. In an earlier work, I used the same image of the "C-major key" to demonstrate how a universal truth could find its incarnation in a plurality of particular manifestations, but not lose its unique sameness. I now doubt it is possible to arrive at any keys that are universal; their apparent 'harmony' still rests on our constructions of their relationality. Cf., David Batstone (1991, 142).

16. Ironically, constructs of transcendence that are emerging at the dawn of the post-industrial society may have more in common, albeit in demystified forms, with animistic concepts of the universe as a constantly changing, changeable place.

17. For conversations weighing the value and relevance of Marxist understanding for the continuing development of capitalism, see Jean-François Lyotard (1986; 1989); Frederic Jameson (1991); D. Sayer (1991); Barry Smart (1992); and Ernesto Laclau (1990).

THE POST-MODERN LOCATION OF BLACK RELIGION:

TEXTS AND TEMPORALITIES IN TENSION

James A. Noel

> We are all embarked on the adventure of modernity; the question is whether we are galley slaves or passengers with luggage who travel in hope.

—Alain Touraine

> I do not remember, will never remember how I howled and screamed the first time my mother was carried away from me . . . yet, what the memory repudiates controls the human being . . . what one does not remember contains the only hope, danger, trap, inexorability of love—only love can help you recognize what you do not remember. . . . My memory stammers: but my soul is a witness.

—James Baldwin

INTRODUCTION

This essay argues that blackness—black culture and black religion—is situated as the inferior sign within the canon of the European Enlightenment project which configured white identity under the category "civilized." Therefore, through juxtaposing Black and Eurocentric texts and temporalities, we can explore the reciprocities signified in the whiteness-blackness, civilized-primitive dialectics. Looking at Nat Turner, W. E. B. DuBois, and Romare Bearden, we argue that black religious texts—rather than constituting anthropological data for the "civilized" to reflect upon its origin—have their genesis in modernity and represent a postmodern "critique of the critique" (Long 1986, 110).

BLACK AND WHITE IDENTITIES: DARK SIDE OF THE ENLIGHTENMENT

During the Renaissance in Europe, reason experienced a degree of emancipation from the Church's authority. This process continued with the

Protestant Reformation's emphasis on the subject and was intensified and made more self-conscious with the rise of science and the Enlightenment. For W. E. B. DuBois the Renaissance marked the transition from the medieval period to what we call modernity. The Renaissance ushered a new form of freedom onto the European scene; it was, however, "not simply freedom of spirit and body, but a new freedom to destroy freedom; freedom of eager merchants to exploit labor; freedom of white men to make black slaves." DuBois' insight into the underside of European progress and the triumph of reason was similar to those of Nietzsche, Freud, Weber, and Foucault. He saw clearly how the West's reason had been subservient to baser impulses—Nietzsche's "will to power," and Freud's "id"—to further the processes rationalizing and bureaucratinizing modern oppressive structures."[1] Like David Theo Goldberg who pointed out that reason was the vehicle for the "European domination of nature, and especially human nature." (Goldberg, 1993, 119) DuBois wrote:

> The medieval world evolved an ideal of personal worth and freedom for wide groups of men and a dawning belief in humanity as such. Suddenly comes America; the sale of men as goods in Africa; the crops these goodsmen grew; the revolution in industry and commerce; the Commercial revolution of the sixteenth century through the opening of new trade routes to India and America, the development of world markets . . . Hence arose the doctrine of race based really on economic gain but frantically rationalized in every possible direction. (DuBois, 1939, 126-7)

Rationality itself was racialized through the counter examples of those whose non-rationality rationalized their subjugation and enslavement by the West. We can also see reflected in the above remarks by DuBois the fact that Africans entered modernity from a vantage point quite different from that of Europeans. For Africans modernity came with the slave trade and then colonialism, whereas for Europeans the Enlightenment represents modernity; which is to say: for Africans the sheer terror caused by their enslavement necessitated a faith transcending the cold logic of their oppression, while for Europeans the break-up of Christendom, the rise of the bourgeoisie, the growth of science, and the autonomy of economics and politics necessitated reason's ascendancy and the discrediting of faith.

DuBois' critique of the Enlightenment project's reason was that it masked the "will to power" and involved more than the disjuncture of faith and reason but also—by valorizing the theme of individual freedom while simultaneously institutionalizing unfreedom—the disjuncture between social-ethical theory and social-ethical practice.[2] One consequence was that black people appropriated Christianity under a set of conditions which subjected them to the categories of the Enlightenment project; this project, however, excluded them as its active participants while signifying them as "empirical others" in contrast to the West's self-identity as Christian, civilized and rational. Within modernity's discourse "primitives" functioned as "a negative structure of concreteness that allows civilization to define itself as a structure superior to this ill-defined and inferior other" (Long 1986, 91). The aforementioned disjunctures were masked by the move which collapsed reason, Christianity and civilization into the West's self-understanding. In other words, the terror inflicted by the West on people of color was dictated by the fact of their being non-rational, non-Christian and uncivilized—in short, non-white.

This was clearly evident in Gines de Sepulveda's argument during his debate in 1550 at Valladolid with Bartolome de Las Casas regarding Spain's treatment of the "Indios." Sepulveda based his rationalization on Aristotle's *Politics* when he argued: "In wisdom, skill, virtue and humanity, these people are as inferior to Spaniards as children are to adults and women to men; there is as great a difference between them as there is between savagery and forbearance, between violence and moderation, almost—I am inclined to say—as between monkeys and men" (Todorow 1984, 153). A similar rationalization was used by English colonists, interestingly enough, to characterize the Irish. John Locke was to defend slavery based on the just war theory in his *Second Treatise* on Government. The practical application of the just war theory can be appreciated when in Elizabeth Donnan's exhaustive *Documents Illustrative of the History of the Slave Trade to America* we come across the account of the exchange which took place between William Snelgrave, a slave trader, and his African captives following their aborted mutiny. When the insurrectionists gave as their reason for rebelling the answer, "I was a great Rogue to buy them, in order to carry them from their own Country, and that they were resolved to regain their Liberty if possible"; Snelgrave informed his captives that "they had forfeited their Freedom before I bought them, either by Crimes or by being taken in War according to the Custom of their country; and they now being my property, I was resolved to let them feel my resentment if they abused by Kindness" (Donnan 1965, 354-7). The outcome of this exchange, which we hesitate in calling a debate, was adjudicated, like the one between Sepulveda and Las Casas, not by reason but by power directed toward economic interest.

The most resounding response to Locke's writings occurred in America where they became the chief source of political ideas expounded by New England clergy and the Founding Fathers.[3] Locke's usefulness had to do not only with the clarity of his exposition on individualism, property rights, and social contract but also in his exposition of just war theory which allowed colonists to simultaneously fight England under the banner of religious and political freedom and enslave blacks. This double ethical standard, subsumed under one comprehensive political theory has its rhetorical roots in Machiavelli's *The Prince* (Hauser 1965, 85).

Ironically, in America, this dualism was not a form of metaphysical manicheanism, nor a generalized ethical ambiguity; it was incarnated and epidermalized at the level of the black-white dialectic. As Bernard Bailyn was to point out in *The Ideological Origins of The American Revolution*, the most frequent metaphor used in fast day sermons and political tracts to characterize taxation without representation was slavery (Bailyn 1967, 232).[4] This reference became an embarrassment to the new nation by the Constitutional Convention of 1787 which signified slaves in the United States Constitution with the term "other persons" to designate them as property (Bell 1973, 42-51; Kahn 24-5).

Christianity did not just exist alongside the mercantilist economic forces which helped generate the moral double standard discussed above; Christianity, rather, became subordinated and conformed to what Weber called the "spirit of capitalism." Under this economic structure religion was relegated to the private sphere. Nature became comprehended under scientific laws, and the economy under economic laws; God became remote and Divine activity more and more restricted to a realm lying beyond a world now "disenchanted" or "deconsecrated." The disjuncture of reason and faith reached its apogee in Immanuel Kant's distinction between "phenomena" and "numena" which rendered metaphysics and philosophical theology impossible and made the notion of "revelation" untenable. Under the gaze of higher criticism the Bible became text—which is to say, an aspect of the phenomenal realm; its interpretation could not tell the reader anything about God in and of God's self but represented only the beliefs and contexts of the Bible's anonymous human authors.

Because of its commitment to modernity and lack of a tradition to control the interpretations of the biblical text, Protestantism adopted two related strategies for finding a basis other than philosophy and revelation: it grounded itself in either history or the religious subject. Among those representing the historical turn were: Harnack, Kahler, Strauss, Baur, Herrmann, Loisy, Weiss, Schweitzer and Drews; while among those representing the subjective turn were: Schleiermacher, Otto, Coleridge, Kierkegaard, and Bultmann. As Hegel was to complain, since they assumed too much from modernity, neither of these turns could satisfactorily secure an intellectual basis for Protestant Christianity against the assault of modernity.

CIVILIZATION, DIS-CONTINUITY, HISTORY AND THE OTHERS

Hegel, for example, concluded in *The Philosophy of History* that Africa "is no historical part of the World" and "has no movement or development to exhibit" since it represents "the Unhistorical, Undeveloped Spirit, still involved in the conditions of mere nature" (Pietz 1985, 5). This verdict, according to William Pietz, was derived from Hegel's understanding of African religion under the category of "fetishism," which had entered European discourse through travel account (Pietz 1988, 105). Later, Karl Marx would also make use of the category of the "fetish" in describing the nature of the commodity; and after that it would enter into the nomenclature of psychoanalytic discourse. Pietz' study lends additional support to this essay's thesis that the fact of blackness is located at the core of modernity and crucial for an explication of modernity's meaning. In Pietz' discussion, Hegel regarded the fetish as unlike the authentic religious object in so far as it enjoyed no independence and was merely an expression of the caprice of its maker. What the fetish brought about in African communities was their subjugation by kings and priests who served as intermediaries between the people and the sacred. Thus, Hegel's characterization of African religion functioned "as an ideology justifying the slave trade by explaining Africans as slavish by nature." Within Hegel's scheme of the Absolute's unfolding, Africans were unconscious beings lacking history and true religion (Pietz 1985, 7). Yet here again, in the above, we see an irony: Hegel's system required the negative signification of blackness in his "master-slave" allegory to dialectically resolve the problem which had become acute in modernity and constituted its primary feature—alienation. The implication of Hegel's thought is that Europe, too, is not fully conscious. This he sought to remedy by revealing the dialectical movement of the absolute through its subjective manifestations in human consciousness and its objective manifestations in institutions such as the Church and the State.

To get back to the historical turn: Hegel, in his *Lectures on the Philosophy of Religion*, after having universally defined religion as "the relation of human consciousness to God" and "the consciousness of freedom and truth," went on to diagnose the problem suffered by Protestant Christianity under the structures of modernity. As the result of historical treatment of dogma, "one is engaged not with one's own cognition but with cognition of other people's representations" (Hegel 1988, 233-5).

The aspect of modernity Hegel was critiquing above was its character of being torn between rationalization and subjectivation (Touraine 1995, 214). Another way of speaking about this is to describe it as the divorce between knowledge and faith which does not suddenly appear in modernity but in modernity becomes more definite and insurmountable. According to

Touraine, "Luther's thought . . . condemned to failure the attempts of the small group of humanists and followers of Erasmus who tried to reconcile the spirit of the Renaissance with that of the Reformation, and faith with knowledge" (Touraine 1995, 214). Touraine wrote: "The divorce between the two faces of modernity is irrevocable. On the one hand, we find a regression to millenarianism; on the other, modernity is reduced to meaning the quest for a utility defined by merchants. Ignoring both these extremes, the history of modernity will be a constant dialogue between rationalization and subjectivation" (Touraine 1995, 38).

Returning to Hegel's statement above, one reason for the material being experienced by African Americans as "the alien truths of others" is that the impact of the West upon the African diaspora during slavery and upon Africans during colonialism has been one of radical dis-continuity which Western texts intensify. From the standpoint of radical dis-continuity, in the West there has not been one modernity but several—for example, the Germanic invasions and eventual collapse of the Roman Empire which since Constantine's conversion many Christians had come to regard as part of God's providential plan.

Later there was the collapse of the Carolingian Empire and the invasions of the Norsemen. These discontinuities have been overcome, however, with the aid of historical reflection and writing which utilized a Christian framework of salvation history for incorporating diverse elements within the social construct called Europe.[5] The diverse tribal groups who subsumed their pagan identities under this broader construct began to refer to themselves vis-a-vis other pagans and Moslems as "a Christian race." Cassiodorus' history contained in Jordanes' *The Origin and Deeds of the Goths* and his *Chronicle*, Isadore of Seville's *On Times, Gregory of Tours' History of the Franks* were produced against the framework of redemptive history found in the biblical text (* see Ernst Breisach). As Ernst Breisach explains:

> *Divorce from the empire, spelled out by Augustine in theory, had become a reality and Christians had to redefine the relationship of the sacred and profane history. . . . The historians of the period, the clergy, were members of the educated elite of the new kingdoms. That group, steeped in the Latin tradition, linked the German past to the redemptive history of mankind, including the Roman chapter of that history. . . . The linkage . . . filled the need for continuity, stability, and legitimacy felt by conquerors and conquered alike. (Breisach 1983, 88-9)*

A new type of history writing was necessitated by the break-up of Christendom and the Protestant Reformation. This history was no longer articulated within the conceptual frameworks of the Holy Roman Empire and the Latin Church but those of two differentiated constructs: the nation state and the church—either Roman Catholic or Protestant. It was only natural that secular histories reflected which side of the Protestant reformation a nation state situated itself on since, as Toynbee pointed out, "An uncritical belief in the divine right of the Apostle at Rome was simply replaced by an equally uncritical belief in the divine right of parochial states" (Toynbee 1956, 185).

The sense of continuity in the West's history, secular histories reified the notion of progress and ecclesiastical histories that of providence.[6] But what do these notions mean for blacks? Could their experience of slavery be made sense of through either of these categories? The answer is obvious.

Although the slave trade was experienced by the African Diaspora as radical disrupture, it was not interpreted by Europeans in terms of discontinuity because blacks were not ushered into the Western mentality as conquerors but as human commodities within the framework of nascent capitalism. Because capitalism but not the slavery attached to it was experienced by the West as discontinuity its intellectuals never fully engaged in a hermeneutic of slavery to discern the practical reason underlying modernity's significations at the level of theoretical reason. Western texts and their interpretations, therefore, impose forgetfulness on the black psyche.

In North America, as Toni Morrison pointed out, the new nation's possibilities were enriched by slavery because in the "construction of blackness and enslavement could be found not only the not free but also, with dramatic polarity created by skin color, the projection of the not-me" (Morrison 1993, 38). At the level of theoretical reason blacks are hidden and obfuscated in Western texts by the theological notion of providence and the secular notion of progress, which are concepts of continuity. Western texts and their accompanying hermeneutic which constitute such a historic turn are inimical to the temporal, subjective and ethical sensibilities of blacks because they deny the possibility and necessity of what Rudolf J. Siebert termed "anamnestic solidarity." He calls for a praxis, a reading of texts, a hermeneutic which is "anamnestic" because

> It does not proceed with its back toward the innocent victims who have been destroyed and with its face toward the always new future into which scientific technological progress drives us with great force and speed as we forget equally fast the innocent other who has died. (Siebert 1985, ii, xiii)

ANAMNESIS: AFRICAN AMERICAN CULTURE AS TEXT

Culture, along the lines of Daniel Bell, can be regarded as the "arena of expressive symbolism" in which human communities articulate their sensibilities regarding life's meaning in "imaginative form." Culture is expressed, among other things, in dance, poetry, visual and literary arts, and both the formal and informal rituals connected with life's major transitions. "Historically...culture has been fused with religion" (Bell 1978, 12). As per Siebert's prescription quoted in the preceding section, African American culture has been oriented both in this backward direction by positing for its constituents a "memory" and also in a forward direction by positing "hope"—the products of this effort, broadly speaking, constitute its texts. African American texts represent, therefore, both forms of survival as well as emancipatory anamnestic praxis.

Elsewhere I have argued that all African-American cultural expressions—the Spirituals, slave narratives, Abolitionist speeches, black prayer, the blues, jazz, African American dance and art, etc.—be regarded as texts (Noel 1990). These are postmodern texts but postmodern from a different location in modernity than the ones we have been discussing thus far. We need, however, to exercise some caution in the way we approach African American culture as text.

Lawrence E. Sullivan makes a very cogent argument against confining a culture's intelligibility and meaning exclusively to the category of "text" construed as a written document or scriptural expression. He points out that prior to Deconstruction and the theories of such thinkers as Jacobsen, Troubetsky and de Saussure, the French Encyclopedist had come to regard all cultural expressions through the model of language. Yet in assessing the results of this approach for the field of religious studies Sullivan feels the analogy has been carried too far because, among other things, "it overlooks the materiality of language," and furthermore, he writes, "The dominance of contemporary talk about 'text' also obscures the performative quality of writing and reading language" (Sullivan 1990, 46-7).

Notwithstanding Sullivan's argument I still wish to give African-American culture the status of text as a strategy for situating it and its religious undergirding within the framework of modernity. This does not mean that African-American texts can all be reduced to "text-talk." Indeed, I have argued elsewhere that the primary data of the New World black religious experience are the moan and the shout which are hardly comprehensible through the categories of rationality (Noel 1994, 72-6).

Above these utterances are other texts—work songs, Spirituals, quilts, folk tales, sermons and slave narratives. What Paul Gilroy said of slave narratives regarding their being more than a mere repetition of Hegel's master-

slave allegory could probably by extension be applied as well to other types
of African American texts.

> *They express in the most powerful way a tradition of writing
> in which autobiography becomes an act or process of simultane-
> ous self-creation and self-emancipation. The presentation of a
> public persona thus becomes a founding motif within the ex-
> pressive culture of the African Diaspora. . . . It is important to
> note here that a new discursive economy emerges with the re-
> fusal to subordinate the particularity of the slave experience to
> the totalizing power of universal reason held exclusively by
> white hands, pens, or publishing houses (Gilroy 1993, 69).*

African American texts as religio-cultural expressions represent objective artifacts of black consciousness or subjectivity. This is applying to the
black experience Heinrich Rickert's definition of culture as "whatever is
produced directly by men and women acting according to valued ends or, if
it is already in existence, whatever is fostered intentionally for the sake of
the values attached to it" (quoted in Arato 1974, 125).

Freedom is the value toward which African American culture's texts
are directed. But African American culture's text also functions in terms of
Georg Simmel's prerequisite that "cultures exist only if man draws into his
development something that is external to him" (Simmel 1971, 230). What
stood external to the black psyche was the all-pervasiveness of whiteness.
For African Americans to have incorporated whiteness into their psyches
unmediated by their own cultural values would have resulted in their having
been ontologically deformed by the definitions whiteness generated about
blackness. Hence African American texts concretized the external values,
symbolic expressions and forms by which black subjectivity could contemplate and live out its own meaning in the world. These texts protected the
black psyche from the brutal impact of whiteness which functioned to de-
form their humanity in a way similar to Fanon's description of colonialism,
in which he said: "By a perverted logic, it turns to the past of the oppressed
people and distorts, disfigures, and destroys it" (Fanon 1968, 210). Thus,
African American texts as expressions of black religio-culture can be
viewed, to borrow from Alain Locke, as "a defensive counter-move for the
American Negro" (Locke 1983, 21-35). African American culture defended
black humanity from the dominant white culture's dehumanizing effects by
positing alternative artifacts by which blacks could represent their collective
values and contemplate their own meanings. In African American texts are
embedded senses of memory, theodicy, and aesthetics—a stylized modality

of being in the world which resists the definitions imposed upon black folks by the dominant culture and its texts. Formed in modernity, these texts also constitute its critique and in this sense African American culture's texts can be said to constitute a counterculture to modernity, and as such their interpretation requires novel approaches from the field of hermeneutics.

NAT TURNER'S BIBLICAL HERMENEUTIC

Numerous examples could be cited in demonstrating this last point but the ones we will focus our attention upon are Nat Turner and W. E. B. DuBois by examining, respectively, their hermeneutic, theodicy, and aesthetic.

Nat Turner led one of the most violent slave insurrections in U.S. history in 1831 at Southhampton County, Virginia, in which ten men and thirty-five children were killed. He related the details of his insurrection, while incarcerated, to T. R. Gray, a lawyer, in what is now known as *The Confession of Nat Turner*. Turner begins his narration by addressing Gray: "Sir, you have asked me to give a history of the motives which induced me to undertake the late insurrection, as you call it. To do so I must go back to the date of my infancy, and even before I was born" (Gray 1969, 6). This is an amazing statement for a slave to make in light of the fact that most were baffled about their origins and had only a vague idea of their day and year of birth. Frederick Douglass recalled in his narrative how slaves reckoned time according to a life cycle of toil—planting time or harvest time. Thus it is remarkable how Turner endeavors to situate his motives—i.e., his subjectivity—within a temporality; not an objective temporality, however, since it was connected with his gift. When as early as three or four years of age Turner related incidents which had occurred on the plantation prior to his birth the older slaves commented that Turner "surely would be a prophet." This was confirmed when as a child he one day began to read and spell without previous instruction. The written word constitutes something entirely different for someone who learns to read in this way than for those who have acquired literacy under Enlightenment mental structures and presuppositions. This is evident when we try to penetrate the opacity of Turner's biblical hermeneutic.

While listening to a sermon, Turner was struck by the passage quoted by the preacher, "Seek ye the Kingdom of Heaven and all things shall be added unto you." When at the plow after daily praying for an interpretation to this passage, the Spirit spoke to Turner by quoting the same passage. This suggests that the African-American hermeneutic is rooted in the rhythms of work and intimately connected with the body. More years passed during which Turner was privileged with additional revelations confirming that he was ordained for a special task.

> *I saw white spirits and black spirits engaged in battle, and the sun darkened—the thunder rolled in the Heavens, and blood flowed in streams—and I heard a voice saying, "such is your luck, such you are called to see, and let it come rough or sooth, you must surely bear it (Gray 1969, 6).*

Following this vision Turner stopped interacting with his fellow slaves as much as the plantation schedule would allow in order to devote himself even more fully to the Spirit, which:

> *appeared to me and reminded me of the things it had already shown me and that it would reveal to me the knowledge of the elements, the revolution of the planets, the operation of the tides, and the change of the seasons. . . . The knowledge of the elements being made known to me, I sought more than ever to obtain true holiness before the great day of judgment should appear; and then I began to receive the true knowledge of faith (6).*

At one point in his narration Turner takes pains to attribute his visions and the influence he had over other slaves to the Spirit and "not to conjuring and other such tricks, for them I always spoke of such things with contempt" (4). Turner's disclaimer regarding the role conjuring played in his hermeneutic is suspicious. One of Turner's lieutenants, Nelson Williams, was known to be a conjurer (Johnson 1966, 73; Drewry 1968, 114-5). Furthermore, Turner was fully aware of the role conjuring beliefs played in the belief system of his fellow slaves as a master code for interpreting the Bible, nature and the symbolic meaning of his own behavior. When we question the possible similarities between conjuring, its related practice of divination, and any act of discursive interpretation we must view Turner's biblical hermeneutic as a form of conjuring and divination. Cowrie shells tossed on the ground require a similar complex task from the divination practitioner as the words written on pages in the Bible demand from the modern biblical scholar—discerning a visual configuration from an arbitrary assemblage of signs to which the application of prescribed rules and conventions is exercised to abstract meaning. In West Africa, for example, among the Fon, the practice of divination entails the priest being able to identify the story from the oral tradition he will recite to his client in one of the two hundred and fifty-six possible combinations formed by the sixteen cowrie shells which have been thrown.[7] An indication of the intricacy involved in divination is evident in Herskovits' and Herskovits' description.

> *The technique . . . therefore consists in knowing the several hundred mythologies associated with these principle and subsidiary Du, and interpreting each in light of that Du identified with the destiny of the individual for whom the Fa is being consulted (Herskovits 1933, 52).*

Both during the consultation and later, as the individual ponders the parables cited by the diviner, he focuses his mature attention and his imaginative faculties on the meaning of the tales and their relevance for his own needs (Herskovits and Herskovits 1958, 27).

For Turner biblical passages were enigmatic signs whose interpretation required additional signs—e.g., the hieroglyphs inscribed in blood on leaves in the woods—which both interpreted the ones preceding them and required yet additional signs in a progression which reached its ultimate culmination in his embodiment of these sign's eschatology. He had no expectation that freedom would accrue to blacks somewhere along the course of Western progress. To overcome the radical disjuncture that ushered slavery into modernity would require the intervention of another radical disjuncture whose agent Turner understood himself to be.

The bizarre visions Turner piles on top of one another in interpreting the passage "Seek ye the Kingdom of Heaven . . ." illustrate Jameson's position that "We never confront a text immediately...as a thing-in-itself." Rather, "our object of study is less the text itself than the interpretations through which we attempt to confront and to appropriate it." Jameson's reason for construing this procedure as allegorical is that it "consists in requiting a given text in terms of a particular interpretative master code" (Jameson 1981, 9-10). This is not entirely true of Turner through whose reading of the Bible a Holy and Personal Other was encountered. Hence for Turner the Bible was not a text in the same objective sense as it was for Protestant exegetes who strove to distance themselves from allegorical readings of the biblical text but with only incomplete success. More recently, in *Memory and Hope*, Dietrich Ritschl discussed Rudolph Bohrern's critique of the schizophrenia of post-Bultmanian exegesis, which winds up

> *doing precisely what it does not want to do, i.e. by trying to gain a "mystical" sense of scripture through existentialist interpretation on the basis of the "literal" sense which was gained through historical-critical interpretation, thus again operating with a twofold meaning of Scripture (Ritschl 1967, 51).*

According to de Man, borrowing from Schleiermacher's insight, this is an inevitable consequence of any and every text which tells the allegory of its own misunderstanding. It is "the nature of language," which

> *makes it unavoidable that texts should be written in the form of a fictionally diachronic narrative or if one prefers to call it so, of an allegory. . . . Accounting for the rhetoricity of its own mode, the text postulates the necessity of its own misreading. It knows and asserts that it will be misunderstood (de Man 1971, 135-6).*

Where this places us, according to Jonathan Culler's discussion of de Man, is in one of those "impossible situations where there is no happy issue but only the possibility of playing out roles dramatized in the text" (Culler 1982, 81). The above insights from de Man and Culler illuminate Turner's narration on several levels. In the progression of his visions is a gradual clarification of an interpretive code for interpreting the passage he was attending to. Constituting this code, which assumed the form of apocalyptic imagery, was an eschatology. He heard a voice saying "the time was fast approaching when the first should be last and the last first." When asked by Gray if subsequent events—namely, his capture—caused him to doubt the veracity of that revelation Turner answered, "Was not Christ crucified?" Turner, in other words, was consciously playing out the role dramatized in his reading of the biblical text and in so doing forced the slave system into playing out an antithetical and repressive role. One of the Hegelian consequences of Turner's revolt was that it became even more difficult for slavery's apologists to deny the slave's humanity and far easier for its opponents to demonstrate the brutality required to maintain slavery. Even after saying all this, however, there is no final resolution to the problem of Nat Turner's biblical hermeneutic—it is neither premodern nor postmodern, and defies the Enlightenment gaze by remaining opaque.

Turner's biblical hermeneutic was neither literal nor historical-critical. At the time of his reading of the text these two possible readings of the Bible were employed respectively by pro-slavery and anti-slavery advocates. Because pro-slavery advocates were able to defend the institution with numerous proof-texts, the anti-slavery camp relied on newly emerging higher critical readings of the Bible in marshalling it into the defense of the anti-slavery position.

One of the legacies of the role the Bible played in the slavery issue is what we observe today in the correlation of higher criticism with Liberal Theology and literalism with Conservative and Fundamentalist Theology.

Although finding themselves in the camps of Liberal, Black, and Liberation Theologies, African American students experience uncomfortableness with their biblical hermeneutical presuppositions.

This problem arises partly from the fact that the method of historical criticism as taught in seminaries fails to historize itself and in so doing it, as William H. Meyers points out, results in "the exaltation of one cultural world view over all others" (Meyers 1991, 41). The historical critical reading of the Bible calls into question the concept of Revelation by identifying the text's meaning and, for all practical purposes, author with its context. God is not the text's author but its ideological construct constituted within the belief system of the text's human protagonists and community of readers. On the other hand, the Literalist Reading, while retaining the Bible's status as Revelation, carries with it the legacy of the Conservative Theologies which justified slavery. Because it is neither a higher-critical nor a literalistic reading the text Turner's biblical hermeneutic is but one of numerous African American texts whose "near-canonical" status in the black community elevates it among the required sources for theological education. As one side of the interplay between religious reflection and cultural analysis, Turner's biblical exegesis links hermeneutics to the eschatalogical implications of signs and codes.

W. E. B. DUBOIS' THEODICY

W. E. B. DuBois was a literary figure in addition to an historian, sociologist, and political activist. In his short stories, poems and prayers are evident DuBois' reflection upon the relationship of the Protestant Deity to Black History. During his student days at Harvard, DuBois engaged in a close reading of Kant under Josiah Royce's guidance and also studied with William James. Later, probably while studying Political Economy in Germany with Smoeller, DuBois absorbed Karl Marx's *Das Kapital*. The importance of these texts for his intellectual formation was reflected in Dubois' comment made in his mid-career that if one could read only three books in one's entire lifetime he would recommend Kant's *Critique of Pure Reason*, Marx' *Das Kapital*, and the *Bible*. It is apparent from this list that DuBois' ongoing intellectual concerns had to do with epistemology, social/historical/economic analysis and religion.

In Kantian fashion DuBois developed distinct tools for exploring phenomena amenable to empirical investigation and those located in the realm of faith. These two realms were related by the question DuBois' historical studies raised concerning the why of black suffering. Facts, while silent on this issue, could be reflected upon as a source for a philosophy of history and a theodicy. DuBois' social activism required an orientation toward the future—if you will, a hope to sustain his commitment. He explored this possibility in his novels, short stories and poems. Through these literary forms DuBois attained a remarkable insight regarding the nature of God. This insight, on the one hand, grounded his struggle in something more than Marxist dialectical-materialism and, on the other hand, overcame Kant's dualism which made God non-sensuous and unknowable.

The lynchings and anti-black riots endemic of US society during the early part of this century occasioned a prayer by DuBois which overcomes Kant's Theistic or Deistic conception of the Divinity with that of a Suffering God. As whites roamed the streets in urban America's black sections to assault and kill African-Americans with impunity DuBois addressed God in the following manner in *The Prayers of God*: Pg. 249-252.

> *Name of God's Name!*
>> *Red Murder reigns;*
>> *All Hell is loose;*
>> *On gold autumnal air*
>> *Walk grinning devils barbed and hoofed,*
>> *While high on hills of hate, Black-blossomed,*
>>> *crimson sky'd,*
>> *Thou sittest, dumb.*

> *Father Almighty!*
>> *This earth is mad!*
>> *Palsied, our cunning hands;*
>> *Rotten, our gold;*
>> *Our argosies reel and stagger*
>> *Over empty seas;*
>> *All the long aisles*
>> *Of Thy great temples, God*
>> *Stink with the entrails of our souls.*
>> *And thou art dumb.*

While addressing God in such manner God reveals to DuBois that God was not dumb and aloof to black suffering.

> *Awake me, God I sleep!*
>> *What was that awful word Thou saidst?*
>> *That black and riven Thing—was it Thee?*
>> *That gasp—was it Thine?*
>> *This pain—is it Thine?. . .*

> *Is this Thy crucifixion, God,*
> *And not that funny little cross,*
> *With vinegar and thorns?*

Then DuBois, in hearing God's cry and God's prayer is put in utter sympathy with God's pathos and suffering.

> *Help!*
> *I sense that low and awful cry—*
> *Who cries?*
> *Who weeps*
> *With silent sob that rends and tears—*
> *Can God sob?*

> *Who prays?*
> *I hear strong prayers throng by,*
> *Like mighty winds on dusky moors—*
> *Can God pray?*

> *Prayest Thou, Lord, and to me?*
> *Thou needest me?*
> *Thou needest me?*
> *Thou needest me?*
> *Poor wounded Soul!*
> *Of this I never dreamed. I thought—*
> *Courage, God,*
> *I come!* (1972, 249-252)

Luther's emphasis on the attribute of Love in describing God is as of little help in explicating the why of black suffering as Calvin's emphasis on the attribute of Will. If God is all loving how can God endure black suffering? If God is all powerful why does God not intervene in black suffering? DuBois posits, as his counterpart James Weldon Johnson does in the poem "Creation" in *God's Trombones*, a needy and suffering God as the answer to the theodicy issue arising from the Black Experience. God is involved in history not as a Sovereign Deity presiding over the workings of Providence but as the victim of history's human sacrifices to the altar of greed and power. In DuBois' prayer victims become subjects and agents of redemptive history; and by placing them at the center of the Divine economy it supplements and enables the historical-critical reading of texts to produce more than mere "alien truths of others," but the key to the victims historical role within the Enlightenment project.

The way DuBois conceives of God being incarnated into human history in the New World in the Philippian (Chap. 2 Vr. 6f) sense of "kenosis" or emptying, can be seen in his short story "Jesus Christ in Texas" (DuBois 1972, 132-3). In this short story Jesus appears incognito in Texas in the racially ambiguous person of a "mulatto." In the New World context of modernity the point of contact between the human and Divine must be contemplated in terms of "creolization" and "miscegenation." DuBois applies the logic of the Chalcedonian formula to the issue that American racism raised for Christian Anthropology. The logos that becomes flesh in the New World defies definition on numerous levels: he is both human and Divine and both black and white but once his blackness is identified not only is his Divinity obscured but his humanity as well. This allowed the Christ to be lynched.

DuBois' mulatto Christ brings to mind what Richard Halpern said regarding the significance of the mestizo Caliban in Shakespeare's *The Tempest*.

> *The racially mixed figure of the mestizo, compounded of native American, African, and European blood, represents a culture that chooses miscegenation over imitation; instead of simply repeating or rejecting metropolitan culture, it assimilates, depurifies, and transforms it with non-European strains . . . the notion of mestizo has clear affinities with certain themes of poststructuralist thought: it denies unique or delimited points of origin, it replaces monological conception of cultural discourse with a dialogical or indeed disseminative one, and it problematizes boundaries and deconstructs binary oppositions, including that of center and periphery. Mestizoization is thus the inescapable condition of culture as such, including metropolitan culture. (Halpern 1994, 263-4)*

From the above we can appreciate how DuBois' short story contains a profound critique of Euro-American Christianity's lack of Christology and the inadequacy of its biblical hermeneutic. What this short story brings to mind is Schleeirmacher's and Dilthey's insight that hermeneutics is only secondarily a problem of interpreting texts—what first occasions the need for hermeneutics is the problematic of understanding the consciousness encountered in another person (Klemm 1986 Introduction); when the other is objectified, the possibility of understanding is precluded. This is precisely what happened in the West through its inability to recognize the Christ in the humanity of one whom its structures had made a "doulous," or slave.

CONCLUSION

Black Religion was the only product produced by black bodies which could not be alienated by the master, and thus the texts articulating the impulse of Black Religion model a subversive mode by which slaves created value within the mercantilist and capitalist context of modernity. This mode was antithetical to the dominant form of Protestantism which was caught up in what Weber termed the "spirit of capitalism."

Our argument is not that African Americans abandon the Eurocentric canon for one which is Afrocentric. Quite the contrary, we have argued for Eurocentric and Afrocentric texts being held in tension so as to, in the words of Gilroy, "represent a redemptive critique of the present in light of the vital memories of the slave past" (Gilroy 1993, 71). If the Enlightenment was a critique of knowledge and if, as Karl Marx said, all critique begins with the critique of religion, then blacks figure into this intellectual enterprise not as representatives of primitive religion—the mythological stage of human evolution which has been surpassed by the West—but as exemplars of a religious impulse instigated by modernity and, therefore, exemplars of a critique of the critique. The fact that Black Religion has remained irreducible to Enlightenment categories of thought—which is to say, remained opaque—while simultaneously being signified under the notion of primitive means that the West never fully and completely encountered it in the radical mode of "difference." Hence blackness has never been configured in the Euro-American mentality as a space where personal and theoretical knowledge can occur. This leaves Hegel's master-slave dialectic unresolved; and it will remain so as long as the nature of the text goes unquestioned and those from the black and white religious experience are not juxtaposed. When theological education gets around to doing this it may be possible to achieve the genuine worldliness and heterogeneity of voices it so desperately needs.

REFERENCES

Arato, Andrew. 1974. "The Neo-Idealist Defense of Subjectivity." *Telos 2* (Fall).

Bailyn, Bernard. 1967. *The Ideological Origins of the American Revolution.* Cambridge, MA: Belknap/Harvard Press.

Baldwin, James. 1985. *Evidence of Things Not Seen.* New York: Holt, Rinehart and Winston.

Bartlett, Robert. 1993. *The Making of Europe: Conquest, Colonization and Cultural Change, 950-1359.* Princeton, N.J.: Princeton University Press.

Bearden, Romare. "A Memorial Exhibit." New York: ACA Galleries.

————.1946. "The Negro Artist's Dilemma." *Critique* (November) 16-22.

Bell, Derrick. 1973. *Race, Racism and American Law.* Boston: Little, Brown and Company.

Bourdieu, Pierre. 1993. *The Field of Cultural Production.* New York: Columbia University Press.

Buck-Morss, Susan. 1989. *The Dialectics of Seeing: Walter Benjamin and the Arcades Project.* Cambridge: MIT Press.

Culler, Jonathan. 1982. *On Deconstruction: Theory and Criticism After Structuralism.* Ithaca, New York: Cornell University Press.

de Man, Paul. 1971. *Blindness and Insight: Essays in the Rhetoric of Contemporary Criticism.* Minneapolis: University of Minnesota Press.

Donnan, Elizabeth. 1965. *Documents Illustrative of the History of the Slave Trade to America* Vol. 2. New York: Octagon Books.

DuBois, W. E. B. 1939. *Black Folk: Then and Now.* New York: Henry Holt and Company.

————. [1903] 1989. *The Souls of Black Folk.* New York: Bantam.

————. [1920] 1972. *Darkwater: Voices from Within the Veil.* New York: Schocken Books.

Ellison, Ralph. 1990. *The Invisible Man.* New York: Vintage International Edition.

Fanon, Frantz. 11968. *The Wretched of the Earth.* New York: Grove Press.

Frey, Sylvia R. 1991. *Water from the Rock: Black Resistance in a Revolutionary Age.* Princeton, N.J.: Princeton University Press.

Funkenstein, Amos. 1986. *Theology and the Scientific Imagination: From the Middle Ages to the 17th Century.* Princeton, N.J.: Princeton University Press.

Gilroy, Paul. 1993. *The Black Atlantic, Modernity and Double Consciousness.* Cambridge, Mass.: Harvard University Press.

Goldberg, David Theo. 1993. *Racist Culture Philosophy and the Politics of Meaning.* Cambridge, Mass.: Blackwell Publishers.

Gray, T. R. ed. 1969. *The Confessions of Nat Turner, Leader of the Late Insurrection in Southhampton, VA.* Miami: Mnemosyne Publishing Inc.

Habermas, Jurgen. 1991. *The Philosophical Discourse of Modernity.* Cambridge, Mass.: MIT Press.

Halpern, Richard. 1994. "The Picture of Nobody: White Cannibalism in The Tempest." In *The Production of English Renaissance Culture*, ed. David Lee Miller, Sharon O'Dair, and Harold Weber. Ithaca and London: Cornell University Press.

Hauser, Arnold. 1965. *Mannerism: The Crisis of the Renaissance and the Origin of Modern Art.* Cambridge: Belknap/Harvard Press.

Herskovits, Melville J. and Frances S. 1933. *An Outline of Dahomean Belief.* Menasha, Wisc: The American Anthropological Assn.

————. 1958. *Dahomean Narrative: A Cross Cultural Analysis.* Evanston: Northwestern University Prses.

James, L. L. R. 1989. *The Black Jacobins: Tousain L'Ouverture and the San Domingo Revolution.* New York: Vintage Books/Random House.

Jameson, Fredric. 1981. *The Political Unconscious: Narrative as a Socially Symbolic Act.* Ithaca: Cornell University Press.

Johnson, F. Roy. 1966. *The Nat Turner Slave Insurrection.* Murfreesboro, N.C.: Johnson Publishing Company.

Kahn, Victoria. 1994. *Machiavellian Rhetoric: From the Counter-Reformation to Milton.* Princeton, N.J.: Princeton University Press.

Klemm, David E. 1986. *Hermeneutical Inquiry, Volume I: The Interpretation of Texts.* Atlanta: Scholars Press.

Klotman, Phyllis. 1977. *Humanities Through the Black Experience Dubuque:* Kendal/Hunt Publishing Company.

Locke, Alain L. 1983. "Values and Imperatives." In *Philosophy Born of Struggle, Anthology of Afro-American Philosophy from 1917*, ed. Leonard Harris. Dubuque: Kendal/Hunt Publishing Company.

Long, Charles H. 1986. *Significations, Signs, Symbols and Images in the Interpretation of Religion.* Philadelphia: Fortress Press.

———. 1995. "Towards a Post-Colonial Method in the Study of Religion." *Religious Studies News*, 10:2,5.

Meyers, William H. "The Hermeneutical Dilemma of the African American Biblical Student." In *Stony the Road We Trod: African American Biblical Interpretation*, ed. Cain Hope Felder. Minneapolis: Fortress Press.

Morrison, Toni. 1993. *Playing in the Dark: Whiteness and the Literary Imagination*. New York: Vintage Books.

Murphy, Joseph. 1988. *Santeria: An African Religion in America*. Boston: Beacon Press.

Noel, James A. 1990. "Memory and Hope: Toward a Hermeneutic of African- American Consciousness." *Journal of Religious Thought*, 47:10.

———. 1980. "Call and Response: The Meaning of the Moan and Significance of the Shout in Black Worship." *Reformed Liturgy and Music*, 28:20.

Ozment, Steven. 1980. *The Age of Reform, 1150-1550* New Haven: Yale University Press.

Pietz, William. 1985. "The Problem of the Fetish I." *RES* 9 (Spring) 5-17.

———. "The Problem of the Fetish IIIa." *RES* 16 (Autumn) 105-23.

Ritschl, Dietrich. 1967. *Memory and Hope: An Inquiry Concerning the Presence of Christ*. New York: Macmillan Company.

Schwartzman, Myron. 1990. *Romare Bearden: His Life and Art*. New York: Harry N, Abrams, Inc.

Siebert, Rudolf J. 1985. *The Critical Theory of Religion. The Frankfurt School*. Berlin/New York/Amsterdam: Mouton Publishers.

Simmel, Georg. 1971. "Subjective Culture." In *George Simmel on Individuality and Social Forms*, ed. D. Levine. Chicago: University of Chicago Press.

Stark, Rodney, and William Sims Bainbridge. 1987. *A Theory of Religion*. New York: Peter Lang.

Sullivan, Lawrence E. 1990. "Putting An End to the Text as Primary." In *Beyond the Classics? Essays in Religious Studies and Liberal Education*, ed. Frank E. Reynolds and Sheryl L. Burkhalter. Atlanta: Scholars Press.

Todorov, Izvetan. 1984. *The Conquest of America: The Question of the Other*, trans. Richard Houtex. New York: Harper Perennial.

Touraine, Alain. 1995. *Critique of Modernity*. Cambridge, Mass.: Blackwell.

Toynbee, Arnold. 1956. *An Historian's Approach to Religion*. London: Oxford University Press.

Woodson, Carter G. 1933. *The Mis-Education of the Negro*. Philadelphia: Hakim's Publications.

NOTES

1. In Weber's theory, according to Schluchter in *The Rise of Western Rationalism*: "the formulation of law, bureaucratization and extension of the market economy were as important as the religious disenchantment of the world. . . . They continue to haunt us in the secularized attitude of world mastery and world domination of impersonality and lack of brotherhood" (1981, 174).

2. For very lucid accounts of Nietzsche's and Foucault's critiques of modernity (which are similar to that of Du Bois) see: Jurgen Habermas' *The Philosophical Discourse of Modernity* (Cambridge: MIT Press, 1991).

3. See Thomas P. Peardon's "Introduction" in John Locke's *The Second Treatise of Government* (1952, xix). See John Locke, *The Second Treatise of Government* (New York: Bobbs-Merrill), edited with introduction.

4. For documentation of the role the black presence had on the political and war strategies of England and the Colonies see: Sylvia R. Frey's *Water from the Rock: Black Resistance in a Revolutionary Age* (1991) and Robin Blackburn's *The Overthrow of Colonial Slavery, 1776-1846* (1988). For an historical analysis of the relationship between Haiti and the French Revolution see C. L. R. James' *The Black Jacobins: Tousaint L'Ouverture and the San Domingo Revolution* (1989).

5. Robert Bartlett said in his *The Making of Europe, Conquest, Colonization and Cultural Change*, 950-1350 that "Europe is both a region and an idea. The societies and cultures that have existed in this western extremity of the Eurasian land-mass have always been highly diverse, and the case for grouping them together as 'European' has varied from period to period" (1993, 1).

6. According to Funkenstein, in *Theology and the Scientific Imagination.* "A respectable family of explanations in social and economic thought since the seventeenth century is sometimes known by the 'invisible-hand' explanations, a term borrowed from Adam Smith. . . . From Vico to Marx . . . whether they speak of providence, nature, or reason as acting directly and invisibly, in all of these constructions the 'finger of God' disappeared from the course of human events" (1986, 202, 204-5).

7. Joseph M. Murphy wrote: "Through the linked concepts of order, creation, and destiny, the number sixteen represents the variables of the human condition, the sixteen possible situations of human life. . . . this means 257 possible combinations of two to the eighth power. The goal of the *babalawo* is to arrive at the appropriate odo for the situation of the querent" (*Santeria: An African Religion in America* (1988), 17).

THEOLOGY AND POPULAR CULTURE

Kathryn Tanner

Recent trends in academic theology attend to what might be called theologies of the people. By that phrase I mean theologies without much textual or even extended verbal expression which are simply found, more often than not, fully embedded in the religious practices and lived relations of those who, with reference to intellectual training, social standing, economic attainment or institutional position, cannot be counted among the elites of church and society. Theologies of the people are the theologies that play out in the lives of those without a great deal of education and certainly without formal training in theology, the theologies of those with no institutional standing in church or academy and/or a far from elevated status in the wider society. In short, these are the theologies of ordinary people, who run a gamut of degrees of marginalization according to their distance from the legitimation that the complex intersection of a number of different factors such as ordination, academic degree, or privileged social location might confer. At the near end of the spectrum are theologies of the lay members of mainstream Christian churches who, even if they are fairly well educated, white and middle class, are without theological training or the privilege of religious leadership roles. At the far end are the theologies of those on the social, intellectual and institutional margins of both church and society: in earlier days, the theologies of black slave and ex-slave converts to Christianity; in contemporary times, Latin American peasants or poor Hispanic women in the United States struggling to make sense of their situation and their Christian faith in light of one another, or the theologies of Haitians practicing, on the outskirts of the Roman Catholic church, a Vodou laced with Catholic liturgical forms and visual representations.[1]

Philosophy, the traditional dialogue partner for theology when it is developed by educated elites or by religious specialists, is obviously far less relevant to academic theology preoccupied with theologies of the people. The social sciences and anthropology have so far taken center stage as interdisciplinary aids to theological inquiry of this latter sort—for example, ethnographic methods are used to elicit belief from lived practice, and Marxist forms of ideology-critique and social analysis help to determine the intersections between Christian faith and socio-political location and organization. Cultural studies—especially recent theories of popular culture within cultural studies—offer another interdisciplinary avenue. What might it mean, from these new theoretical vantage points, to consider theologies of the people as forms of popular culture?

The first aim of this paper is to explore this question in a programmatic way. A second aim is to broaden the question so as to encompass inquiry into the nature of theology in its traditional associations with educated and religious elites. After investigating the light that recent theories of popular culture throw on popular religion and theology, I attempt to draw out broader implications for theology in general—that is, implications for theology in both its elite and popular forms. In this connection I inquire about the extent to which an account of theologies of the people that is informed by theories of popular culture might also hold for theology more traditional-, ly conceived. By calling them "theology" and serving to give them voice, recent trends in academic theology elevate the commonly ignored religious beliefs and practices of ordinary and marginalized peoples to a level equal in importance to that of Christian theological "classics." Perhaps a cultural studies treatment of theologies of the people would have a similar leveling effect by the opposite route. Traditional theology might, so to speak, be brought down to the level of popular theology should one be able to demonstrate, by way of theories of popular culture, that many of the characteristics of popular theology also hold for the theologies produced by educated and religious elites.

POPULAR THEOLOGY AS A FORM OF POPULAR CULTURE

In current religious studies literature some consensus on a descriptive level exists concerning the general features of popular theology and religion (see Schreiter 1986; Scott 1990; Brown 1991; and Rabateau 1978—the last two works are not concerned to summarize such features but offer richly detailed accounts of particular cases). Popular religious practices, and therefore the theologies embedded within them, are, first of all, eminently practical. The various aspects of popular theology and religion—e.g. what is worshipped and how—serve the everyday needs of people. They help make sense of, or, better, serve as psychological and even hoped for real remedies for, the everyday distresses which tend to multiply in degree and severity with the extent of one's marginalization. The object of worship is someone or something that helps—someone or something that, especially in times of trouble, hears and responds to the believer and to the forms of worship and appeal in which he or she engages.

A number of other features follow from this practical character of popular theology and religion. To better serve the end of succor in everyday life, popular theology and religion are hospitably inclusive. "Syncretistic" is the more common and somewhat perjorative term for this; popular theology and religion bring together beliefs and ritual forms that are not considered compatible in elite theologies or in organized religions under the control of religious specialists. Questions of logical coherence or purity of religious identity—typical concerns of theologies developed by educated or religious elites—are, moreover, overridden by a quest for functional coherence. What holds all the apparently theoretically inconsistent and wildly disparate elements of popular theology and religion together is the hope that all of it "works." A certain isolating selectivity and attention to form over content are, furthermore, the prerequisites for the mixed forms of religious belief and practice that result from such hospitable inclusivity. Statements of belief, images, prayers, etc. are incorporated without the rest of their ritual or theological trappings. For example, an image of krishna can stand on a Vodou alter only insofar as it has been isolated from the rest of Hindu worship and belief (see Brown 1991, 13). The form of beliefs, images, or ritual practices is retained but almost always with some alteration of content. For example, black slaves would tell the Exodus story but for them Egypt referred to the very United States that white preachers identified with the promised land. Again in virtue of their practical function, the significance of the various aspects of popular theology and religion cannot be separated from the specifics of the circumstances they address; the meaning of beliefs and ritual action is closely tied to the incidentals of everyday life. One cannot, for example, recount the meaning of black spirituals without attending to what is going on in the lives of the people who sing them. Finally, the theological and ritual productions of popular religion—the stories, the songs, the street festivals that people regularly enact—are not fixed, closed, or rigidly defined; they instead take flexible and open-ended forms that are responsive and adaptable to the changing particularities of situation and need.

In this general description, garnered from works on popular theology and religion, I have unified what might otherwise have seemed a disconnected set of separate features—practicality, hospitable inclusiveness, selective attention to form, situational responsiveness—around the point or end of popular religion and theology: the effort to make do. Theories of popular culture, while not by any means dismissive of the importance of the plight of the people for making sense of popular culture, contribute to an understanding of popular religion and theology by organizing these features along a different axis: as moments of a particular form of productive and relational cultural process.

The words "productive" and "relational" are especially important here. Recent theories of popular culture (Hall 1981, 1988; and de Certeau 1984) are designed to move beyond the inadequacies of two previous theoretical perspectives. The first of these sees popular culture in terms of passive receptivity. A Marxist variant of this perspective interprets popular culture as the production of dominant classes interested in generating the consent of the lower classes to social, political, and economic arrangements that disadvantage them. Here the people are the cultural dupes of the dominant classes who, through control of the means of cultural production and distribution, manage to impose cultural forms—beliefs, values, attitudinal outlooks—upon them. Frankfurt school theories of mass culture are another variant of this same perspective. The passivity of the people is highlighted by simply identifying popular culture with the productions of the culture industries that are run by moneyed and educated elites—movies, television sitcoms, pulp fiction.

The second general understanding of popular culture that recent theories avoid isolates popular culture from the power dynamics of elites struggling for control and views popular culture instead as the autonomous, completely authentic production of the people. Popular culture is romanticized along the lines of an anti-elitist populism—e.g., in the view of the United States as a nation unified by a democratic culture enjoyed by all without regard for class or social distinction—or along the lines of an anti-modernist search for an alternative to the cultural forms of industrial capitalism—e.g., an alternative to a profit driven bureacratic ethic. This theoretical outlook has its roots in the preoccupations of late eighteenth and nineteenth century European intellectuals with the "folk" (as in the work of Herder and the brothers Grimm), which spearheaded nationalistic and anti-Enlightenment currents in modern European thought about manners and customs (see Burke 1978, chap. 1).

In contrast to these two general perspectives, new theories of popular culture regain a sense for the creative agency of the people (missing in the first perspective), while (pace the second) refusing to consider popular culture independently of a tension-filled relationship with elite cultural productions. Popular forms of culture only exist vis-à-vis elite cultural productions, but this relationship with elite cultural productions is not typified by passive consumption. It is instead considered a creative, productive relation in its own right.

Popular forms of culture only exist vis-à-vis elite cultural productions because, in the first place, popular forms of culture presume a polarized dynamic of cultural forms in which relations of dominance and subordination are being set up. However much they may be the product of activities rooted in the social and material lives of the people, popular forms of culture are also, in other words, essentially bound up with efforts on the part of elites to maintain a distinction between more and less valuable aspects of culture, attempts to police a boundary between what counts as an elite cultural activity and form and what does not, by way of such institutions as the educational system and literary and scholarly productions. These efforts to set off popular from elite culture are combined, at least in the modern period, with efforts to control popular practices—efforts to reform, marginalize, or eliminate them altogether. The monopolization of the culture industries by elites under conditions of modern global capitalism puts the final touches on such efforts to control: indigenous forms of cultural production by non-elites are increasingly replaced by popular consumption of mass-marketed cultural commodities. This is, then, a second and stronger sense in which popular culture only exists vis-à-vis elite cultural productions. Popular culture lives off those cultural productions of elites that are intended for them; popular culture is itself the product of their consumption.

According to these new theories, what elites produce for mass consumption (popular and commercial culture) and what the people make of it are not, however, the same. Popular appropriation—how mass-produced culture enters into the lives of non-elites—is never entirely manipulable by those commercial cultural productions. Popular consumption is therefore its own kind of cultural production. In other words, popular culture in this sense of popular use or consumption—what I usually mean by "popular culture" in this paper—is a *creative* process of working with the materials provided by cultural elites, materials that it finds rather than produces for itself, materials provided to it by elites with the power over the means of cultural production and distribution that non-elites lack.

Thus the cultural creativity of the people is displayed not in artifactual productions that are distinctively their own, but in the novel ways they make do with the cultural productions of others. The creativity of popular culture exists *as* a process of cultural transformation in the in-between. What popular culture works with has its own structure and definition, acting as limits on popular creativity: popular culture cannot just make anything it likes out of the material it employs. Elite cultural productions often effectively convey preferred meanings which any popular cultural process is forced to struggle against, either directly (in the hard task of altering relatively taken-for-granted denotative meanings) or indirectly with reference to their valuational associations (an easier task but one that remains circumscribed by popular culture's acceptance of the denotative senses of the cultural forms communicated by elite productions) (see Hall 1980, 133-5; Condit 1991). Popular culture often regains, however, its interpretive license by taking a special interest in elite cultural productions that allow some free play: for example, elite productions that are not entirely coherent, productions that include internal tensions (e.g., television programs that both mock and laud working class lives); productions that are not characterized by complete or highly detailed expositions (e.g., images—the Virgin Mary has a child in her arms but perhaps it is a girl? (see Brown 1991, 228); or productions in media that can exercise little control over the way they are heard or seen (e.g., radio and television programs which cannot keep listeners from leaving the room or switching channels). The techniques of cultural transformation employed in the processes of popular culture tend, moreover, to make any elite cultural production susceptible to the novelty of popular use. Selective attention breaks apart or interrupts whatever coherence the forms of elite cultural productions might attempt to achieve. Popular culture also typically employs in episodic and ad hoc ways the elements into which selective attention has broken down elite cultural productions, in order to bring out their relevance for the changing circumstances of everyday life—its struggles and conflicts. Popular culture in these ways takes advantage of the very potential for shifting or floating signifiers that post-structuralist thought posits as an ever-recurring threat to attempts by elite cultural productions to achieve coherence and closure (see Laclau and Mouffe 1985, chap. 3).

Because popular culture is understood by this new theory as a productive process in relation to elite cultural productions, what matters is not so much what the people say and do, but how they say and do it. In its efforts to describe and analyze forms of popular culture, the theory is therefore interested in the characteristics of the processes of cultural transformation themselves, in the types of operations on elite culture that the processes of popular culture involve. Most generally, one could say those operations are diversionary; they turn elite cultural forms in new and unexpected directions. More specifically, these processes involve the inventive recombination of cultural elements drawn from very different elite cultural sites (e.g., the eclectic assemblage of dead symbols and industrial commodities—from swastikas to safety pins—in punk style), the superimposition of foreign cultural forms within the spaces of elite cultural productions so as to produce a kind of cultural palimpsest (e.g., the way Haitian immigrants insert within the system of space imposed by low-income housing in the United States a manner of dwelling typical of their native land); an almost parodic use of the terms and forms of elite culture that subjects them to new and different intentions (e.g., a drag queen's use of high fashion), and an improvisational playing with the opportunities that the elements of elite culture provide to address in a fitting way the exigencies of particular situations (e.g., the selection of supermarket products to create the appropriate meals for an ethnic festival) (see de Certeau 1984, 1-44). When this theory of popular culture looks for the message of popular culture it therefore does not look for explicit statements but for a message conveyed inarticulately in the manners by which popular culture makes do. Some sort of resistance to a disempowered life occurs in and through such processes of cultural transformation, in the sense that the people can carve out thereby a life of their own that is significantly different from the preferred meanings of their existence conveyed by elite cultural productions. Refusal to consent to a life in which struggle and trouble are to be one's lot need not therefore be sought primarily in the content of what it is that ordinary and marginalized people do, say, and value.[2]

Besides adding transformative cultural process to practical orientation as a unifying focus for the various aspects of popular theology and religion, this theory of popular culture suggests some important directives for the study of popular religion and theology. First, there is little point in trying to distinguish popular and elite forms of belief and practice according to content. Considerable overlap is likely in what it is that ordinary and marginalized people, on the one hand, and religious specialists and trained theologians, on the other, say and do. Elite and popular forms of theology and religion cannot be distinguished, therefore, by distributing cultural objects or forms between them. Second, the commonly employed external perspectives of quantitative social science are inappropriate for the study of popular theology and religion; indeed, any method that merely tallies up or classifies aspects of popular theology and religion is inappropriate to the extent that it extracts them from the field of cultural operations, the historical context, or the tensive relations to elite culture that characterizes their use. Finally, if, as we have said, the message of popular culture is conveyed in the very ways it makes do, then those who study popular theology and religion are best able to make that message clear by simply recounting those doings (de Certeau 1984, chap. 5). Forms of popular culture "say exactly what they do. They constitute an act which they intend to mean" (80). Those who study popular theology and religion should therefore eschew the interpretive efforts necessary to gloss a supposedly hidden depth of meaning, and practice the more straightforward "art of telling about ways of operating" (89); the interpretive task becomes to narrate those ways of operating.

IMPLICATIONS FOR THEOLOGY GENERALLY

Interpreting popular theology and religion according to these new models of popular culture makes it easier to see elite and popular forms of theology as similar enterprises, and makes it easier to produce thereby a kind of "unified field theory" for theology generally—in both its elite and popular forms. The practical orientation, highlighted in other views of popular religion and theology, is perhaps not also characteristic of elite theology, although one might try, with social scientists such as Max Weber, to interpret traditional theology as an effort to give meaning in the face of the trials and tribulations of life, and therefore as a way of providing at least some sort of intellectual succor. If, however, as new theories of popular culture suggest, certain discursive processes of cultural formation are important indicators of popular theology, similar processes might turn up in elite theology, whatever the difference in aim between the two.

Indeed, it is characteristic of recent theories of popular culture to problematize any sharp distinction between elite and popular culture. As an historical matter, the distinction is far from clear, coming to the fore perhaps only in the last several centuries with the efforts of cultural and socio-political elites to set off their own ways of life from those ways of the lower classes that they hope to control or suppress. Recent theories of popular culture also question whether the distinguishing features of elite culture—e.g., the unity and completion of high-culture novels—are really essential or intrinsic to elite cultural forms themselves; this is the usual assumption when elite and popular cultural forms are sharply distinguished in a way that devalues the latter. Recent theories of popular culture instead devise a unified method of approach to both popular and elite forms of culture using a single system of categories (such as sign system and ideological function) that relativizes the differences between popular and elite culture and puts them on an at least initially level playing field of potential value (see Easthope 1991).

These recent theories of popular culture do differ among themselves to an extent on the degree of difference marked by the continued employment of a distinction between popular and elite forms of culture. De Certeau, for example, describes the operations of popular culture using the foil of a very different set of high-culture operations—ones that, unlike popular culture, are totalistic, homogenizing, coherent, and abstract. Yet, he clearly also blurs the distinction between popular consumers and high-culture producers by talking of consumption as a particular form of production in its own right—this is indeed one of his most important contributions to the study of popular culture. He recognizes, moreover, that a sharp distinction in form between popular and elite culture is itself in great part a creation of high culture's own ideological self-presentation; such a sharp distinction in form is in the interest of a high-cultural devaluation of the popular.

Stuart Hall (following the socio-cultural theories of Ernesto Laclau and Chantal Mouffe) carries through on these more innovative aspects of de Certeau's work (Hall 1981, 1988; see Laclau and Mouffe 1985). While not overlooking the power differences reflected in a distinction between elite and high culture or the differences of means and aim into which those power differences translate—the culture of elite groups working, for example, towards hegemony with the help of schools and print and electronic media the culture of the people resisting, through processes of creative consumption, what elites would like them to believe—Hall nevertheless brings out the structural similarities in their respective productive cultural processes. Just as popular cultural production occurs in and through a tensive relation with elite culture, so elite cultural production often exists in and through a tensive relation with popular culture. Elite cultural productions that are intended for popular consumption, or that are designed to influence what the people say and do, work on popular culture in much the same way that popular culture works on elite culture. One can therefore say that "elite culture is itself constituted in large measure by an operation on materials that do not properly belong to it. It is also a very subtle game of appropriations, of reusages, of misappropriations" vis-à-vis popular processes of cultural production (Chartier 1982, 34).

Like what popular culture does to it, but this time with the advantages that money, power, and social prestige afford, elite culture arrests cultural elements from their usual flow in popular cultural usage and diverts them to new uses within its own productions. It disorganizes popular cultural productions and reorganizes at least some selection of these now dislodged elements so as to bring them into line with its own preferred outlooks. The result is a mixed and oddly compound discourse, bringing together as it does elements from very different cultural sites. Theoretical consistency is hereby sacrificed to the end of wide-spread popular acceptance; the point of encorporating elements from popular culture would be lost if in being transformed within elite cultural productions they became unrecognizable to the people to whom they already meant something. Elite cultural productions, if they are to be popular—consumed, that is, by large numbers of the people— have to successfully reference popular experience even as they transform it. This structural tension in elite cultural productions between elements from popular culture and an elite use of them, while it helps make elite cultural productions popular, also renders them susceptible in turn to the ultimately uncontrollable transformations of popular cultural processes. For example, television sitcoms may present a certain preferrred image of working-class life by reorganizing and reshaping what working-class people themselves say and do; but what working-class people get out of watching such programs is another matter. They need not passively accept that image since it contains within it, in virtue of its efforts to be popular, elements of internal contestation. Finally, when managing well their efforts to be consumed by the masses, these elite cultural productions, like those of popular culture, make the most of the opportunities provided by the particulars of the changing cultural scene.

Hall suggests, moreover, that much the same general types of cultural operation, which we now see hold for both directions of the vis-à-vis between popular and elite culture, extend to relations *among* elite cultural productions—in situations, therefore, where power differences are not by definition as stark at the start as those between elites and the people (see Hall 1988). Various forms of elite culture—say, various political philosophies—are not entirely discrete cultural productions but vie with one another in a kind of cultural contest over the meanings, associations and "inferential logics" of shared terms (46). Across the wide field of competing elite cultural productions, one elite cultural production gains credibility and acceptance over others in much the same way that an elite cultural production gains popular acceptance: by successfully turning to its own uses the cultural forms employed by other cultural productions. "Nationalism," for example, might be turned from the associations it has in one elite political philosophy with a consensus in beliefs and values and aligned, instead, in a new cultural formation with a healthy complementarity among people of markedly different backgrounds and opinions. Or, what was secondary and subordinate in one cultural formation becomes the primary nucleus for a new organization that covers much the same cultural terrain (Gramsci 1971, 195). For example, when economic weakness in Britain and the United States imperiled the achievement of both profitability in the private sector and state sponsored welfare programs, the new political right of the 1980s was able to disorganize a previous political consensus in which social needs were beginning to have a say over market forces and then to reorganize many of the same elements of political discourse around the preeminent needs of the market and the value of privatization (Hall 1988, 35-41).

Unlike popular culture, elite cultural productions in their struggles with one another are working toward intellectual coherence and multi-contextual pertinence; victory over elite cultural competitors is often indeed measured in such terms. But the internal tensions and relevance to particular situations typical of popular culture have their place here, too. The cultural terrain over which such elite cultural battles are fought is often tensive and contradictory, prompting elite cultural productions to contain an awkward mixture of different discursive fields—e.g., in the last example of the political right, tales of hardship in working class family life intermingling with the cold calculation of the conditions for maximum profit in industries. "Thatcherism, as a discursive formation, has remained a plurality of discourses—about the family, the economy, national identity, morality, crime, law, women, human nature . . . [it] has stitched together a contradictory juncture between the logics of the market . . . and organic conservatism" (53). This tensive quality of the cultural terrain is indeed what enables a cultural struggle among elite discourses to take place: because the terrain is tensive, no final or uncontestable settlement is possible concerning the way to put it all together intelligibly. These cultural contests among elites have a situational character, moreover, in that the fights tend to be fiercest over the meaning and associations of terms with the greatest cultural currency at a particular moment. Finally, the tension-filled relation of production and consumption that holds between elite and popular culture has its analogue in cultural struggles among elite cultural productions. Although the playing field is more level here than in the case of elite and popular cultural processes, there are certainly analogous differences in cultural power in contests among elite cultural productions, which therefore have discursive effects comparable to those involved in the relation between elite and popular culture. Elite cultural productions that have established for themselves some degree of cultural dominance have gained thereby an initial "inertial authority of habit and instinct" (44). These elite cultural productions are usually the ones with the greatest say in politics, educational institutions, or media outlets, and through such means they set the terms of elite cultural contest: other elite cultural productions must respond to them. Therefore, just as popular culture works with and makes over whatever it is that elite cultural productions provide to it, so non-dominant elite cultural productions are forced to struggle against the preferred meanings of the cultural terrain provided by dominant elites.

These suggestions by Hall about the ways in which popular and elite culture might be structurally similar as processes of cultural transformation have important implications for an understanding of theologies produced by educated elites and religious specialists. For example, from the very beginnings of Christianity, the theologies of classically trained clergy were directed at a very wide audience; they were meant to be popular in the statistical sense of the word, consumed by many and not simply by members of elite cultural or religious classes. "One of the greatest advantages of Christian over pagan literature was precisely this, that it could break out of the mold of traditional elite culture and develop types of writing that could be diffused far more widely, and yet that did not lose the essential appeal to the elite audience" (Cameron 1991, 147). By way of sermons and the writing of apocryphal acts and lives of saints, Christian theologians used their classical training to propogate the Christian faith across the stratifications of Greco-Roman society. Like any elite cultural productions designed for more widespread consumption, these Christian cultural productions exhibit a mixed, internally tensive character. Using all the techniques of classical rhetoric, they nevertheless proclaim their simplicity of expression; the productions of classically educated theologians, they nevertheless make the virtue of saints without formal education their subject matter (e.g., Athanasius' *Life of Anthony*); breaking through the usual preoccupation of classical biographers with public figures (that is, great men), Christian theologians narrate the lives of women or the poor, those who are closely identified with the private sphere according to a classical distinction between public and private.

If Stuart Hall is right about the nature of elite cultural productions that are designed to be popular, then what is happening here cannot simply be understood as a subsequent, secondary adjustment of a theological message for popular consumption via innovative media. The theological message itself is the product of a negotiation with popular forces; it is formed from the beginning in a vis-à-vis with popular culture. In the process of producing a theological message, the theologian performs a balancing act between the desire, on the one hand, to reshape and reorganize popular belief and action, and the need, on the other, to establish a broad popular appeal. The theologian performs a balancing act between what he, as a classically trained member of the clergy, might like something to mean and what significant numbers of lay and formally uneducated people might be willing to accept. What most scholars recognize about Christian festivals and rituals—they essentially involve negotiations with popular forms of culture—should therefore also be expected of the beliefs and concepts of elite Christian theology. Like those festivals and rituals, Christian theology arises from the very first in a kind of local, ad hoc, relational process of adjustment to the demands of popular cultural practice. Finally, despite the intention to meet theoretical aims such as coherence, clarity, and completion, elite theological productions are pulled by the demands of popularity toward polyvalent ambiguities of sense. For example, theological discussion of divine kingship may suggest to elite classes that God is a king like any other and therefore properly represented on earth by human potentates; to the ordinary and the marginalized, however, God may be the only king, replacing in ultimate authority all the earthly lords before whom they are forced to bow. Elite theological discourse cannot winnow down the meaning of divine kingship to the first sense, and thereby remove this sort of ambiguity and inconsistency in its cultural productions, without threatening its base of popular support, without threatening its plausibility with the ordinary and marginalized people that make up the rank and file of Christian adherents.[3]

What, however, about elite theologies with no intention of broad appeal, the elite theologies of arcane and learned treatises, theological productions whose subject matter, style, and genre presumably restrict their public to similarly elite groups? One might be led by the historical associations of theology with philosophy to think that the structure of these sorts of elite theological productions has little in common with the mixed, ambiguous and situational logic of operations typical of popular forms of culture. One might think that these elite theological productions (say, the publications of contemporary theologians based in research universities) would be preoccupied with the ends of good theory, the ends of science understood as *Wissenschaft* (e.g., consistency, coherence, and the comprehensiveness afforded by abstract thought) in a way that would preclude the possibility of strong structural similarities with popular cultural processes.

The general nature of theological discourse, whatever its audience, provides, however, an analogy with popular culture. The general nature of theological discourse is such that, like popular culture, it does not provide for itself the cultural resources out of which it is constructed; the process of elite theological production works with and makes over cultural productions that are not its own. Elite theological productions, no matter how impervious to popular consumption, form no insular body of simply self-referencing arcana, but, like popular culture's relation to elite culture, essentially exist in a tensive relation with wider cultural spheres (whether elite or popular is immaterial here). Rather than being a self-sufficient sort of cultural production formed in isolation from the wider culture in which theologians participate, theological discourse is a kind of parasitic cultural production living off the host cultures that it finds and does not produce. Theologians, for example, do not create from the bottom up their own language of God, or their assumptions about the world and the human beings in it; they do not create them out of whole cloth. The general nature of theological discourse is such that theologians create their own distinctively Christian theological productions by working instead with what the wider culture gives them, altering these cultural productions of the wider society— selecting from them, reorganizing them, diverting the usual meanings of their terms—in accordance with their own particular religious perspectives and interests.

One can therefore say that elite theology plays the part of popular culture vis-à-vis the practices of the wider culture in which its creators participate. If the distinction between production and consumption is the basis for the structural differences that remain between elite and popular culture, then elite theology is like popular culture in its own relation to the wider culture since it depends on the productions of that wider culture to provide it with the materials with which it works. Elite theology is in this way distinguished from other elite cultural productions which are only forced into the popular cultural operation of creative consumption when trying either to be popular or to wrest the cultural ground from more dominant elite cultural productions. Because the analogy with popular culture exists in virtue of the general nature of theological discourse, the structural operation that elite theology shares with popular culture—creative consumption—holds generally and across the board; it is not an occasional matter of particular aims (say, the desire to appeal to popular tastes) or a matter of special circumstances (say, situations of relative non-dominance vis-à-vis other elite cultural productions). Thus, one can expect elite theological productions to show this similarity with popular culture whether or not those elite cultural productions and their authors are culturally or socially marginalized in relation to the wider society. The analogy here with popular culture is not predicated on power differences but on the general nature of theological discourse—the structural insufficiencies of theological discourse discussed above. The power imbalances that are ordinarily essential to the formation of popular culture are therefore not a prerequisite for elite theology's showing a structural similarity to popular culture in its cultural operations.

If, therefore, elite theology always bears at least this analogy with popular culture, then the operations of popular culture become the model for understanding theology as a whole. Given such a model one should, first of all, not expect elite theological cultural productions to be distinguished from those of the wider culture primarily by differences in content. Like what we saw in the case of the relation betwen elite and popular culture, considerable overlap may exist between what theologians and others do and say. Of much greater significance for the distinctiveness of theological cultural production is the how, the particular shape of the use that theologians make of the wider culture—the style of that use (to use a term from aesthetics) or its logic of transformation (to put it more abstractly and less colorfully). "Nature" and "hypostasis," for example, are not the monopoly of the early Christian creeds; but the oddity of their uses when speaking of Jesus Christ and the Trinity is.

In such processes of cultural production vis-à-vis the cultures of the wider society, theology becomes, one could say, double voiced.[4] Theology makes what is said in the wider culture its own, but only by twisting it in new directions, to serve different intentions, so that the wider culture speaks with a new intonation and syntax. The audience hears what is commonly said in the wider culture but in and through the voice of the theologian who now utters it in some novel way from a different point of view. The process of theological production issues therefore in a kind of palimpsest: what is said in the wider culture is visible underneath the surface of a theological production so as to produce a kind of transformative and reevaluative commentary on the wider culture. At one end of the spectrum of degrees of possible transformation and reevaluation that this involves, the new twist might mean the simple identification of an aspect of the wider culture with the truth of Christ (e.g., in theological statements in which Christian salvation is equated with the transcendence of nature aspired to by a nineteenth-century bourgeois ideal of progress); at the other end of the spectrum, the transformation might amount to outright antagonism (e.g., in theological statements that conform with the programmatic dictate of Tertullian, "What has Athens to do with Jerusalem?").

Even in the case of the greatest antagonism, however, the polemic to be found in such double voiced theological productions is indirect or hidden (Bakhtin 1984, 195-7). The polemic or apolegetic occurs here within the very formation of theological statements and not by way of subsequent argument in which the assumptions of the wider culture are made the object of explicit debate. Although the theologian can of course go on to produce an explicit apologetic or polemic, here the theologian makes no direct reference to what is said in the wider culture with the intent of arguing with it, showing its faults or fine points from the novel perspective of belief in Christ; an address to the wider culture is instead contained from the first within the very construction of theological meaning. Such a hidden polemic or apologetic has certain advantages over direct argument: it amounts to a kind of apologetic or polemic by stealth. Because theological productions that are constituted by an odd use of the wider cultural field do not leave that wider cultural field but insinuate themselves within it, because these theological productions seem on the face of it, therefore, to start where everyone else starts, they work so as to seduce the adherents of the wider culture into following along, undefensively, a track of cultural transformations which holds unexpected surprises in store for them.

Such a tensive relation with the wider culture, written as it is into the very processes of theological cultural production themselves, is missed when attention is directed simply to the theologian's subject matter. For it to be seen, the rhetorical surfaces of elite theological productions—their "figures" and "turns"—have to be taken more seriously than they usually are. For this tensive character with the wider culture to be seen, the situational character of elite theologies also has to be acknowledged. There are not so much perennial topics of theological discourse as there are situationally variant materials which theological productions rather episodically rework using their tools of cultural subversion. Far from being a majestically abstract discussion of the nature of God and the world, theological productions drift, so to speak, from one particular situation of cultural contest, with its host culture or cultures, to another. The material which the wider culture provides to theology varies, but perhaps the tactics of cultural transformation in theology remain.[5] Those persistent tactics are, however, situation sensitive; they have the persistence of a tireless wiliness, rather than the persistence of timelessly true propositions. Like rhetoric, one can say that theological productions "are manipulations of language relative to occasions," with the intention thereby "to seduce, captivate or invert the . . . position of the addressee" (de Certeau 1984, 39).

Theological production does not just arise in and through a relationship with the cultures of the wider society but also with reference to other past and present theological productions. Past theological productions often have some claim, as authorities, to respectful treatment. (For example, biblical texts, early ecumenical creedal statements, and theological treatises by the "fathers" of the church, often fall into this camp.) Present ones more often than not figure as simple rivals in a competition for credibility and acceptance from the same audiences.

Following what was said above about relations among elite cultural productions generally, popular culture as a model for these relations among elite theological productions suggests that such theological productions involve the disorganization and reorganization of shared cultural elements. Theological productions appropriate the wealth of past theological productions selectively, often breaking them apart in the process, so as to redirect their senses and associations within new discursive organizations according to judgments of value which are often, though not necessarily entirely, premised upon present day concerns. For example, spurred by the worry that past theologies of the cross merely served to confirm the sufferings of this life by viewing them as the demands of an oddly un-Christian, hard-hearted God, recent theologies of the cross selectively appropriate, from among the great variety of positions made possible by past theological interpretations, those that comport with God's compassion rather than God's justice, changing thereby the sense of that divine compassion in the direction of a willingness to suffer with others. Contemporary theological productions, moreover, compete among themselves in a contest over the meaning, associations, and inferential logics of the terms they share in virtue of this theological past, as well as in virtue of their participation in the wider cultural scene. The tension-filled character of these diverse cultural materials (e.g., what has God's grace to do with God's wrath, or the power of God to do with a world that runs according to its own laws?) is never fully overcome by any one theology in its competition with other theologies to establish coherence and closure, setting the stage thereby for further cultural contests over the meaning and organization of the same cultural terms.

If processes of theological production are like this, then they do not require the mechanical virtues of accurate repetition or reproduction often associated with abstract theory; that is, they do not require the ability to follow predictably the prescription of formal rules, or the ability to translate the same meaning across accidental circumstances of situation, or the ability simply to apply a general theory to the particulars that are properly seen to fall within its scope. Theological production instead requires more complicated and subtle skills: "a kind of 'tact', the apprehension and creation of a 'harmony' among particular practices, the ethical and poetic gesture of *religare* (tying together) or making a concordance through an indefinite series of concrete acts" (de Certeau 1984, 74, following John Henry Newman). The theologian has to have the skills of a tight-rope walker, balancing by means of innumerable ad hoc adjustments the tensions to be found both within the irreducible diversity of Christian theological productions and between any selective appropriation of elements from these past theological productions and the wider cultural scene (see de Certeau 1984, 73; also Barth 1978, 207. This idea, as a programmatic statement, however is perhaps more Troeltschian than Barthian—see Troeltsch 1991, 97).

THEOLOGICAL CONCLUSIONS

The above description of theology, especially the description of elite theology, is not theologically neutral. Although it is designed to cover, and therefore to be true to, what all sorts of different theologians are doing (whatever their philosophical, theological, or denominational commitments), the description itself would not be acceptable to all of them. Not all of them would affirm that such a description makes good theological sense. Theological objections would no doubt settle around the account of elite theology as a mixed discourse in an essential, albeit tensive, relation with both popular practices (religious or otherwise) and the cultural forms of the wider society generally. This idea does not sit well with assumptions about Christian identity that base it upon a sharp distinction between what is Christian and what is not, assumptions about Christian identity that make it, so to speak, a boundary issue—the more impermeable the boundary the better.

Certain answers to a number of classic theological issues are aligned with such a concern for purity.[6] For example, the account of sin will often locate it outside the person or community transformed in virtue of faith in Christ; and the correlative idea of God's grace sees it as issuing in a completely holy life. A very sharp separation is drawn between Jesus Christ and the God of nature and history, and between their respective goals and purposes. A narrow view is therefore taken of what is included within the purview and influence of Christ's grace. Allegiance to Christ, as a result, does not readily translate into responsibilities beyond the borders of Christian community; it tends to have no implications, either, for the whole of one's life. Christian commitments, moreover, are either not viewed as culturally conditioned at all, or they are thought to establish their own distinctive form of life, sitting next to, so to speak, a bevy of others—religious, ethnic, political—and to be chosen instead of them. Being true to one's Christian identity consequently involves stripping oneself of one's other identities and loyalties.[7]

A theology that finds the description of theology offered in this paper acceptable would form the contrary theological judgments on the same issues. For such a theology, the distinction between what is sinful and what is not does not fall at the boundary between Christian and non-Christian. Christian perfectionism is rejected. The comprehensiveness of Christ's transformative grace is affirmed, along with the comprehensiveness therefore of a Christian way of living. That way of living, insofar as it *is* genuinely comprehensive, is to be identified with an altered—perhaps radically altered— way of living all one's other commitments and allegiances, and not with some separately localized alternative to them.

One could muster theological arguments to support the latter conjuncture of theological claims rather than the former, and in that way bolster a theological judgment in favor of the application to theology of the theories of popular culture discussed in this paper. The former set of theological claims, a theologian could argue, is insufficiently trinitarian. Or it does an injustice to the way the original gospel message of Jesus Christ broke through the barriers of his own culturally divided world—cultural divisions between the religious worlds of Jew and non-Jew or the public and private worlds of free men, on the one hand, and women and slaves, on the other (see Elizondo 1990). Making such arguments would involve one in contests over the meaning, associations, and inferential logics of terms like sin and grace or creation and salvation, the sort of contests whose general structure it has been one aim of this paper to sketch in light of recent theories of popular culture. If such theories of popular culture are plausible in their own right, it may be that theological productions never in fact escape the mixed and tensive character of cultural productions as those theories describe them—whatever the desire on theological grounds for self-sufficient purity.

REFERENCES

Bakhtin, Mikhail. 1984. *Problems of Dostoevsky's Poetics*. Minneapolis: University of Minnesota Press.

Barth, Karl. 1978. "The Word of God and the Task of the Ministry." In *The Word of God and the Word of Man*. Gloucester, Mass.: Peter Smith.

Brown, Karen McCarthy. 1991. *Mama Lola: A Vodou Priestess in Brooklyn*. Berkeley: University of California Press.

Burke, Peter. 1978. *Popular Culture in Early Modern Europe*. New York: Harper and Row.

Cameron, Averil. 1991. *Christianity and the Rhetoric of Empire*. Berkeley: University of California Press.

Chartier, Roger. 1982. "Intellectual History or Sociocultural History? The French Trajectories." In *Modern European Intellectual History*, ed. D. LaCapra and S. Kaplan, 13-46. Ithaca and London: Cornell University Press.

Condit, Celeste. 1991. "The Rhetorical Limits of Polysemy." In *Critical Perspectives on Media and Society*, edited by R. Avery and D. Eason, 365-86. New York and London: The Guilford Press.

de Certeau, Michel. 1984. *The Practice of Everyday Life*. Berkeley: University of California Press.

Easthope, Antony. 1991. *Literary Studies into Cultural Studies*. New York and London: Routledge.

Elizondo, Virgil. 1990. *Galilean Journey: The Mexican-American Promise*. Maryknoll, N.Y.: Orbis.

Fiske, John. 1989. *Understanding Popular Culture*. London and New York: Routledge.

Gramsci, Antonio. 1971. *Selections from the Prison Notebooks*. New York: International Publishers.

Hall, Stuart. 1980. "Encoding/Decoding." In *Culture, Media, Language*, edited by S. Hall, P. Willis, D. Hobson, and A. Lowe, 128-38. London: Hutchinson.

———. 1981. "Notes on Deconstructing 'the Popular'." In *Peoples History and Socialist Theory*, edited by R. Samuel, 227-40. London: Routledge and Kegan Paul.

———. "The Toad in the Garden." In *Marxism and the Interpretation of Culture*, ed. C. Nelson and L. Grossberg, 35-58. Urbana and Chicago: University of Illinois Press.

Laclau, Ernesto, and Chantal Mouffe. 1985. *Hegemony and Socialist Strategy*. London: Verso.

Niebuhr, H. Richard. 1951. *Christ and Culture*. New York: Harper Colophon.

Rabateau, Albert. 1978. *Slave Religion*. Oxford: Oxford University Press.

Scott, James. 1990. *Domination and the Arts of Resistance*. New Haven: Yale University Press.

Schreiter, Robert. 1986. *Constructing Local Theologies*. Maryknoll, N.Y.: Orbis.

Tanner, Kathryn. 1994. "The Difference Theological Anthropology Makes." *Theology Today* (January): 567-79.

Troeltsch, Ernst. 1991. "The Dogmatics of the History-of-Religions School." In *Religion in History*, ed. J. L. Adams and W. Bense. Minneapolis: Fortress Press.

NOTES

1. "The people" is thus a collective term with a loose and shifting reference that may span or cross in complex ways common factors of social division such as class, gender, age and ethnicity; it is defined in opposition to the elites who make up the "power-bloc" on the grounds of a marked difference in social, economic, political, and cultural influence. See Hall (1981, 238-9).

2. This rather minimal sense of resistance does not necessarily imply, of course, active mobilization with others to work for social change. One might argue, however, that it forms the psychological prerequisite for a more activist contestation of that sort. See Fiske (1989, chap. 7).

3. Compare Scott (1991, 96-103), for similar ambiguities in elite cultural productions concerning monarchy generally.

4. Concerning this idea of double voiced texts and the features of texts associated with it, see Bakhtin (1984, 185-204).

5. For an example of what these tactics of cultural transformation might amount to, at least in the case of theological anthropology, see Tanner (1994).

6. H. R. Niebuhr (1951), though dated in certain respects, is still helpful in formulating these positions.

7. I have listed the above theological positions in such a way as to bring out their logical or associational connections, but such connections are not unbreakable; a theology that stresses purity of identity might include some of these positions and not the rest.

two

METHOD

TRACKING SPIRIT:

THEOLOGY AS CULTURAL CRITIQUE IN AMERICA

MARK MCCLAIN TAYLOR

> *I heard God whisperin' in my ear:*
> *"You better watch what's goin' on*
> *when the lights go out, when the night is dark*
> *when there ain't nobody lookin' around*
> *Down in this dirty little town."*

—Bruce Springsteen

> *I guess that's why I get spiritual*
> *spirituality supports reality*
> *no not Catholic, no not Baptist*
> *no not passive*
> *very active!*

—Speech, of Arrested Development

Two American singers invoke a notion of spirit in these verses, even though much of their lives has involved alienation from traditional religious forms and institutions. This essay begins by problematizing precisely this invocation.

Troubadour and rocker Springsteen, who works predominantly white audiences in the United States (when not touring other continents), sings of the "whisperin'" in his ear that he dares attribute to "God" when exploring the personal and social betrayals that reveal the "American dream" to be dangerous illusion. See, for example, "When the Lights Go Out," an un-recorded song, performed at the Christic Institute Benefit Concert, The Shrine Auditorium, Los Angeles, California, November 16 and 17, 1990. Todd Thomas (Speech), the major lyricist and vocalist for the African American musical family named "Arrested Development," has been "fishin' 4 religion" in white supremacist U.S.A. since the group's first Grammy-winning album (Arrested Development 1992). As the lyrics quoted here from the later 1994 release suggest, he seeks a "very active" liberating spirit, one that creates a "united front" among all oppressed peoples of the Americas (Arrested Development 1994).

Both of these singers are masterful interpreters of the corruptions in American bedrooms and boardrooms that prompt anguish and fury, or that create hearts always hungering for more. Amid it all, both know too the necessity of celebrating, "rockin' all night long" (Springsteen), and of giving not just concerts but public "Celebrations" of "Life Music" (Arrested Development). The personal and political rise and fall together in Speech and Springsteen, as do the pain and the celebration. Amid it all, the references to spirit abide.

Speech and Springsteen are not isolated cases. The imaginaries of cultural[1] expression regularly feature uses of some notion of spirit. Established religious traditions in United States history may have provided a part of the conditions that make available a notion like "spirit," but I am here referring to the uses of such notions as they persist outside established religious traditions.

The "spirit" at issue is a notion that is variously invoked in the midst of cultural practices like popular artistic expression (not only Springsteen and Speech, but also Madonna, Public Enemy and many others), political movements, or debates over urban policy—all expressions and developments that are rarely termed "spiritual" or "religious." Cultural critics themselves can also employ the notion, as does Joel Kovel in "Marxism and Spirituality" or Sut Jhally in "Advertising as Religion" (Kovel 1995, 42-50; Jhally 1989, 217-29). In cultural and political domains, in social action and intellectual discourse, therefore, some notion like "spirit" often persists. To observe this entails no claim that the users' concerns are only or primarily "spiritual." Nor do I intend any kind of defense of the spiritual in cultural domains or for the benefit of anyone else. I begin simply by noting the persistence of the reference to spirit in diverse cultural spheres.

I do not pretend that my selected references to spirit are impartial or exhaustive. Other references are possible. I can clarify at the outset why I have chosen to talk of spirit in culture by referring first to Springsteen and Arrested Development, and then, below, to Derrida.

First of all, with their references to spirit, these cultural discourses wrestle with numinous or mysterious senses in cultural expression. As such, they occasion theological interest. Second, as a theologian working in the culture of the United States, I am interested especially in those discourses that develop extensive critique of American traditions and cultures. These references to spirit—*in* culture but *critical* of its pervasive distortions—are instructive for developing views of theological discourse as cultural critique. Third, all three develop their references to spirit alongside a certain suspicion of, and alienation from, explicitly spiritual traditions. Their potential for saying something about "spirit" which is appropriatable outside the circles of established or explicit spiritual traditions would seem greater.

They are, in this sense, more helpful for developing *cultural* critique than would be, say, Presbyterians or tele-evangelists, whose spiritual interests are to be expected. Fourth, to varying degrees, all three can lay claim to developing a discourse that can be termed "popular"—two in "popular music" (Springsteen and Arrested Development), one representing widespread interests across academic subcultures in the United States (Derrida).

I will argue that by studying the cultural contexts of these invokers of "spirit," we can forge an understanding of spirit in culture and of its key characteristics. This will then provide a context for situating theology as a kind of cultural critique, whose distinctive character I portray as "tracking spirit" in culture. I underscore here that this essay's particular view of spirit in culture, and its consequent understanding of theology as cultural critique, will need to be tested in light of study of other references to spirit that might be selected for examination.

SPIRIT IN CULTURE

Cultural voices that invoke a notion of spirit may seem only to be utilizing a casual figure of speech. As such we might set aside the term, "spirit," as a bit of hyperbole functioning only as an exclamation mark for more important discourse about cultural, economic, political or other intellectual perspectives and events. Or, we might see references to spirit as signaling only high-energy, liveliness or vitality, as in "He sure has spirit." Sometimes spirit functions as a kind of cipher for something unknown or mysterious, as in the U2 song, "Spirit moves in mysterious ways/She moves with it" (U2 1991).

I contend that these meanings do not fully account for the invocations of "spirit." The meanings take on fullness when we reflect on the contexts within which the notions are invoked. Other cultural critics have also noted this. Joel Kovel, writing about a spiritual dimension in Marxist discourse, and Michael Dyson about spirituality in Michael Jackson's performance art, may be talking about two very different kinds of figure *and* two very different types of "spirituality." Nevertheless, as cultural critics exploring such a phenomenon, they both interpret the spiritual by means of a contextual analysis of how the term is invoked.

When Kovel writes, for example, about a radical "spirituality" in Marxism, he is not simply employing a rhetorical device to accent Marx's intense commitment at the heart of his critique. No, he is suggesting, as he himself stresses, a "fourth, indispensable source" for Marx's synthesizing of diverse resources in his context, like German philosophy, French political theory and English economics (Kovel 1995, 42).

Similarly, when Michael Dyson writes of pop-music king, Michael Jackson and his postmodern "spirituality," Dyson means more than the present-day remnants of his youthful family-based Jehovah Witness's religion (Dyson 1993, 38). Dyson is not suggesting that any new "religion" is being born with Michael Jackson, but he does argue that something unique and forceful, moving through Jackson's contexts and cultural practices, warrants the references to it as "spiritual."

In analyses by both Kovel and Dyson, the "spiritual," although taking very different forms, has the status of being a *distinctive* dimension of the cultural practices in question, but the spiritual is surely not *separable* from cultural practice nor operative in some terrain "above" or "outside" of cultural practice. The distinctiveness of something called spirit/spirituality which is yet also a dimension *in* culture can be affirmed without "essentializing" spirit. Spirit, that is, may distinctively be sought in culture, without presuming it to be a homogeneous, unchanging, or core ("essence") of culture. To the contrary, spirit is like all religion generally, I argue, always being constructed and reconstructed amid practical conditions, produced and maintained in different contexts, variant and in process of change (Asad 1993, 27-54; Wuthnow 1994, 21-39). The distinctiveness of the notion of spirit emerges, I will suggest, not so much in terms of a definition of its essence, as by presenting and discussing certain shared "family resemblances" that occur in the dimension of cultural practices where "spirit" is often invoked.

Dyson's analysis of Michael Jackson's work exemplifies such an approach to study of spirit and spirituality. Dyson avoids any presentation of spirituality's essence, or even "common property." Rather, he keeps the focus on cultural art and performance, and allows Michael Jackson's "postmodern spirituality" to emerge as a configuration of distinctive dynamics, which in Jackson's case involve "social ramifications . . . at minimum linked to expressing authentic and concrete concern for other human beings." Dyson goes on to contrast Jackson's material and enfleshed spirituality with any "abstract mysticism," records Jackson's sense of sacred calling, and notes the power of his concert-carnivals to create ecstasy and a "secular koinonia" (Dyson 1993:40-42).

Dyson still leaves readers uncertain, however, as to what precisely the "spiritual" means in this configuration. Perhaps, for him, any remedy for that uncertainty risks an essentializing definition. Dyson's own understandable and telling critique of all esentializing trends is appropriately presented in his book, *Reflecting Black* (1993, xiii-xxxiii). I want to suggest here, however, that while respecting Dyson's hesitance to essentialize, we can nevertheless "stylize" our reflection about spirit in cultural practices, in a way that allows "family resemblances" to appear, and so grant greater clarity to the notion of the "spiritual." Such an attempt at "stylizing," while producing no essential definition of spirit, does yield a mobile form, a temporary carrying frame for discerning and discussing dynamics of cultural life that we might refer to as spiritual. In the following section, I discuss the three dynamics of this mobile form.

SPIRIT

It should be clear now that this study of "spirit" does not focus simply on specific beliefs or convictions, though such beliefs and convictions could be part of the cultural practices that feature the family resemblances I term "spiritual." Neither beliefs generally, nor specific beliefs (in Allah, a divine plan, Christ, et al.) are in themselves key marks of the spiritual. What matters most are the kinds of dynamics playing within the cultural configuration in which such beliefs occur. Here, then, are three dynamics of cultural practices which I propose as signaling a spiritual dimension.

First, where "spirit" is invoked in cultural practice and expression, there is often an experience of *liminality*. This term is frequently used among scholars of religion, who borrow it from the anthropologist Victor Turner, who in turn appropriated it from French ethnologist Arnold Van Gennep (Turner 1969, 94-130; 1974, 13-15).

I invoke the term here merely to describe a key trait of the configuration of cultural practices that are "spiritual." A cultural practice attended by liminality is one somehow wrestling with being "betwixt-and-between." Between what? There can be uncertainty in responding to that question, but it could mean between places in some geographical matrix, or between phases of a temporal development. Both spatial and temporal liminality were evident in Turner's study of Ndembu initiates who were between puberty and adulthood and isolated in the village sacred hut. Being "liminal," then, might mean being between some here and there (spatially) or between some then and now (temporal). Or, perhaps, it means somehow even slipping between the temporal and spatial matrices themselves.

Liminal experiences are not experiences outside temporal and spatial matrices, but betwixt-and-between typical ways of organizing both. They exist, in other terms, in the interstices or within some overlapping of these domains, within some dense, textured interaction of them.

We might also link "liminal" to senses, generally, of being "at the limit." Again, we might ask, "of what"? We might name a variety of senses of intensification, of life-settings at the edges, our pushing against or resting in margins, frontiers, boundaries. These have been explored before by religion scholars as "boundary situations" (Jaspers 1948, 469-70), "limit situations"

(Ricoeur 1975, 107-48), "limiting questions" (Toulmin 1950, 202, 204-11), or "limit-to/limit-of experiences" (Tracy 1981, 158, 160-1, 163-5). In these, again, we find not definitions of religion or of spirit, but signals nevertheless of cultural practices *in extremis*, marching on faith, limning the spiritual.

Whether as betwixt-and-between or as "at the limit," this trait of liminality can be variously seen in contemporary culture. Let me return to my examples from popular culture.

Springsteen invoked his, for him, ghostly god-talk, amid haunting reflection on the boundaries between life and death, between the hidden threats and revealed fears sensed in the beds and towns of violation. Moreover, the whole song, "When the Lights Go Out," from which I quoted at the start of this essay, was performed for an organization, the Christic Institute, working very much "at the limits"—up against a hostile and elite crew of United States government leaders, court officials, businessmen, and military personnel, all accused by the Christic Institute lawyers of illegal drug trafficking between the United States and Nicaragua (DeCurtis 1991, 15f.).

Springsteen's corpus, more generally, feeds off a striking liminal consciousness, as heroes and heroines move continually along streets in cars, between town and edge of town, hovering between the day and the night, always seeking some kind of something in a luminous darkness. Cultural practice and expression here are strikingly liminal, and usually offer the intensified contexts for spirit-talk.

Arrested Development's "spirituality," as in the song "Tennessee," is forged amid the boundary situation created by the deaths of Speech's grandmother and only brother (Arrested Development 1993), but forged also by the death and continuing legacy of enslaved and lynched ancestors who now make his people's "eyes as hard as a million tombstones" (1992; 1993). His song's pleas are cried out from somewhere between this time and place of pain, and past ones. Yet, the "Tennessee" in question is not only past and present, but also future, and Speech's song is thus also stretched toward a future Tennessee that needs to be built here to replace the one whose land and history bring so much violation.

Make the leap now from this sphere of popular culture (i.e. popular music) to another sphere, that of academic subcultures where a figure like Jacques Derrida has taken on notoriety and popularity. Although an academic world is different from popular culture, its emergent discourses can be viewed as popular strains, surely as cultural practices (Harvey 1989, 116-8). We have learned to be suspicious of the policed boundaries between the academic and "the popular." It is appropriate, therefore, to move to academic culture and watch, there also, for invocations of spirit that may have similarities to those occurring in more popular contexts.

Derrida's talk of spectral "ghosts" or "spirits" can be found in his recent re-readings of Marx's *Manifesto* (Derrida 1994). As is typical of him, Derrida reads Marx from between the lines, from the margins, between the said and not-said. But this working from margins is not the only kind of "liminal" domain in Derrida I wish here to spotlight. Rather, the "learning to live with ghosts" that Derrida stresses, the kind of "learning spirits" he seems even to advocate, is conjured up from his own liminal sensibilities. By the liminality of Derrida's own work, I mean his self-avowed working be-twixt-and-between himself and others, between life and death. His advocacy of "learning spirits" arises from his need to speak now of "certain others who are not present, nor presently living either to us, in us or outside us. It is in the name of justice that Derridas speaks . . . where it [justice] is not yet, not yet *there*, where it is no longer . . . (xix)."

We cannot here pursue further how, for Derrida, spirit's work of "mourning," of "localizing the dead," emerges from such a sensibility. Here it suffices to note the "liminality" of his sense—between self and other, be-tween inside and outside, between conditions of justice and injustice. Although Derrida writes in worlds seemingly far removed from a Springsteen or Arrested Development, he, too, invokes spirit-language in the context of dynamics of liminality. Derrida's liminal spirit-language, as in Springsteen and Arrested Development, has additional complexity due to two other traits.

A second trait of spirit is *a penchant for the integrative*, a drive that seeks some holistic vision. In many of the established religions there is re-liance on a narrative to provide this, to tell a story from beginning to end. In such traditions there may also be a cosmology that gives an etiology of the cosmos, of its traumas and beauties, and which orients believers toward cer-tain ends. The integrating drives may produce not only unities of the long ago with the long-awaited/not-yet, but also the unities of levels of creation, whether the "three-story universe" in forms of Christianity or the thirteen stages of heaven and the nine stages of hell that make up a structured but mobile underworld and overworld in Mayan systems.

In what I am here exploring as culture's "spiritual" dimension, the in-tegrating vision is rarely as cosmic, hardly as "totalizing" as in more devel-oped religious systems. There often does remain, however, a penchant for the whole, a wonder about the fullness of things. There may be no compul-sive need to make every particular fit into some cosmic pattern, but there often persists a questioning search for a center amid the many, which preserves integral wholeness or which nourishes vitality at the heart of one's manifold of experiences. Often, certain senses of an organically connected "nature" provide spirit's sense of integrative vision; at other times, it is the felt need for coalitions or for larger perspective amid the vicissitudes of history and culture that prompt spirit to its broader visions. Most usually, nature, history and culture play together for the human imagination to spawn its integrative reach.

For a Springsteen, there is only the barest suggestion of such an integrating vision. In fact, any whole—whether town (hometown), city, or land—tends to be more a place to leave by moving into liminal intensity (in the car, on the street, into the night, et al.) than a place to get to and find fulfillment in. There is, however, a sense of being on the way toward some place where conflict and pain are somehow dealt with through human connection. Springsteen's work, for example, features an uncompromisingly fierce effort to focus some communal place (some "Club Soul City") where the broken-hearted can go to find friends, some space for all those who have broken free from whatever holds them down so as to just "walk in the sun" (Springsteen 1975). In such places, new connections can be forged and a little of that "human touch" can be shared (1992). No master narrative here, no cosmology; just life lived toward a healing in community with others, under one sun.

Again, Arrested Development and Derridean deconstruction, though very different sorts of cultural expression, both display a reach for holistic vision and relation.

Amid the liminal intensity of "Tennessee," spirit and god-talk are invoked by Arrested Development in relation to a search for broad historical perspective. Being at the edge ("Why does it have to be so damn tough?"), Speech utters, "Let me understand your plan." Then, at the song's crucial bridge, the lead female vocalist soars high over the song's vista with a controlled and insistent, wailing demand, "Won't you help me?/Won't you help me?/Won't you help me?/Understand your plan?" Again, there's no totalizing holism here, but a reach for breadth, a desire for a holistic standpoint—laboring against all odds to put some things together, to make a little bit of sense of things.

Arrested Development's holist vision is evident also in the kind of revolutionary practice advocated, built from "united minds of the Americas" and a "united front." The active "spirituality" quoted at the outset of this essay is announced just before the song moves into a call for a unity of minds, drawn from Africa, the Carribbean, Europe, Asia and Australia. "Its not just race, we're all in this together" (Arrested Development 1994).

Holistic perspective and united revolutionary practice, then, rise together in their work. Speech calls for the "united front" of the "red and the black and the green," and this call comes from a vantage point where his "soul" has reached "newer levels," working now from a "mountain top so I can better see/step back and see the whole mighty picture."

But holism in Derrida? In the master of differance, dissemination and dispersion? To claim to find a penchant for integration in this realm of culture may seem a "category mistake" of the most blatant sort.

To be sure, when writing of spirit and spirits or of specter and specters, Derrida is true to usual form and plays out endlessly the celebration of "pure and simple dispersion, without any possible gathering together" (Derrida 1994, 3). There is, however, an intriguing dimension evident in what he terms the "spectral moment." This is a dimension of his reflective struggle which he conjures up, most notably when he wrestles with the "ghosts" and "spirit/spirits" that haunt him at the liminal edges already discussed. Any notion of a whole, of one, may seem discardable only if Derrida is seen simplistically as some mere champion of contemporary fragmentation and nihilism. But his talk of "many" and "more" continually feeds off of a sense of "one." Derrida admits this and is aware of it, as in his constructions like "more than one/no more one [le plus d'un] (3).

As I read Derrida, however, the holist reach is most apparent amid that kind of liminal intensity forged by a particular kind of lack—the lack of justice for victims of wars and exterminations.[2] Or better said, this liminal tension occurs between the justice that is there and not there. To be sure, Derrida's integrative reach from amid such tension entails no mountain climbed, no asking for a plan, as in Arrested Development. There is, however, amid sensed injustice, a call for "responsibility" that seems to entail invocation of a whole (even if it's not a whole in any typical sense!), something Derrida tends to call a "spectral moment." This is an orienting realm beyond "all living present." It is such that it "disjoins the living present" (xix). Or maybe, it disjoins the present because it is not.

Derrida is typically indirect and obscure, but along the way of his writing in Specters, he does signal the importance he sees in this larger perspective, this "spectral moment" that "secretly unhinges" the living present with all its victims (xix). It is a spectral moment that no longer belongs to time, but seems to haunt (like spirit or ghost) the living present.[3] This integrative reach for a spectral moment yields, again, far less than the figurative place Speech sought at the mountain top. Derrida's spectral moment seems also less than Springsteen's barely glimpsable hope for "a place in the sun." The integrative reach or a holist presumption, however, seems to be at work in even Derrida's "spirit" discourse.

The third trait of spirit in culture is a dynamic prefigured in my discussions of the previous two: *a drive toward liberation*. Whether hungered for, dreamed of, struggled for, enacted or celebrated in cultural practices, I suggest that crucial to spirit, and playing in relation to liminal intensity and holistic searching, are emancipative transformations.

Emancipative concern, or a drive for freedom, is a way to describe the *dunamis*, the power and energy, at work amid the various kinds of liminal intensity which, in turn, prompt the reach for some integrative vision and practice. Joel Kovel has interpreted spirit as *that which surpasses the immediate given properties* of the self; that is, the relation of the self to the expanded kind of being encountered *as its boundaries give way* (Kovel 1995, 42-50, emphasis added). To focus spirit as emancipatory is to highlight this as another distinctive dynamic, playing in relation to those of liminality and the integrative reach.

In the diverse cultural spheres I have already sampled— Springsteen, Arrested Development, Derrida—the interest in emancipative freedom is clear. Moreover, the language of "spirit," when invoked by these cultural figures, is especially constructed in a way that foregrounds emancipative concerns. It will be important to note the special role played by the foregrounded, emancipatory interests.

Return to Springsteen. His liminal movement toward the "edges of town," in the darkness, and into other liminal spaces, was almost always intended as a move toward freedom—and away from a town that is like a death-trap that "rips the bones from your back" (as in "Born to Run"), from a place full of losers (as in "Thunder Road"), from a house where women can just melt way "like the scenery in another man's play" (as in "Jackson's Cage"). Even the U.S.A., reputed home of the free, is rendered an emblem of unfreedom, overshadowed by the image of the penitentiary, leaving even its heros with "Nowhere to run/ . . . nowhere to go" ("Born in the U.S.A."). Confinement by internal fear and external, oppressing constraints prepares one for the many drives toward freedom, toward some future sunny place—a place where "every fear you've felt" can "burst free" (as in "Janey, Don't You Lose Heart").

If we shift from this marginalized-but-still-mainstream troubadour to Arrested Development, we find, of course, an even clearer emancipative concern bound up in the language of spirit. The liminality and holistic search so dramatically present in "Tennessee" is all about the deprivation of freedom, the hunger for it, the dream of attaining it, in face of the conditions posed by a racist United States. Further, the "active spirituality" proposed by Arrested Development is named as such by Speech in a song, "United Minds," which insists that we "start servin' liberty," a kind of liberty that bursts on the scene by freeing political prisoners in the United States. Freedom or emancipation is a theme carried by the all-pervasive ache for revolution in Arrested Development's music and lyrics—a revolution that will come like rain to heal social and personal pain, to mitigate rifts everywhere, even between nature and non-nature. Spirituality, for Speech and Arrested Development, perhaps would come to its culminating moment in the revolution that works such freedom. Being between non-revolution and revolution (or on the way between them) becomes the crucial liminal way of being, and the revolutionary life becomes the most significant integrative whole of life. The liminal and the integrative thus abide, but the greatest is the emancipatory concern, pulsing as the power in both. For Speech, it's all in the rain:

> *I feel the rain enhances the revolution, and reminds us*
> *of a spiritual solution, and reminds us of a natural*
> *yet unnatural*
> *solution*
> *It's raining revolution.* (1992)

Emancipation in Derrida is a topic already inviting book-length treatments. Here, however, we can simply ask if emancipation is a dynamic at work amid the liminal intensities and spectral moment that are part of the "haunting" at work in his language of spirits. I argue that such a dynamic *is* visible in Derrida's movements from an awareness of justice as "not there" to his sense of demand, some "responsibility" to redress injustice. This is strongly implied when Derrida acknowledges the legacy of those who evoke "mourning." This work of mourning, as calling for responsive action, comes as Derrida stands

> *before the ghosts of those who are not yet born or who are al-*
> *ready dead, be they victims of wars, political or other kinds of*
> *violence, nationalist, racist, colonialist, sexist, or other kinds of*
> *exterminations, victims of the oppressions of capitalist imperial-*
> *ism or any of the forms of totalitarianism."* (Derrida 1994, xix)

In this segment of *Specters*, Derrida sets out these traumatic configurations of power and abuse as so many intensifiers of his own liminal sense.

It is not difficult, therefore, to read Derrida's play between such liminal intensifiers and his spectral moment (by which injustices in the living present are unhinged) as a movement between oppresssive and constraining conditions to dynamics of release and emancipation. This movement is a type of transformation which, as Derrida says about transformation more broadly, is a sign that "the spirit works." Or again, "whether it [the "single thing, spirit"] transforms or transforms itself, the spirit, 'the spirit of the spirit' is *work*" (9).

Derrida's notion of "working" spirit, and the direction of his own working in *Specters*, presume and cultivate, we might say, a "practical wish to be free," which Kovel argues is crucial to spirit. Spirit in humanity and culture is "characterized," says Kovel, "by a tendency to define itself expressively and in conflict" with constraint (Kovel 1995, 109). Especially under conditions of domination, within the kind of oppressions and totalitarianisms catalogued by Derrida, where peoples' beings are being expropriated by others, spirit tends to "work" emancipatively. So, in Derrida, we note that in spite of many indeterminacies, and in spite of the impermanences of ghosts and spirits, these latter have to do, in a profound sense, with the coming and going, the wanting and the seeking, of *freedoms* from oppressions. In this way, Derrida's invocation of spirit(s) also exemplifies a dynamic emancipatory drive occuring between his liminal sensibilities and his reach for the spectral moment.

Whether in a Derrida, Arrested Development, Springsteen or some other cultural voice or group, it is especially with its emancipatory feature that spirit's power as cultural *critique* becomes apparent, thus bringing the various implications of critique to the fore—negation, resistance, drive to restoration.

To be sure, critique is significantly present in liminal sensibility and in integrative vision. As liminal, for example, spirit hovers between all established lines, categories, sectors, groups, cultures, phases, places, times—and so, prompts at least a questioning, if not also a "deconstructing," of the adequacy of any of these designations. In these ways, critique emerges from liminal positions and sensibilities. Similarly, as integrative reach, spirit seeks some embrace of a manifold, and so ennervates multiple tasks of connecting and reconnecting, if not outright reconstructive projects of reparation. The integrative move can also thus be a contributor to critique.

Critique in the fuller sense, however, comes to the fore in the power of diverse emancipatory motion and movement. As emancipatory movement, spirit breaks out from dominative forces which "press down upon" lives or which surround and "press in upon" them. As emancipatory, spirit not only "breaks out from" places of oppression, but also "breaks out toward" alternative life where the negativities of domination are eradicated or mitigated in actions of reparation, restoration, and connection. The liminal sensibility and the integrative reach, of course, remain crucial, but they are catalyzed into a critical force by the emancipatory concern.

These three traits of liminality, integrative reach and emancipatory concern, and their dynamic interplay, provides a "stylized mobile form" that might enable cultural critics to know when they are encountering distinctively spiritual dimensions.

THEOLOGY AS "TRACKING SPIRIT"

With this understanding of "spirit in culture," it is possible to refocus a view of the discourse that has traditionally been termed "theology." This essay's subtitle announces theology as "cultural critique." I can propose now a theology that becomes such critique as it participates in spirit in culture.

"Theology" allows for this relation to something like spirit in the very construction of the term. It is discourse (*logos*) about, or following after, something else, i.e., whatever is taken as mystery or sacral presence of some sort (*theos*).[4] Theology that participates in spirit, as spirit has been rendered in this essay, will therefore be discourse about experiences of spirit that are not only liminal or integrative but also, especially, emancipating. Theology, as discourse, has its cognitive and literary disciplines that make it "critical" in the sense of formulating arguments or developing and comparing positions. As *cultural* critique, however, this is not enough.

In addition, and in order to be "critical," theology, needs to *participate in* the spirit of critique at work in cultural practices. Let me develop theology's participation in spirit by working with a metaphorical depiction of theology as "tracking spirit."

The metaphor "tracking," while remaining helpful for interpreting theology's relation to spirit and critique, also possesses some negative meanings. I myself sense the force of this negativity, but I preserve the term to dramatize some key points about theology becoming cultural critique in our contexts.

First, the metaphor could suggest that theology is only at a distance from spirit. It connotes spirit as external to theologians' work, as present "out there somewhere" in culture and world, seeming to imply that the theologian is somewhere else, needing to go on an expedition, of sorts, to find spirit. Clearly this obscures the diverse ways that theologians might contemplate how they are already steeped in spirit, how theological selves in diverse locations are already implicated in spirit, with potential for developing resources for spirituality that are ready to hand.

While acknowledging these points, I employ the tracking metaphor because, as spiritually aware as some might think theologians to be, the fact remains that insofar as we are located in academic subcultures, we often *are* at a remove from spirit—especially from the kind of spirit in culture that I have sketched above. If theology is to be *cultural* critique, there must be a "going out" toward spirit, a repositioning of one's discursive work that often involves journeying toward the margins of the academy, into other related but often different cultural spheres. I understand the claim that academic campuses are significant spheres of culture, scenes of contestation, challenge and resistance. But I write with a sense that they are also small places, isolated scenes. Theologians need not abandon academies as social locations of struggle, but if engaging in *cultural* critique, we must at least shuttle between cultural worlds, be ready for some searching and journeying. The "tracking" metaphor seeks to respond to that demand.

Second, the tracking metaphor can conjure up some of the most oppressive parts of United States life and history. Especially when thought in a paradigm of tracking and hunting prey, "tracking" connotes for some not only a process for killing animals, but also for pursuing human prey—above all the runaway slave hounded by vicious forces of white supremacism. At other times, we may hear tracking as "stalking," and so find ourselves burdened by images of the all too real world of men stalking women (Morgan 1988, 23-4). Or again, maybe the tracking metaphor casts up the picture of a whole nation appropriating a continent to itself, presuming its "manifest destiny," and hence leaving tracks across western lands stolen from Native American communities. Still others may hear in "tracking" the sinister monitoring and surveillance of people in national security state systems, as in the COINTELPRO project of the FBI that sought to destroy dissent in this country by using techniques for tracking every move and speech made by activists like Assata Shakur, Mumia Abu-Jamal, Angela Y. Davis, Martin Luther King, Fannie Lou Hamer, Malcolm X and a host of lesser known "security threats."

In spite of the weight of these negative connotations I persist with the metaphor. There are simply too many positive meanings raised by it, which when used to speak of theology suggest a purposeful wandering and journeying, theologians' taking to trails and pathways, seeking out things hard to find because they are hidden, things kept in hiding often by dynamics of oppression. Might not the following of trails through nature's canyons, woodlands and prairies, and our tracking of wind-marks in sand, along streams and riverbeds—might not all these be understood as a matrix of "pilgrimages" giving theological discourse one of its crucial contexts?

Similarly, in the cultural and political spheres, the tracking image is not all, or even primarily, negative. Runaway slaves were not simply victims of pursuing trackers, but also trackers in their own right, reading signs and trails, planning cunning strategies, all toward a hoped-for freedom. Moreover, a resistance to oppressive "trackers" today often requires tracking skills of one's own. We need to conduct our own investigations and searches to expose the systems of lies and plans of devastation that are made to look normal. Women, "stalked" though they be by agents of patriarchy, need not relinquish the tools of a tracker as they make their way through, maybe out of, the master's house. Is there not a sense in which all cultural critics, theologians or not, need something of the tracker's art to discern the goings on around them? Cultural critics as trackers might use, say, Freedom of Information Act appeals to help expose abuses of power and to prevent similar ones from occurring. These are just a few suggestions as to how theologians as culture critics need to do more than simply "take a look at" culture, even more than just creatively interpret its dynamics. Also required is a going out, a searching, a critical wandering on new terrain, a testing—an art of tracking spirit.

We can highlight the following features, then, of a theology that is tracking spirit, and doing so as a form of cultural critique in the United States today. First: if we envision a tracking person or group that seeks another person or group, the latter being lost in a woods or at a distance but leaving tracks, then we know that tracking entails searching and investigation. We can begin with the already-noted feature of the metaphor, and recall that *theology is a searching and investigating reflection, attempting to discern the tracks of spirit*. It searches for tracks left, for example, by liminal dwellers and spinners (as labyrinthine as these may be!), by integrative visionaries, and by those fighting and hoping for liberation.

As any good tracker knows, this searching and investigating is not a simple matter of just "taking a look" at tracks. Here we can note that tracking is an interpretive art, requiring that one make guesses and fill in blank spaces, and allow one's process of discernment to shuttle between what is observed and what is imagined both about what is sought and about the conditions under which the search transpires (e.g., conditions of land and weather).

Searching, investigating and interpreting spirit in United States culture is an exceedingly complex task. I made one attempt in the previous section of this essay. The field seems broad because there are so many instances of each type of spiritual dynamic. Liminal experiences are innumerable. America itself is a liminal place in many senses. Further, integrative visions abound and compete in our pluralistic milieu. Surely, also, almost everyone talks of freedom and seems to insist on some type of liberation for themselves or their group. The field of the "spiritual" even as I have defined it, then, seems unmanageably broad.

Yet, the field narrows considerably, even in the United States, if critics seek out and track spirit in those places where the liminal, integrative and liberating dynamics *occur together*. I propose that such a conjunction will be found especially in those cultural practices where people acknowledge (whether from personal necessity or out of solidarity with others) a privilege of the liberation dynamic. In contrast, where there is a primacy of liminality alone, or of integral vision alone, then it is far less likely that these two dynamics will come together in dynamic interplay with the third one, emancipatory practice. The presence of the emancipatory interest is often what unites the liminal and the integrative sensibilities to one another, and then galvanizes them in an emancipatory direction.

Among the cases of cultural phenomena represented by Springsteen, Arrested Development, or Derrida, for example, it is Arrested Development, I suggest, with its emancipatory drive amid the longstanding exploitation of African peoples in the Americas, which best expresses and enacts the creative interplay of the three dynamics. To be sure, each dynamic can be found in Springsteen and Derrida, but not as intensely. In Arrested Development, the emancipative practice toward revolution demands a strikingly liminal dwelling and an integrative vision and organizing.

"Liminoid" figures (Turner 1974, 14-7), who share in the cultural phenomena built up around Springsteen and Derrida, by contrast, tend (because of having certain socio-political entitlements) to be content with drifting, "hiding on the backstreets," or with carnival play in the liminal interstices of culture. The "hiding" and "carnival play" can, indeed, make a way for emancipatory practice (Dyson 1993, 41-2), but this does not usually happen without an explicit and forthright commitment to such practice.

Further work in the cultural criticism of spirit in United States culture needs to search out other phenomena where the three dynamics of spirit occur together. In this way, we might test my proposal that giving primacy to the liberation dynamic is what most usually catalyzes an interplay of all three. Such searching investigation and alternative interpretation is part of the first sense of theology "tracking" spirit. Second: the notion of "tracking" also allows us to stress again that *theological reflection is a second move or act. Spirit has already gone before theology.* Whether moving liminally, integratively or in a liberating way, spirit in culture, with respect to theological reflection, already has taken flight, already is indwelling, or already is breaking forth. Theology "follows after" such spirit. Theology is, as Gustavo Gutierrez has said about Latin American liberation theology, a "second act," following after and depending on the primary acts of spirit working amid cultural practices.[5]

Given the way I have portrayed spirit, a theology that "follows after" has a certain character. It seeks out the liminal, integrative and liberatory, and thinks after observing and experiencing their various combinations.

Theology may be as diverse as are the various combinations of the liminal, integrative and liberatory features of a particular cultural setting.

It may be thought that describing theology as a "following after" is to consign theology to an essentially conservative role, suggesting that theology just works in the tracks (well-worn trails, "ruts") of traditions. To be sure, the image of theology following spirit in culture and history allows for the important notion of theology living and working in relation to "spiritual traditions." But the traditions I propose that theology follows after may or may not conform to the great religious traditions that have been taken as "spiritual" and which have often demanded for themselves conservation, maintenance and reinforcement.

In fact, the particular notion of "spirit," as presented here (integrative, liminal, emancipatory), suggests "traditions" that are crafted by subjugated and revolutionary peoples. If these are the traditions "followed after," then this would lead us to the worlds of the forgotten, the repressed and danger-ous ones who have been forced to appropriate liminal, integrative and liber-ating spiritualities. In the United States, this implies a "following after" the movements of resistance and hope now underway among, and on behalf of, the growing numbers of poor women and children, disenfranchised work-ers, environmentalists seeking restoration of our threatened ecosphere, the diverse ethnic groups suffering the scourges of white supremacism, and those consigned to outlaw status for their gay or lesbian practice.

This is a crucial point for theologians in the United States today. Theologians as cultural critics tracking spirit in America can be viewed as very much the respecters of historical traditions, even though these tradi-tions are usually not the ones of established religious bodies (Protestant de-nominations like Baptist or Presbyterian, or churches such as the Roman Catholic and Orthodox ones). Nor are the "traditions" of theologians, as culture critics, composed of typically-identified examples of spiritual phe-nomena (evangelistic campaigns, cultic activity, meditation circles, et al.). None of these need be dismissed or ignored by cultural critics. They, too, *might be* expressions of liminal, integrative and liberating spirituality. In the United States today, however, the established religious traditions often seem to be ways to shore up mainstream systems of entitlement, or to be modes of opting out of consciousness about culture and politics. The discrimen of the spiritual, however, is not simply a matter of comparing establishment or anti-establishment credentials. It is more important to ask whether and how the conjunction is evident, that is, whether or not there appears that inter-play of liminality, integrative vision and liberating practice. "Following after" the tracks of traditions featuring *that* conjunction is a task I have pro-posed here for theology.

Note also that because of the way I have formulated this "following" by theology, and in light of the particular way I have understood spirit, this "following" cannot become merely a drifting into the latest cultural style, revolutionary agenda (of right or left) or toward poses of "radical chic" and "postmodern cool." It cannot be co-opted either by establishment spiritualities (which are usually non-liminal and non-emancipatory), or by simple "alternative" spiritualities. Whether drawing from "establishment" or "alternative" legacies and trends, a theology follows with a searching that focuses the sustained, vital interplay of liminal, integrative *and* emancipative forces. Many "alternative" cultural "trends and fashions" can lack that interplay as often as can reputed "establishment" forces. Third: the notion of "tracking" suggests that *theology entails a certain body politic as a dimension of its participation in spirit.* Theology is formulated by those who seek to walk and go along the way where critical spirit has been at work. The crafters of theological discourse, "theologians," then, do well to put themselves, body and mind, in the ways of spirit. I do not refer simply to a "body action" of practical involvement in spiritual movements, although that is an essential connotation of the metaphor of tracking that I develop here. By a "body politic" I mean also participating in public practices that are forged out of a consciousness of where one's body and life are in relation to the spirit being tracked. It means that theologians, those engaged in tracking spirit, cultivate their *own* senses of liminality, integrative vision, and liberating practice, especially as these are viewable at work in their own natural and cultural settings. We theologians are ourselves inhabitants (physically, socially, culturally) of the liminal, integrative, and liberating places of spirit. In fact, being such is necessary to tracking spirit.

Good trackers do not simply think about or imagine the ones sought after as at a distance; they need also to read and feel themselves as distinct but in relation to the sought ones, and then set their feet and bodies in motion along the way they discern the ones sought after to have gone. They rarely imitate exactly the ways of the distant ones, but with their motions and presence, they seek to approximate those ways.

The invocations of spirit by Springsteen and Arrested Development, which I recorded in this essay and then situated within liminal, integrative and liberating dynamic settings, were selected by me because they are two of many popular art forms playing in the communities of struggle and hope through which I experience spiritual community. From different vantage points, they are artists wrestling with the internal and external complexities of the vicious dominations pervading life in the U.S.A. today. I have been in attendance at performances by these artists, but more importantly, have long found communal listening to these artists in spiritual community to be ways of focusing on the dynamics of liminality, integrative vision and liberating practice in American life today. For others, it may be Derrida's deconstructionist strategies and spirit-talk that can invite not only academic, discursive practices, but also boundary crossing practices that move one into other spheres.

The point here is not to champion these particular artists, either Springsteen, the white troubadour of the "marginalized mainstream," or Arrested Development, the Grammy-celebrated African musical family later commercially suppressed, perhaps as a dangerous threat amid the resurgent racism and nihilism of contemporary culture (White 1994, 25). My major point here, instead, is that theology as "tracking spirit" suggests some participation by theologians which invites placing their bodies and beings along the way of spirit's trails.

There are, of course, many modes of such participation. As I have portrayed spirit, following after such groups as these will mean moving outside as well as inside the academic spheres usually inhabited by theologians. Spirit's trails may at times be tangled and labyrinthine, at times singular and lonely. The point is that "tracking spirit" suggests that theologians be on those trails. Fourth and finally, theology as "tracking spirit" has another implication. Assuming a relation to spirit in the ways I have suggested in this final section, *theology and theologians themselves can "leave tracks" in culture.* They "track up" the house of culture with spirit. If theology searches, follows after, and goes the way of spirit, then, while never catching or containing spirit, its discourse itself can become "inspirited" and leave tracks of spirit in culture. The primary media of spirit, and its critical practice, remain the liminal, integrative and liberating dynamics at work in culture generally. Theology need not pre-empt or co-opt the dynamism of spirit in culture, even if it successfully becomes inspirited discourse. But theology can also become a kind of "discursive practice,"[6] which itself leaves tracks of spirit because and insofar as it lives and works in spirit's trails.

As participants in an inspirited discourse that "tracks up" culture, theologians may need to experiment with a variety of genres and styles of discourse. Late-twentieth-century theological expression already shows theologians involved in such experimentation, through the short essay, the poem, the photographic essay, the journal, the protest rally or march, and increasingly, film, dance, theater, and other artistic forms—all ways to "act up" with spirit. Many of my theologian colleagues have followed spirit to the point of experimenting with such alternative genres, and have found themselves unable to get jobs as "theologians" or to be recognized as such. If theology as cultural critique needs itself also to be inspirited discourse, their loss is theology's loss.

Using alternative genres need not mean the end of the book and the systematic text in theology. The systematic and synthetic operations of traditional "systematic theologies" (whether those of Thomas Aquinas, John Calvin, Karl Barth, or Paul Tillich) are not so much wrong as they are incomplete; that is, they may satisfy a certain kind of integrative reach of spirit, but not so much spirit's liminal and liberating desires. The verdict is still out on whether or not the system-building integrative reach in systematic theology can work with, and not squelch, liminal intensity of spirit or the urgencies of liberating practice.

Alternative styles might accent aesthetic expression to "track up" culture with the liminal dynamic of spirit. Or perhaps new styles will employ a combative or confrontational polemic about abuses of power (entrenched patriarchy, exploitation by the few who control wealth, white supremacists), and thus "track up" culture in the United States with spirit's liberatory dynamic. These activities may occur in neighborhoods, families, relationships, the university classroom, the seminary chapel, and also in the labor union hall, city street, shopping center, or the Lacandon jungle of Chiapas, Mexico. A theology that moves into these scenes, finding new ways to be inspirited discourse, will not only contribute to the critical force of spirit in culture, but also might help to revitalize theological disciplines in the academy.

REFERENCES

Arrested Development. 1992. *3 Years, 5 Months and 2 Days in the Life of . . .* , music recording. New York: Chryslais Records.

————. 1993. Interviews, Concert Footage, Vignettes, Behind the Scenes. In *Eyes as Hard as a Million Tombstones*, video cassette. New York: Chrysalis Records.

————. 1994. *Zingalamaduni*, music recording. New York: Chrysalis Records.

Asad, Talal. 1993. *Genealogies of Religion: Discipline and Reasons in Christianity and Islam*. Baltimore: The Johns Hopkins University Press.

DeCurtis, Anthony. 1991. "Springsteen Returns." In *Rolling Stone*. (January 10).

Derrida, Jacques. 1992. "Force of Law: The 'Mystical Foundation of Authority.'" In *Deconstruction and the Possibility of Justice*, ed. Drucilla Cornel, Michel Rosenfeld and David Gray Carlson, eds., New York: Routledge.

————. 1994. *Specters of Marx: The State of the Debt, the Work of Mourning, and The New International*. Trans. P. Kamuf. New York: Routledge.

Dyson, Michael Eric. 1993. *Reflecting Black: African-American Cultural Criticism*. Minneapolis: University of Minnesota Press.

Foucault, Michel. 1972. *The Archaeology of Knowledge*, trans. A.M. Sheridan Smith. New York: Harper and Row.

Grossberg, Lawrence, Cary Nelson, and Paula A. Treichler, eds. 1992. *Cultural Studies*. London and New York: Routledge.

Gutierrez, Gustavo. 1988. *A Theology of Liberation*. Maryknoll, New York: Orbis Books.

Harvey, David. 1989. *The Condition of Postmodernity*. Cambridge: Basil Blackwell.

Jaspers, Karl. 1948. *Philosophie, Zweite unveranderte auflage*. Berlin: Springer-Verlag.

Jhally, Sut. 1989. "Advertising as Religion: The Dialectic of Technology and Magic." In *Cultural Politics in Contemporary America*. New York: Routledge.

Kovel, Joel. 1995. "Marxism and Spirituality." In *Marxism in the Postmodern Age: Confronting the New World Order*, ed. Antonio Callari, Stephen Cullenberg, and Carole Biewener. New York: The Guilford Press.

Morgan, Robin. 1988. *The Demon Lover: On the Sexuality of Terrorism*. New York: W. W. Norton.

Ricoeur, Paul. 1975. "The Specificity of Religious Language." *Semeia* 4:107-48.

Schüssler Fiorenza, Elisabeth. 1994. *Jesus: Miriam's Prophet, Sophia's Child*. New York: Continuum.

Springsteen, Bruce. 1975. *Born to Run*, music recording. New York: CBS Records.

————. 1992. *Human Touch*, music recording. New York: SONY/CBS Records.

Toulmin, Stephen. 1950. *An Examination of the Place of Reason in Ethics*. London: Cambridge University Press.

Tracy, David. 1981. *The Analogical Imagination: Christian Theology and the Culture of Pluralism*. New York: Crossroad.

Turner, Victor. 1969. *The Ritual Process: Structure and Anti-Structure*. Ithaca and London: Cornell University Press.

————. 1974. *Dramas, Fields and Metaphors: Symbolic Action in Human Society*. Ithaca and London: Cornell University Press.

U2. 1991. "Mysterious Ways." In *Achtung Baby*, music recording. New York: CBS Records.

White, Armond. 1994. "After Despair: Arrested Development Still Dreams." *The City Sun*, 10: 42, 25.

Williams, Raymond. 1976. *Keywords*. London: Fontana.

Wuthnow, Robert. 1994. *The Production of the Sacred: An Essay on Public Religion*. Urbana and Chicago: University of Illinois Press.

NOTES

1. About the terms "culture," or its adjectival form "cultural," Raymond Williams' comment remains true: it "is one of the two or three most complicated words in the English language" (Williams 1976). This remains so whether we think of the social science field of "cultural anthropology" in the United States or the more recent field initiated in Britain as "cultural studies."

   In this essay, "culture"/"cultural" will be used as referring to a "whole way of life" (including attitudes, ideas, languages, practices, institutions and structures of power) which is constructed and continually negotiated within and sometimes between specifiable populations. It is possible also to speak, as I do in this essay, of a whole range of "domains" or "spheres" of culture, which make up different "cultural practices"—spheres or domains such as texts, canons, artistic forms, popular music, mass-produced commodities, advertising, kinship organization, architecture and so on.

   For discussion of the complexities of the culture concept, in anthropology and "cultural studies", respectively, see Talal Asad (1993, 248-53), and Grossberg, Nelson and Treichler (1992, 4-6).

2. This is not unlike the way Derrida's memories of the horrific "Final Solution," in mid-twentieth century Europe, compel him to put limits on embracing the violence of play he sees endlessly occurring in the notion of "justice." He seems to accept a "demand," precisely because of the pressure of this kind of memory. (Derrida 1992, 61-3)

3. A search for such a spectral moment, in relation to which the "spirits" are invoked by Derrida, is underway in a passage like the following: "But the irrefutable itself supposes that this justice carries life beyond present life or its actual being-there, its empirical or ontological actuality: not toward death but toward a *living-on [sur-vie]*, namely, a trace of which life and death would themselves be but traces

and traces of traces, a survival whose possibility in advance comes to disjoin or dis-adjust the identity to itself of the living present as well as of any effectivity. There is then *some spirit.* Spirits. And *one must* reckon with them" (Derrida 1994, xx).

4. I here leave unaddressed the questions of how *theos* is to be rendered in images—as pervasive spirit "force," in various anthropomorphic images, across a series of "divine acts in history," et al. Central to such questions is the usability of the very term "God," which some scholars refuse to use because they see it so inextricably bound up with, and so reinforcing, systems of oppression (patriarchal, elitist, white supremacist). Elisabeth Schussler Fiorenza's approach to this is to write the sacred as "G*d" and yet still refer to her liberationist reflection as "theological" (Fiorenza 1994, 178-82).

5. I interpret my notion of "acts of spirit (liminal, integrative, liberating)," which work amid cultural practices, as further elaboration of Gutierrez's notion of "historical praxis," and as analogue to what he terms "ecclesial praxis" (Gutierrez 1988, 5-12).

6. Recall this as Michel Foucault's term. Discursive practices may include texts, theories, ideas, etc., and still be "practice," and thus have impact on the historical and material matrices that also shape them. Here, Foucault takes up a "task that consists of not . . . treating discourses as groups of signs (signifying elements referring to contents or representations), but as practices that systematically form the objects of which they speak. Of course, discourses are composed of signs; but what they do is more than use these signs to designate things" (Foucault 1972, 49).

PASSING ON THE SPARK:

A WOMANIST PERSPECTIVE ON THEOLOGY AND CULTURE

Karen Baker-Fletcher

BLACK WOMEN'S CULTURE AS A RESOURCE FOR WOMANIST THEOLOGY

Black women's culture is a primary resource for womanist theologians and ethicists. Womanist methodology looks to primary resources that are authentic to Black women's religion, culture and lived experience. Womanist theology and ethics draw extensively on Black women's culture, particularly as it is found in narrative (written and oral, historical and contemporary). By narrative I have in mind all kinds of texts: scripture, intellectual essays, autobiography, fiction, poetry, and song. Scholars like Delores Williams, Katie Cannon, and myself have argued that Black women's narratives preserve much of the moral wisdom and symbolizations of God in Black women's culture that give meaning to life historically and today (Cannon 1989, 281-92; Williams 1989, 179-86; and Baker-Fletcher 1994, 185-9). Black women's religio-cultural thought in narrative resources represents a diversity of African American women's voices. Womanist theologians and ethicists have dusted off forgotten and neglected texts, recovered the memories of living Black women in the aural-oral tradition, and lifted theological and ethical themes from such cultural resources.

A contemporary cultural critic whose work is foundational for developing womanist methodologies for theology that take seriously Black women's culture is Alice Walker. Before Alice Walker coined the term "womanist," most Black women theologians and ethicists referred to themselves as "Black feminist" or "Black women" ethicists. When Walker coined the term "womanist" in 1983, a number of Black women religious scholars quickly adopted it. Walker's definition of "womanist" emphasizes love of Black women's history and culture. Most simply, a womanist is "a black feminist or feminist of color." The term "womanist" comes from the black cultural understanding of *womanish*, which is the opposite of "girlish" irresponsibility, frivolousness, lack of seriousness. It refers to "outrageous, audacious, courageous or *willful* behavior." A womanist is "Responsible. In charge. *Serious*." She "loves other women, sexually and/or nonsexually." She "*appreciates and prefers women's culture, women's emotional flexibility (values tears as natural counterbalance of laughter), and women's strength"* *[emphasis mine]*. A womanist *"Loves* the Spirit" (Walker 1983, xi-xii). In this essay I focus on a Christian womanist understanding of theology and culture with particular attention to a womanist as one who loves *women's culture and the Spirit*.

WALKER, WOMANISM, AND WOMEN'S CULTURE

Walker does not define what she means by "women's culture" in her definition of womanism. One can gather from her writings that she has in mind Black women's creativity in language, writings, religious and political understandings, moral values, ways of relating to creation, and making articles of beauty for everyday use. She suggests such an understanding in "In Search of Our Mothers' Gardens," in which she speaks of her appreciation for her mother's "love for beauty" and "respect for strength" (Walker 1983, 231-43). This love for beauty and respect for strength is evident in Walker's description of her mother as one who received praise from those who came from three counties to be given cuttings from her flowers "because whatever rocky soil she landed on, she turned into a garden. A garden so brilliant with colors, so original in its design, so magnificent with life and creativity, that . . . perfect strangers and imperfect strangers . . . ask to stand or walk among my mother's art." She describes her mother as one "who literally covered the holes in our walls with sunflowers" (Walker 1983, 231-43).

Womanist theologian Delores Williams is well-known for emphasizing the black cultural saying that "God makes a way out of no way." Building on the meaning of the biblical story of Hagar in the lives of historical and contemporary Black women, Williams describes God as "a God of Seeing" who provides Hagar with new vision "to see survival resources where she saw none before" (Williams 1993a, 197-9). Likewise, Walker describes her mother as one who has the power to make a way out of no way and as a woman of vision. I would say that the source of that vision is "a God of Seeing" who empowers the dispossessed with vision and a "creative spark" to make a way out of no way. This "creative spark" makes possible the creation of positive, life-affirming, Black women's cultures even in the midst of dominant, oppressive cultural strategies in the larger society. While white Southern culture and American culture in general deemed that Black women, children, and men were fit only for shacks with holes in them, women like Walker's mother moved and acted out of cultural norms that were resistant to dominant cultural expectations. So powerful was her mother's "creative spark" that Walker was strengthened to move from the shacks of segregated Georgia to the halls of great American writers. Walker became one of several black daughters who transformed America's understanding of its own culture and who its great contributors are.

By surrounding her family with beauty in the midst of scarcity, Walker asserts, her mothers and grandmothers *"more often than not anonymously, handed on the creative spark, the seed of the flower they themselves never hoped to see"* (Walker 1983, 240) [emphasis mine]. For me, Walker's words suggest that culture and spirit are within each other. The "creative spark" or "seed of the flower" she refers to is spiritual and concrete. It is empowering and sustaining in palpable ways. Within Black women's culture there is enormous creativity, often passed on by anonymous women whose names are not preserved in history books or museums. For me, this "creative spark" is God's creative power within Black women. Black mothers and grandmothers who are aware of this shining well of strength and creativity in the desert of oppression pass on the empowering wisdom it offers to humankind spark by spark. It is not limited to Black women, although it takes on particular forms in Black women's culture. That Walker points to black mothers and grandmothers as the most visible source of passing on a creative spark among Black women suggests that the power of creativity, which Christians associate with God, is in culture.

While Walker's mother was not a famous artist, she passed on the gift of creativity through Black women's everyday culture. She expressed her love of beauty in ordinary acts like gardening, quilting and canning food. Walker explains that her mother encouraged her to value language, words, and writing by encouraging her love for poetry, literature, and writing. She inherited respect for strength through her mother's example of creating beauty in the midst of some of poverty's ugly situations. Walker's mother overcame the conditions created by the power of evil, oppressive systems of racist, sexist, and classist injustice dominant in Euro-American culture (especially in the South) by the strength of her creative power. Walker is not clear about the source of this creative power in "In Search of Our Mothers' Gardens." However, the character Shug, in Walker's novel *The Color Purple*, describes God as powerful in Creation (Walker 1982, 164-70 and 242). Also, in her definition of "womanist" Walker connects "Spirit" with culture and creation:

> *Loves music. Loves dance. Loves the moon. Loves the Spirit. Loves love and food and roundness. Loves struggle. Loves the Folk. Loves herself. Regardless.* (Walker 1983, xi-xii)

Delores Williams has expounded briefly on what it means to "love the Spirit" from a Christian womanist perspective, identifying it as a very important religious value in Black women's culture. "Walker's mention of the black womanist's love of the spirit," Williams explains, "is a true reflection of the great respect Afro-American women have always shown for the presence and work of the spirit." As examples, she notes that in the Black church, the congregation (predominantly female) judges the effectiveness of the worship service on whether or not "the spirit was high" (Williams 1989, 185-6). The spirit has been effective if it was:

> actively and obviously present in a balanced blend of prayer, of cadenced word (the sermon), and of syncopated music ministering to the pain of the people . . . In relation to the Christian or New Testament, the Christian womanist theologian can refocus the salvation story so that it emphasizes the beginning of revelation with the spirit mounting Mary, a woman of the poor: (" . . . the Holy Spirit shall come upon thee . . . " Luke 1:35). (185-6)

Williams goes on to argue that refocusing the salvation story to emphasize the spirit coming upon or mounting Mary has roots in nineteenth-century Black women's culture. For example, black feminist and abolitionist Sojourner Truth proclaimed that Christ came from God and a woman; man had nothing to do with him. Harriet Tubman, who often "went into the spirit" before her liberation activities, Williams argues, is another of many sources for "a womanist theology of the spirit." What is significant about Williams's suggestion is that she indicates that in a womanist theology of the spirit, God, who is spirit, is in women's culture and provides strength for liberation activity. "Each womanist theologian," in Williams' view, "will add her own special accent to the understandings of God emerging from womanist theology" so that "womanist theology will one day" reflect "the divine spirit that connects us all" (185-6).

Among womanist theologians there are diverse pieces of a vision of God as Spirit. God as Spirit is at the heart of much of historical and contemporary Black women's understanding of God. While Williams is careful to note that "Walker's way of connecting womanists with the spirit is only one clue "to the Christian womanist question 'who do you say God is?', it is nonetheless a foundational clue" (Williams 1989, 186). Building on Walker's understandings of Spirit[1] and Creation, as well as on Williams's suggestions, I find it important to develop a concept of God as Spirit. God as Spirit, as I understand it, is intimately connected with Creation. It acts and moves through human culture most visibly when we choose to participate in the creative, loving, empowering, and justice making activity of Spirit. This is consistent with Walker's understanding of Spirit which is connected with womanists' love of *struggle* for spiritual, political and economic freedom.

Both Walker, who describes herself as pagan, and Christian womanists find loving the Spirit an important aspect of Black women's culture. This love of the Spirit is not separate from love of self, struggle, Folk (others), or the music, dance, and food in women's culture. Nor is it separate from love of the cosmos (the moon) or of one's own body (women's natural round-ness). Love of creation, Spirit, and Black women's culture are deeply inter-twined and interrelated. Walker, a novelist, essayist, and poet, does not write about the relationship between Creation, culture, and Spirit in a systematic way. While one can tease out her understanding, it is not easily placed into systematic categories. Spirit, Creation, and culture are dynamically interrelated.

I would say that in its best, nonoppressive forms, culture can reveal Spirit. Spirit moves within culture when human beings choose to participate in the life-affirming, creative, loving, and justice-making activity of Spirit. These are qualities of God that I derive from the works of various Black women and womanist writers. For example, Walker emphasizes the loving, creative and freedom-fighting activity of God. Jacquelyn Grant emphasizes the liberating activity of God in the lives of the least of society's members (Grant 1989, 209-22; 1995, 129-42). Williams emphasizes the empowering activity of a God of vision, freedom-fighting and survival strategies.

Womanist theologians and ethicists to date have tended to focus on Black women's culture as described in contemporary and historical writings by and/or about Black women.[2] In her definitions of womanism, Walker refers to historical black Christian women like Harriet Tubman, who freed three hundred slaves and Rebecca Cox Jackson, whose love for women and women's culture included female visions of God (Walker 1983, xii; 71-82). An exploration of diverse aspects of Black women's culture, historical and contemporary, has been at the heart of womanist scholarship in religion for the last decade and more. Theoretically, Walker includes the cultures of other women of color as well, although the characters in her novels are pri-marily black and white American, African, and European. It is important, however, not to ignore Walker's inclusion of women of color besides black American women in her definition of "womanist." In her writings she often refers to Black women's Native American ancestry and the wisdom living Indians continue to pass on. Such inclusion indicates to me that black wom-anists ought to be open to and in solidarity with cultural perspectives of other women of color. While the vast majority of those who call themselves womanist are of African descent, some theologians, like Rita Nakashima

Brock, who is Asian, Native American, and Hispanic, have called themselves womanist. Hispanic and Latin American feminist theologians, such as Maria Isasi–Diaz employ the term *mujerista* to refer to their distinctive understanding of feminist theological issues. *Mujerista* means *womanist* in Spanish. There is at once a sense of solidarity with other women of color and self-naming in the use of the term *mujerista*. Although I focus on the relationship between theology and culture from a black Christian womanist perspective in this essay, I find it important to acknowledge that there are other voices with distinctive perspectives on this subject.

TOWARD A WOMANIST APPROACH TO THEOLOGY AND CULTURE

Delores Williams is an important resource for exploring a womanist approach to theology and culture. Her article "Womanist Theology: Black Women's Voices" (1989) is perhaps the earliest article on the subject. In her discussion of the meaning of the term "womanist" Williams observes that Walker's concept "contains what black feminist scholar bell hooks in *From Margin to Center* identifies as cultural codes." Williams explains that:

> *These are words, beliefs, and behavioral patterns of a people that must be deciphered before meaningful communication can happen cross-culturally. Walker's codes are female-centered and they point beyond themselves to conditions, events, meanings, and values that have crystallized in the Afro-American community around women's activity and formed traditions.* (Williams 1989, 180-1)

As a paramount example of such a cultural code, Williams builds on Walker's emphasis on the wisdom passed from mothers to daughters. She observes that black mothers historically have passed on wisdom for survival, not only to their daughters, but "in the white world, in the black community, and with men." Female slave narratives, folk tales, and some contemporary black poetry and prose reflect this tradition (Williams 1989, 180). I would emphasize that such narrative forms are primary cultural resources that womanist theologians can and do draw on to develop theologies that are authentic to Black women's culture and experience. Within such narratives, one finds the types of cultural codes reflected in Walker's definition of "womanist." Williams, for example, observes that Walker's "reference to Black women's love of food and roundness points to customs of female care in the black community (including the church) associated with hospitality and nurture." As an example of such care she refers to the description in *The Book of Negro Folklore* of rent party practices during the

Depression, which reveal that "black folk stressed togetherness and a closer connection with nature" (Williams 1989, 180-1).

Williams finds that Walker's allusion to skin color, which she highlights in her description of the colored race being like a flower garden with rich colors from white to yellow to black, indicates tensions over skin color and some Black men's preference for light-skinned women. This too is a cultural code, specifically a behavior pattern, that may not be obvious to dominant culture and is complex enough in its relationship to interlocking forms of oppression that it is not easily deciphered by or for dominant white culture. I would add that even in intercultural communication among African Americans, it is important and valuable for such codes to be deciphered so that we more clearly understand how certain beliefs, words, and behavior patterns reflect our concepts of the sacred in relation to self and community. Is not preference for light-skinned women, for example, a disparagement of the sacredness and beauty of difference? If, as Walker suggests, God is in Creation, do not such attitudes disparage not only Creation but God? Overall, I agree with Williams's conclusions about cultural codes:

> *These cultural codes and their corresponding traditions are valuable resources for indicating and validating the kind of data upon which womanist theologians can reflect as they bring Black women's social, religious, and cultural experience into the discourse of theology, ethics, biblical and religious studies. Female slave narratives, imaginative literature by Black women, autobiographies, the work by Black women in academic disciplines, and the testimonies of black church women will be authoritative sources for womanist theologians. (Williams 1989, 180-1)*

Williams argues that Walker situates her understanding of a womanist in the context of nonbourgeois black folk culture, which has "less rigidity in male-female roles and more respect for female intelligence and ingenuity than is found in bourgeois culture." Williams is careful to describe "nonbourgeois black folk culture," but could more clearly describe bourgeois culture. For example, are all black middle class women and men "bourgeois" by virtue of economic and educational status? Or by bourgeois black culture does she have in mind attitudes, customs, beliefs, and words that are disparaging of traditional, African-based black culture and that give preference to Western socio-economic, political, and religious values? I suspect she has in mind the latter, since otherwise it would be difficult to treat the works of Black women scholars as serious reflections of Black women's nonbour-

geois culture, given their economic and educational status. I appreciate
Williams' suggestion that it is important to differentiate between different
types of Black culture. Not all black cultures are the same. Even "nonbourgeois Black women's culture" is diverse. I agree that the wisdom of black
folk culture is a rich resource for the black community intellectually and
academically. I also find it important to note, however, that the writings and
social justice activity of women like Anna Julia Cooper, Mary Church
Terrell, Ida B. Wells-Barnett, and Frances Ellen Watkins Harper reflect the
justice-making values of Black women's folk culture to varying degrees, although they also reflect values that are more assimilating to white bourgeois
culture. From the narratives of these women also must be gleaned values
that reflect freedom-fighting, vision for survival strategies, and life affirming
activity that forwards survival of the masses of black Americans. It is important to look at a complex mix of cultures that make up what one calls Black
women's social-historical context. This context must be dealt with in all
its complexity.

Womanist theology is *contextual* theology. Contextual theology is an
inductive approach to theological construction. It takes seriously theological
analysis of the social-historical and religio-cultural context of a people.
Theological perspectives are never purely objective. They are shaped by the
cultural and historical contexts we humans belong to. Contextual theology
considers the influence of culture(s) in shaping a people's worldview.
Womanist theology takes seriously Black women's culture as a resource for
theological reflection. I have given examples of Black women's cultural resources and an overview of Williams' understanding of *cultural codes*.
Perhaps it would be helpful to further outline my understanding of culture.

I understand *culture* as the ways in which people make meaning of the
"world" they find themselves in (Geertz 1973, 126-41; Kaufman 1993, 32-
47, 301-40). It has to do with how they define and describe their environment—how they make sense of it, and the kinds of social structures they
create in response to it. Building on the work of hooks and Williams, I also
find it important to consider the customs, habits, words, and beliefs of a culture and how these reflect a people's worldview. I am interested in what a
culture's habits, beliefs, words, customs, and behavioral patterns reflect
about a people's concepts of God, self, and community. As a womanist theologian, I am particularly interested in the contributions Black women's culture makes to the black community and the other cultures with which it
is connected.

While culture is based in large part on human interpretation of a particular environment, culture also shapes human interpretation. The world
we enter as babies, children, teenagers, adults, workers, parents, thinkers,

clergy, and believers is not a vacuum. We are born into societies that already are comprised of complex systems of political, social, economic, and religious rules, laws, beliefs, and customs. These systems and natural environments shape our understanding of our experience. At the same time, cultures are not static. But rather they are in a continuous process of construction, deconstruction, and reconstruction. We continually reinterpret them over various historical periods in response to new, previously unnamed experiences. Culture has to do with human habits, customs, beliefs, the creation of systems of law, rules, government, economics, religion. It includes art, philosophy music, dance, mythopoetics, narrative, architecture, agriculture, technology, beliefs, practices, and understandings of relationship to or dominance of the earth, skies, and waters. Like the air we breathe, culture so permeates and underlies our everyday consciousness that we tend to be aware of only its most superficial aspects in our daily living. All too often we become aware of culture in the midst of conflict as we realize that other groups have practices, beliefs, customs, and traditions, that are different from the ones we are familiar with and take for granted as normative. Womanist theology asserts the value of Black womens' cultures in a society that often disparages them. It relates concepts of the sacred to culture within the conflictual interstices of White feminist, Black male, and Eurocentric theologies.

Womanists take seriously written and oral-historical narratives regarding the experience of God's activity in the history of a people. This is considered a valid starting point for theological construction. Moreover, womanist theology tends to examine overlapping forms of oppression such as racism, sexism, classism, heterosexism, and environmental racism. Womanist theologians analyze such forms of oppression, I would say, with the presupposition that dominant cultural norms in Euro-American society regarding goodness and evil, black and white, men and women, humankind and nature, and superiority and inferiority lead to systemic socio-economic injustice.

We live in a society in which blacks are considered inferior to whites, women are considered inferior to men, and the earth is subjugated by humankind. Such oppositional, disparaging, dualistic understandings and the oppressive behavior that results from them are affirmed by dominant culture. Attitudes of racism, classism, sexism, heterosexism, and environmental racism are learned through a process of inculturation. This is theologically important because traditional Euro-American concepts of God have tended to affirm oppressive behaviors that are accepted as cultural norms. Moreover, God has tended to be imaged as white to the exclusion of other races. The dominant cultural image of full humanity in North America and

Europe is whiteness. The dominant image of God affirms Euro-American aesthetics and cultural values.

Alice Walker portrays this problem in *The Color Purple*. Shug debunks Celie's notion that God is an old white man in the sky. Sympathizing that it is hard to read the Bible without thinking that God is white and a man, Shug explains that "My first step from the old white man was trees. Then air. Then birds. Then other people. But one day when I was sitting quiet and feeling like a motherless child, which I was, it come to me: that feeling of being part of everything, not separate at all" (167). Womanism as envisioned by Alice Walker seeks to move beyond such exclusivist imagery of God. It recognizes that God is beyond all images. Therefore, the character Shug explains to Celie that God is not a "he" or a "she" but an "it" (Walker 1982, 164-168). She goes on to describe God as immanent in Creation—trees, air, birds, and all kinds of people. For Shug, God transcends gender and is not limited by the images humans construct in various cultures. For womanists like myself who build on Walker's narratives, God transcends the gender, racial, and humanocentric categories.

CULTURAL RESOURCES FOR WOMANIST THEOLOGIES

The narrative resources womanist theologians and ethicists draw on are connected with the religio-cultural values, beliefs, and practices of African-American women and men. Written and oral narratives are resources that womanist theologians and ethicists draw on for gaining access to Black women's interpretation of their religious, social, historical, political, and economic experiences. In Black women's interpretations of such experience we find certain cultural patterns reflected. One's cultural context influences one's interpretation of experience. Womanist theology sees Black women's experiences as a valid starting point for theology. I would suggest that Black women interpret these experiences through a complex set of cultural codes. People from different cultures might respond to similar situations differently.

For example, Walker turns to her mother's cultural heritage of creating beauty out of ugliness. While Walker's mother placed sunflowers in the holes in her shack, another response might be to despair about the lack of finances to build new walls. Indeed, scientists from dominant culture have registered surprise at such creative, strengthening responses to oppression. Harvard psychologist Robert Coles observes that he determined to devote his entire psychological research to studying children after he observed six-year-old Ruby Bridges, the lone black child ordered to integrate an all-white elementary school in New Orleans in 1965 amidst a chorus of racial taunts and slurs, defying theories in his clinical background that she would disintegrate under the pressure (Getlin 1995, E1, 4). Ruby Bridges explains that rather than try to explain racism to her young child, her mother instructed her to do what she always did when she was afraid, pray. Everyday, surrounded by crowds hurling cruel, racial epithets, six-year-old Ruby would pray:

Please, God, try to forgive these people,
Because even if they say those bad things,
They don't know what they're doing.
So you could forgive them,

Just like you did those folks a long time ago
When they said terrible things about you.
(Getlin 1995, E1-4)

Ruby Bridges's prayer gave her strength and courage to meet her situation with a positive and creative spirit. She did not fall apart. The references to Jesus' activity and power of loving to the point of forgiving even his enemies suggests creative interpretation and application of Christian biblical principles in Black women's culture. That the narrative of Jesus informs her interpretation of her situation of persecution for doing what is good and right is significant for Christian womanist analysis. For womanists from other religious traditions (Walker does not describe herself as Christian), Ruby Bridges's application of her mother's teaching indicates a tradition of strength and creativity in the face of great odds. Her narrative points to Black women's cultural beliefs about the power to walk with strength in the midst of terror. Her words reveal a sense of walking a similar path to Jesus, who Christians claim embodied God. Mrs. Bridges passed on a "creative spark" to her daughter so that she was able to make a way out of no way, finding healing in hostile circumstances. Young Ruby's prayer suggests Black women can imitate Jesus, embodying the creative Spirit that Jesus embodied.

Ruby Bridges's story stands in sharp contrast to the response of Shannon Faulkner, a Southern white woman, who recently struggled to be the first woman to integrate Citadel Naval Academy. Amidst hazing and taunts, Faulkner found that she was emotionally and psychologically unprepared to complete her task. While this is understandable, it is striking to many in the black community that she seemed not to have received from her mothers and grandmothers the kind of preparation that young girls like Ruby Bridges received from their mothers. While racism is abominable, the creative response of black mothers and their daughters to this insidious social sin reveals empowerment resources in Black women's culture. As Walker's definition of womanism indicates, such creative response has historical roots in the narratives of figures like Harriet Tubman who freed herself, her family, and hundreds of other slaves by belief in the power of the "spirit."

His expectations that Ruby Bridges would shatter and fall into psychological disintegration proven wrong, Robert Coles came to see Bridges as an example of "the power of the human spirit" (Getlin 1995, E4). I would argue that she is an example of the power of God as Spirit, creativity itself, in human culture. Bridges's mother, like Walker's mother, defied white cultural norms and expectations of how human beings respond to disparagement, abuse, dispossession, and oppression. There are numerous accounts of such responses of creativity and strength by Black women historically and today. As Williams suggests, such responses point to a cultural code. Ruby Bridges's mother passed on the kind of strength and creative spark to her daughter that Walker discusses. She engaged in the tradition of passing on wisdom for freedom and survival strategies that are the basic building blocks of womanist culture.

I see Bridges's response as a testament not only to the human spirit, but to God, Spirit-Itself, which for me is the source of Walker's "creative spark" and "strength." Accounts like Walker's and Ruby Bridges's that emerge from Black women's culture make an important contribution to other cultures as well. As Coles' response suggests, peoples from different cultures can learn something about the diverse potential of Spirit in humankind from each other. For Christian womanists, Jesus Christ is the most complete embodiment of Spirit, which is creative in its activity and effects in human culture. Historically, Christian Black women have sought to walk in the power of the Spirit. Ruby Bridges inherited such a practice. While it is not exclusive to Black women's culture, it is a distinctive cultural code that takes on particular meaning in the context of a dominant, racist, sexist culture. Her narrative, as well as the narratives of diverse historical and contemporary Black women, is an important resource for constructing womanist theology.

Womanist theologians have turned to the narratives of such women to examine concepts of God, Christ, Spirit in Black women's culture. Jacquelyn Grant, for example, turns to the narrative of Sojourner Truth as a resource for womanist understanding of the nature of Christ. Truth's assertion that Jesus came from God and a woman with man having nothing to do with him points to Black women's emphasis on the *humanity* of Jesus (Grant 1989, 220). Katie Cannon refers to the life and work of Zora Neale Hurston to discuss the moral values of *invisible dignity, quiet grace,* and *unshouted courage* that Black women pass on from mother to daughter (Cannon 1988). Delores Williams refers to Black women freedom fighters who fought against injustice and against the odds with belief in the power of the "spirit" (Williams 1989, 181-2). Early-twentieth-century black church-woman Lucie Campbell wrote a hymn symbolizing God as "Something Within" (Dodson and Gilkes 1986, 80-94). I have drawn on turn-of-the-century black feminist Anna Julia Cooper's metaphor of a "*Singing* something" that makes humankind "*anthropos*" and "justifies the claim to equality by birthright to the inheritance from a common Father [sic]" (Cooper 1945, 5; Baker-Fletcher 1994, 65-7, 190). Cooper described a *Singing* Something as a "divine spark" that "is capable of awakening at the most unexpected moment." It "never is wholly smothered or stamped out." For this reason, any racial group or nation "that undertakes the role to play God and dominate the earth, has an awful, a terrific responsibility" (Cooper 1945, 5). Such metaphors are diverse examples of creative responses to the evils of racial and gender oppression.

THE RELATIONSHIP BETWEEN GOD AS CREATIVITY AND CULTURE

When one examines narratives from Black women's culture, one finds diverse symbolizations of God as a source of strength for freedom-fighting, sustaining, liberating, and healing activity. I understand such symbolizations as referents to God as Spirit, which is both *creativity itself* and the empowering source of humankind's creativity. Given that one can find creative responses to evil in Black women's culture and human culture generally, a fundamental question is: What is the relationship of God to the kinds of creative responses and patterns human beings construct in their symbolizing activity? Is God utterly transcendent of this symbolizing process? Is our symbolizing activity an entirely *human* activity, separate from the activity of God?

If God is involved in our symbolizing process, then God is involved in human cultural activity. The problem is that not all cultural activity is life affirming. Much of it is sinful and participates in the evils of classism, racism, sexism, imperialism, greed, and selfishness. And yet, if humankind has the capacity to be moved by the Spirit, then God nevertheless must also be present in our cultural activity, in spite of our limitations. There is something in the strength and spiritual creativity of a Ruby Bridges that indicates the presence of something greater than ourselves, whether we call it a "creative spark," "something within," a "Singing Something," or a "divine spark." I understand God as creativity. This metaphor is often used by process theologians. However, I am not a Whiteheadian. While I appreciate process theology's grounding in the philosophy of Alfred North Whitehead as a way to develop a metaphysics that moves beyond a Newtonian mechanistic interpretation of the universe to consider the interrelated nature of all life, I draw my own understanding of "creativity" from African and African American cultures (Suchocki 1989; Young 1990). Also, I find Gordon Kaufman's discussion of God's function helpful because he cautions against reifying any particular set of symbols or images of God. While Kaufman describes God as "serendipitous creativity," which moves dynamically in human history, his theology is open-ended (Kaufman 1993, 46, 319-20). He presents "serendipitous creativity" as a helpful symbolization of God, but takes painstaking care to clarify that no symbolization of God is absolute. My focus is on *creativity* as a particular *symbolization* of God. While I find Kaufman's discussion of serendipitous creativity intriguing, I move beyond it, to consider understandings of such dynamic creativity in human history that are authentic to Black women's culture and experience. For me, *creativity* symbolizes the kind of powerful, positive response to everyday life with its joys, beauty, oppressions, and vicissitudes represented by Walker's "creative spark."

In my work, when I use terms like "creativity," "creative spark," "strength," or "a Singing Something" to describe God I am mindful that these are *symbolizations* of God that refer to the real, ultimate, ineffable, compassionate, mysterious, life-affirming and empowering presence in the universe that provides hope, meaning, sustenance, vision for survival strategies, and strength to struggle for freedom and justice. I employ God-language from African American women's culture and American culture generally, with the understanding that such language is not final. A diversity of womanists and peoples from other cultures are rich resources for diverse symbols of God that represent such life-affirming, liberating, creative activity. Such language helps make meaning of experiences of faith in sustenance, healing, empowerment, and strength to struggle for freedom and justice. Walker's use of the metaphor "creative spark" reflects a symbolization of spiritual empowerment from Black women's culture. But again, what does God have to do with such symbolizing activity? Is God involved in such activity? My understanding of these questions is influenced in part by the thought of Richard Reinhold Niebuhr and Gordon Kaufman.

Niebuhr suggests an integrative concept of divine and human cultural activity. He highlights a dynamic, mutual relationship between theophanous experiences and the theological symbolizations that emerge from them. Such symbolizations are ongoing and incomplete. We require a multiplicity of symbolizations because they inform and correct one another. Theophanous experiences inspire mythopoeic works of prophets, the primary and invaluable resources upon which religious traditions, doctrines, and formal theological treatises are built. This occurs in a whirlwind of rich, creative, processive, symbolizing activity. Multiple theological symbolizations found in mythopoeics, doctrine, sermons, graphics, photography, and systematic theologies inform one another in a continuous process. Mytho-poeics is a kind of soil from which systematic theology emerges. Conversely, systematic theology inspires new symbolizations of God (and Christ for Niebuhr) from which new mythopoeics emerge.[3] Niebuhr uses the term theographia to refer to the multiplicity of writings and graphics that inform our theological understanding. Included among forms of *theographia* are letters, sermons, myth, narrative, autobiographies, personal narrative, hymns, markings and graphics, as well as the traditional formal theological treatise. Formal theological treatises and religious narrative are types of theographia that exist in a complex environment of multiple symbol systems. Narrative, sermons, graphics, etc. form the soil for formal theological treatises; but formal theological treatises also form a soil from which emerge new narratives, sermons, and graphics. One might say that writings by and/or about Black women are forms of theography (Niebuhr 1977-78, 9-22; Baker-Fletcher 1994, 21-2, 187). The varied genres of writing and their content point to a multiplicity of theological symbolizations among Black women.

Kaufman describes the situation somewhat differently. For Kaufman, "in human imaginative and critical activities of this sort...the cosmic tension toward the human began to express itself *within* human consciousness and culture" (Kaufman 1993, 351). Through the construction and reconstruction of God-Talk humans become aware of who we are and what is going on in the world. For Kaufman, God makes Godself "known to humankind: in and through the emergence and development of God-talk." However, one must not take such language so literally or absolutely as to reify the notion of "God as speaker" (Kaufman 1993, 352). Kaufman warns that all of this ultimately has to do with *mystery*. We would be mistaken to take our imaginative constructs of mystery as real and absolute. What I find most helpful in Kaufman's work is his argument that "theology as imaginative construction . . . demands that we clearly distinguish our ideas—especially when we speak of God—from the mysteries to which we intend them to refer" (Kaufman 1993, 353). This keeps theologians honest about God's independence from our God-language. It is important to recognize, as Kaufman argues, that all of our language is an *imaginative constructive activity*. We seek to name that which we *cannot* claim to know absoultely. For Kaufman, God's activity is humanizing on the one hand, relativizing (transcendent) on the other. God is the "ultimate mystery of life," because no one has seen God (315, 319-21). Such mystery relativizes all of our God-language, including "serendipitous creativity," "creativity," "creative spark." All of our language about God in human culture is limited. To believe otherwise results in self-idolatry.

Kaufman's and Niebuhr's theories about the relativity of symbolizing activity is not incongruous with Black women's thought. The writings of black feminist and Social Gospel writer Anna Julia Cooper (1858-1964) are a primary resource for my understanding of the rich but relative interpretations of God's activity that humankind engages in. Cooper argued that while she did not deny the reality of absolute and eternal truth, she did understand faith as neither "the holding of correct views and unimpeachable opinions on mooted questions," nor "the ability to forge cast-iron formulas and dub them TRUTH." Rather, "truth must be infinite, and as incapable as infinite space, of being encompassed and confined by one age or nation, sect or country—much less by one little creature's finite brain" (Cooper 1988, 298). There are limits to what we can claim to know about God. Humankind's knowledge of God—infinite, ultimate, and absolute truth—is always partial and incomplete. For Anna Cooper, this meant that reformers thought God's thought after God. Even when human beings seem to gain some glimpse of God's thought which moves them toward fuller human potential, their understanding is incomplete. No one generation receives or works out the full revelation of God's intention for human freedom and equality. "Not unfrequently has it happened," Cooper contended, "that the impetus of a mighty thought wave has done the execution meant by its Creator in spite of the weak and distorted perception of its human embodiment." In her view, so incomplete is human envisionment of God that "it is not strange if reformers" have often "builded more wisely than they knew;" and while fighting consciously for only a narrow gateway for themselves, have been driven forward by that irresistible "Power not ourselves which makes for righteousness to open a high road for humanity" (Cooper 1983, 118-119).

For Cooper, God is not separate from human culture and history, but works within culture to empower human beings to resist domination and move toward freedom. God, as the very source of such empowerment, is beyond and something more than culture. As one struggles for reform, one has only a narrow view of the larger idea one is fighting for. Humanity, thinking God's thoughts after God, is an instrument of a larger power, a grander concept of social reform or social salvation (Baker-Fletcher 1994, 148-50). Cooper's thinking has something in common with Kaufman's concept of the relativizing nature of God and with Niebuhr's argument for a multiplicity of theological symbols that inform and correct each other. A Womanist theology of culture can build on such understandings of God's relativizing activity to consider a diversity of symbolizations of God. A multiplicity of theological symbols can offer a fuller concept of God than one perspective alone can contribute. Womanist theology, like Black theology, Asian theologies, and Latin American theologies, adds yet another set of voices, images, and concepts to the ongoing conversation regarding the relationship between theology and culture.

FURTHER CONSIDERATIONS FOR A WOMANIST THEOLOGY OF CULTURE

An area for further consideration is the relationship between Creativity, culture, and *creation*. One of the problems in approaches to the study of theology and culture is that Spirit and culture tend to be separated from nature. For Alice Walker, Spirit moves not only in culture but in creation. Womanist theologians like Emilie Townes and Delores Williams have made important steps in recognizing the interrelationship of God, culture, and creation (Townes 1995, 55-7; Williams 1993b, 24-9). In considering the metaphor of a *Singing* Something that rises forth in humankind to resist domination, which I derive from the writings of Anna Cooper, I now find it important to ask, "Is there a Singing Something in all creation?"

People of color and the poor are disproportionately affected by toxic waste which industries site in their communities. Environmental justice is directly related to socio-economic justice. What are some of the cultural codes in Black women's culture that provide important insights and strategies for developing a religious culture that gives strong recognition to the connections between human survival and the earth's survival? As director of the United Church of Christ's Commission for Racial Justice, Rev. Ben Chavis was instrumental in the release of a 1987 landmark study, "Toxic Wastes and Race in the United States." Since the 1980s, African Americans and other people of color have increasingly sought environmental justice (Bullard 1994; Grossman 1993). It is important that womanist theology give increased attention to this phenomenon among African Americans and other communities of color. Concepts of culture that are discontinuous with nature are inadequate. For contemporary womanist theology to move more fully into a wholistic vision of survival, liberation, freedom, and healing it is necessary to self-consciously construct concepts of God that move explicitly toward an integrative understanding of theology, culture, and creation.

REFERENCES

Baker-Fletcher, Karen. 1994. *A Singing Something: Womanist Reflections on Anna Julia Cooper*. New York: Crossroad.

Bullard, Robert. 1994. *Dumping in Dixie: Race, Class, and Environmental Quality*. Boulder, Colorado: Westview Press.

Cannon, Katie G. 1988. *Black Womanist Ethics*. Atlanta: Scholars Press.

———. 1995. *Katie's Canon*. New York: Continuum.

———. "Moral Wisdom in the Black Women's Literary Tradition." In *Weaving the Visions: New Patterns in Feminist Spirituality*, ed. Carol P. Christ and Judith Plaskow. San Francisco: Harper and Row, 1989.

Collins, Patricia Hill. 1991. *Black Feminist Thought: Knowledge, Consciousness, and the Politics of Empowerment*. New York: Routledge.

Cooper, Anna. 1945. *Equality of Races and the Democratic Movement*. Washington, D.C.: Privately Printed.

———. 1988. *A Voice from the South*. Xenia, Ohio: Privately printed, 1892. Reprint, New York: Oxford University Press.

Dodson, Jualyne E. and Cheryl Townsend Gilkes. 1986. "Something Within: Social Change and Collective Endurance in the Sacred World of Black Christian Women." In *Women and Religion in America: A Documentary History, 1900-1968*, ed. Rosemary Radford Ruether and Rosemary Skinner Keller. New York: Harper and Row.

Getlin, Josh. 1995. "A Profile in Courage." *Los Angeles Times* (11 September), E1-4.

Geertz, Clifford. 1973. *The Interpretation of Cultures*. New York: Basic Books, Inc. Publishers.

Grant, Jacquelyn. 1989. *White Women's Christ and Black Women's Jesus*. Atlanta: Scholars Press, 1955.

———. "Womanist Jesus and the Mutual Struggle for Liberation." In *The Recovery of Black Presence*, ed. Randall C. Bailey and Jacquelyn Grant. Nashville: Abingdon.

Grossman, Karl. 1993. "Environmental Racism." In *The "Racial" Economy of Science: Toward a Democratic Future*, ed. Sandra Harding. Bloomington, Indiana: Indiana University Press.

Kaufman, Gordon. 1993. *In Face of Mystery: A Constructive Theology*. Cambridge: Harvard University Press.

Niebuhr, Richard R. 1977-78. "The Tent of Heaven: Theographia I." *Alumnae Bulletin, Bangor Theological Seminary* 2 (Fall/Winter): 9-22.

Suchocki, Marjorie [1982] (1989). *God, Christ, Church*. New York: Crossroad.

Townes, Emilie. 1993. *A Troubling in my Soul: Womanist Perspectives on Evil and Suffering*. Maryknoll, NY: Orbis.

———. 1995. *In A Blaze of Glory*. Nashville: Abingdon.

Walker, Alice. 1982. *The Color Purple*. New York: Harcourt, Brace, Jovanovich.

———. 1983. *In Search of Our Mothers' Gardens*. New York: Harcourt, Brace, Jovanovich.

Williams, Delores. 1989. "Womanist Theology: Black Women's Voices." In *Weaving the Visions*, ed. Carol P. Christ and Judith Plaskow. 179-86. San Francisco: Harper and Row.

———. 1993a. *Sisters in the Wilderness: The Challenge of Womanist God-Talk*. Maryknoll: Orbis.

———. "Sin, Nature and Black Women's Bodies." In *Ecofeminism and the Sacred*, ed. Carol J. Adams, 24-9. New York: Continuum, 1993.

Young, Henry James. 1990. *Hope in Process*. Minneapolis: Fortress.

NOTES

1. While Williams employs lower-case letters, I prefer to spell "Spirit" with upper case letters, as Walker does. For me, this distinguishes *God* as Spirit from the *human* spirit.

2. See, for example, Emilie Townes (1993); Katie Cannon (1995); Jacquelyn Grant (1989); and Delores Williams, (1993a).

3. Notes from Richard R. Niebuhr's course, "Symbolizations of Christ," Harvard Divinity School, Fall 1988.

THEOLOGICAL METHOD AND CULTURAL STUDIES:

SLAVE RELIGIOUS CULTURE AS A HEURISTIC

Dwight N. Hopkins

This essay uses the culture of enslaved African Americans' religious experiences to explore how theological method can learn from cultural studies. The history of enslaved blacks in North America offers a fertile site for the development of a theology which originates out of a particular set of cultural expressions about beliefs, and, furthermore, can serve as a heuristic for all genres of theological methodology, especially liberation theologies. Theological methodology and cultural studies warrent a mutual investigation because they both adhere to at least two basic principles. First, both claim that people are the ones who are involved in creating their respective objects of study. For instance, black and other liberation theologies immediately confess that their enterprise centers around humanity's involvement with some divine or ultimate or spirit. And though traditional, mainstream theology often gives the impression that "God" does theology—with the consequent implication that humans are acted upon only by "God"— even the most conservative theologians are struggling with the notion of how humans should relate to the conservative's "God." Similarly, cultural studies by definition engages the multiplicity of cultural representations and formulations—such as popular, mass, high, etc.—dynamics which humans undertake (Agger 1992; Milner 1991; Dirks et al. 1994).

Second, both theology and cultural studies are concerned with transformations of the human: they are engaged enterprises. Again, black and other liberation theologies tend toward religious movements as radically altering systems and structures on earth as a foreshadowing of a novel future instance of just social relations. And mainstream theological endeavors, especially conservative, are dedicated to defeating the entire world of "Satan" in order for the new world to emerge. Similarly the origin of cultural studies grew out of a sociological concern for the plight of the working class vis-a-vis social inequality and political issues (Simon During 1993, Intro.; Easthope and McGowan 1993).

A common comparison of theological methodology and cultural studies does not obviate clarity of definitions. Culture, in this essay, is defined as Raymond Williams' "total of way of life."[1] Furthermore, from the cultural

life-styles of enslaved African Americans, I would modify Williams' definition in two ways. Culture is religious in so far as the way of life of all human
beings entails some yearning for, belief in, and ritualization around that
which is ultimate—that which is both part of and greater than the self.
Culture is religious because the ultimate concern is both present in the material (tangible manifestation) and transcendent (the imagination of the ultimate is not limited to the self). Therefore, in this essay, culture refers to
religious culture as a total way of life.

A second modification of Williams' perceptive analysis is my specification of four component parts of the totality of a person's or community's reality. Here too cultural studies insights are pertinent.

Part of life is political economy; that is to say that the production,
ownership, and distribution of wealth (in contrast to income) impact one's
way of life. Though one would not subscribe to an epiphenomenal causation
like the base-superstructure paradigm, Marx is helpful with political economic investigations. Here one would accept the inciteful Marxian analysis
with the following caveat: there exists a mutual penetrating and fluid interaction between superstructure and base.

Life is not only a macro picture but, and at certain times more importantly, is constituted also by micro considerations, such as space and time,
body and sexuality, fun and laughter, pleasure and desire, architecture and
geography, etc. Here Foucault's work bears fruit: his technologies of power
and (his later) ethics or techniques of the self. One would however posit the
same caution about using Foucault as one did with Marx. To employ aspects
of the works of Foucault and Marx is not to submit to their entire programs
and their alleged "essentialism" (Foucault) and "totalitarianism" (Marx).

In addition to the micro analysis in cultural studies, language is a third
important slice of culture as a total way of life. We communicate with and
make ourselves known to others through language, either verbal, silent,
body, or textual. In a sense, the language of life is so important that it defines what it means to be alive and a human being—the ability to articulate
the self to the self, and the ability to articulate the self in community. But
language in life is never transparent because it does not simply passively reflect thoughts, ideas or objects. Language, indeed, formulates and fashions
reality. Thus it embodies codes and signs, as well as symbols and metaphors.
Parts of the systems of Eco (semiotics) and Ricoeur (hermeneutics) can help
us unpack and grasp the receptivity and creativity of language.

Fourthly, culture circumscribes identity. What are the processes of
identity formation, of the production of "who I am" and "who we are"?
One of the most important American intellectuals to grapple seriously with
this issue was Malcolm X, who persistently pondered why and how a group

of people could lose their identity and why and how to craft a new identity. Identity, however, is not a static reality forged once and forever, but a contestable terrain to be negotiated in the face of continual influences and spaces differentiated from oneself. In other words, identity is dynamic because time changes people. Malcolm X's life and teachings are testimony to the persistent quest for identity formation.

For this essay, then, culture refers to a total way of life which is religious and constituted by a dynamic, non-hierarchical interplay of macro, micro, linguistic, and identity concerns. Theological method details the path by which people develop a conscious and intentional understanding of a community's belief in and practice with the ultimate as it is envisioned by their religious culture. We now turn to enslaved African American religious experiences as one methodological window.

The question of theological method in religious culture is complex, even when one engages the coherent and consistent thought of an academically trained theologian. The question becomes even more pressing when posed in a situation of unlettered slaves whose cogency in theological matters is not readily apparent. African Americans, from the period of 1619 to 1865, did not attend divinity schools or seminaries. Thus, on the one hand, the task of theological methodology is made more difficult by the lack of recognizable road signs which are missing in this strange and unfamiliar land of religious thinking and practice of the chatteled blacks. On the other hand, a creative challenge presents itself because the poetic and painful experiences of enslaved African Americans offer ample opportunity for deciphering theological insights from the faith environment of primary religious resources for research. In other words, one does not have to filter through established systems of doctrinal theology when dealing with these accounts; hence the problem and the possibility of the endeavor.

A critical engagement with slave religious culture—their total way of life—suggests that theological methodology should consist of several parts. In particular it should include: diverse sources, guidelines for approaching the sources, a relatively consistent norm, reoccurring theological patterns, and a theoretical framework to assist in the interpretation of the sources.

SOURCES

A major development of cultural studies is an emphasis on the people and events that have fallen between the cracks of history and official recordings of human societies. Perspectives with bourgeois interests, in contrast, perceive human interactions from the top down; hence dominating definitions narrow the multiplicity and vibrancy of the majority of humanity's activities, particularly the striving and strength of the "folk," the "masses" or the "oppressed."[2] On the other hand, a more democratic cultural studies allows for the possibility that the earth's voiceless populations and communities can speak, even from beyond the grave. To hear them talk requires a deliberate excavation into terrain labeled unorthodox and, in certain cases, heretical. But again, the question is, terrain irreverent to whom? The terrain of the unspoken pauses and hidden revelations become anathema primarily to those who prefer a linear, positivist perspective on life circumscribed by a "great man of history" attitude, thereby truncating the intellectual contributions of society's pyramidal bottom.

Consequently, for my purposes, the opportunity to conceptualize a framework (e.g., theological method) afresh is enhanced by the disparate sources and myriad testimonies given by enslaved blacks. For instance, there are forty-one volumes of interviews with ex-slaves living in the previously known Black Belt South of the southeastern United States (Rawick 1972, 1977, 1979). There are also over one hundred autobiographies of former chattel who ran away, purchased their own freedom, or were manumitted.[3] And fragments and shorter accounts of slave religious life appear in denominational publications and abolitionists' materials (Blassingame 1977). Perhaps among the more enigmatic, intriguing, and revealing sources for devising a theology are the Spirituals, the faith songs uniquely created by black Americans under slavery (Fisher 1978; Lovell Jr., 1986). The intellectual contributions of ebony bondwomen and men were intentionally locked out of conventional accounts of America's formation or included as entertainment or pathos propaganda. Rarely have oppressed and illiterate blacks taken center stage in any discipline's substantive academic endeavors. A multilevel approach within cultural studies opens up these voices.

Moreover, the claim that theological sources emerge from religious culture (as described above) is aimed at two onesided and false analytical postures. One is that of the traditional religious person or community which narrowly positions normative sources within the confines of a church or organized established religious institution. It is a mistaken scholarship that limits belief expressions only to ecclesial formations and palatable doctrinal categories in order to privilege religious organizations, thereby denying the fecund, syncretistic ways of thinking about (immanent and transcendent) ultimate concerns throughout human culture. This latter tendency is common not only in mainstream liberal and conservative Christianity but even to liberation theologies. The second underestimators of a more far-reaching religious culture are those so-called secular modernists and postmodernists who speak of reason and particularities but do not take religion seriously. For the modernist, reason enables freedom from religion; and for the postmodernist, the accent on particularities frees one from any meta-narrative, including religious assertions about normative freedom.

The experiences of enslaved African Americans, in line with our understanding of religious culture, indicate that questions of ultimate concern are embodied, embedded, or incarnated, if you will, in the everyday life represented by manifold sources. The presence of the divine reality or that which was greater than themselves was manifest in the material and visible world of the enchained African Americans. How one negotiates time, space, and one's being in the world signifies one's religious sensibilities. Being religious or connecting to one's ultimate is, therefore, a pervasive, personified mood and manner. Hence, rarely is there a separation between the reputed secular and sacred worlds; instead, all life is religious. Ultimate concerns reside in the flesh of everyday life.

GUIDELINES

In addition to the glaring reality of ultimate convictions in the crucial as well as mundane exigencies of life, turning to slave religious thought (as one heuristic site for the interplay between cultural studies and theological method) reveals a necessity for guidelines in the investigation of the different sources. How does one approach these seemingly opaque experiences of religious culture so that the resulting theological method will reflect a faithful depiction of the root religious concerns embedded in the sources? A journey into the world of the sources presents possible guidelines. In other words, the sources themselves contribute to the appropriate guidelines. When one enters the world of slave religious culture and allows it to introduce new insights, one can posit at least four guidelines or dynamic dimensions of life. They are dynamic because they come in pairs, such that to view only one part of the pair in one's investigation of the sources would not be faithful to how the sources themselves keep the pairs in a dynamic interconnection. The "dimension of life" aspect means, once again, a reaffirmation of the permeation of the ultimate in the life of these ebony chattel.

The first pair speaks to the importance of viewing the sources from the perspective of both males and females. Whether the slave narratives recount women and men enduring the same types of labor, whether the Spirituals sing stories of the male and female nature of Jesus, or whether autobiographies indicate the role of female and male leadership in the secret religious worship services of the slaves, one has to acknowledge gender complementarity.

The second dynamic entails the consistency of holistic ultimate beliefs; that is, the appearance of both Christian and non-Christian ingredients in the unfolding world view and dynamic belief system of bondwomen and men. For instance, there are striking testimonies of slave conversion experiences where the convert praises the role of Jesus in the move from the old self to the new. And later on in the testimony, the Christian convert will easily resort to discourse regarding haints, ghosts, or subject matter often referred to as witchcraft. The consciousness or unconsciousness of Christian and non-Christian features of the ultimate was a given.[4]

The third guideline in religious culture to which one must be sensitive is the interconnection between political and cultural intricacies—that is, the relation between the chatteled blacks' political attempts to determine the space around them and what little resources they were able to access and their concomitant cultural attempts to claim themselves by naming their own identity and their own ordeals and joys of life. (Culture, in this instance, serves the limited role of pondering "who am I?") For instance, one discovers a political motif in the Invisible Institution—the surreptitious religious meeting held by chattel late at night in the woods or an appointed cabin. Here, under the moonlight or deep in the forest, the enslaved faithful seized sacred space in which to think through and act out their religious convictions and theological beliefs. On this ground where the holy nearness met the gathered bondmen and women, one finds African Americans implementing their political right to determination of the space around them. Likewise, black people pursued a religious quest for their right of cultural self-identity (Hopkins 1993, chap. 1). One encounters this fact in several African American accounts of why they continued to seek freedom by running away. As one former slave wrote in his autobiography, not only was he running away to break the chains around his body, he also sought his freedom to have the right to name himself: a faith statement implying that the African American refused to continue bearing the names of various slave owners because an individual's name is a free choice between him or her and ultimate concerns (Osofsky 1969, 217).

The church and non-institutional religious organizations mark the final pair of guidelines suggested by a study of chattel culture. The church, and here I refer mainly to the secret Invisible Institution, provided the only free space where enslaved blacks could be themselves without surveillance or restrictions. This underground Invisible Institution was not merely a sacred space and time for normal religious worship; it was also the arena in which the makings of an incipient alternative community were evident.[5] At the same time, because African Americans believed in no sharp separation between sacred and secular, non-church institutions developed parallel to the Invisible Institution church. A classic example would be the non-church tradition of passing along folk tales to each generation of the enslaved. What is interesting about these stories of the unlettered is the faith and theological dimensions embodied in the fictional narratives. At this point, one discovers the appearance of divine-human encounters in folk "lies" which are explicitly non-Christian (Hopkins 1993, chap. 3).

NORM

If we are to enter religious culture, the heuristic of chatteled black life especially, the above guidelines facilitate a dynamic mapping of balanced pairs—a sorting–through mechanism, so to speak. In addition, an investigation of the disparate sources points to a consistent norm in the type of theological thinking held by African Americans in their religious culture. Within each paired guideline, put differently, the majority's liberation and the quest for full humanity become the consistent conviction and major motivation. Both in the bondmen's and women's usage of the biblical narrative and their creation of a sacred world in the realm of folk tales, one perceives a continual emphasis on the weak surviving and overcoming imposed limitations in life. The explicit Christian sources rely heavily on a biased and mediated interpolation of the biblical texts. In particular, from the vantage of the African Americans' life dilemma, the Hebrew and Christian testament stories were accounts corresponding to black people's stories. The prophetic Moses paradigm and the Hebrew exodus tale especially drew chatteled blacks more deeply into the Christian mythos. Despite the standard catechisms, sermons, and rituals proclaiming "slave obey your master," African Americans, in their illiterate state, were somehow able to filter through the dominant theological discourse and create their own reappropriated biblical text. In a sense, because black chattel faced a reality of an apparent irreversible human predicament (that is, one of bondage), and because the Hebrew community of the Old Testament endured a similar suffering but achieved ultimate salvation, the possibility of earthly (as well as heavenly) liberation was hoped for and would someday be certain. In a word, the Christian biblically based community embraced a freedom motif in both their interpretations of the Hebrew slaves' Old Testament story and the New Testament's tales of Jesus.

A similar norm of freedom and justice pervades the convictions of seemingly non-Christian slave folk tales. When one investigates rigorously such slave folk talk as the Brer Rabbit cycles, one encounters a whole novel world of God-talk about righting incorrect relationships between the weak and the strong. Wholeness in community results from a rectification of communal and ecological imbalances. Trickster heroes such as Brer Rabbit appear literally to save the day and the host of fallible, broken, panicky creatures of the forest who shudder in terror, captured by the prospect of a threatening larger beast or oftentimes fenced in by their own thought about fear. The movement from paralysis and hopelessness to a new state of both free individual initiative and free accessible forest space signifies a return to a pristine scene of harmony with the self, community, nature, and the ultimate. The liberation of the self—from both external and internal restraints—represented in the Christian world view complemented similar scenarios in the philosophical and linguistic prerogatives of folk discourse. The same norm of freedom was evident.

Normative discourse in the area of cultural studies is seen as contested currency and polarized polemic. Norm suggests the possibility of certainty and a non-relativity in one's position. My advocacy of a norm of freedom hails from that trajectory in cultural studies which has been engaged historically and presently, taking sides and naming names.[6] This cultural studies trend dovetails with a black theology of liberation which interprets those faith communities who wage efforts for life over death as symbolizing one strand working for full humanity within the African American religious cultural experience—both Christian and non–Christian practices and beliefs in freedom. What slave religious culture and cultural studies tell us is that theological methodology is committed and concerns power.

THEOLOGICAL PATTERNS

The sources of religious culture, as we have seen, present us with various guidelines for negotiating the abundance of slave religious experiences and intimate a relatively consistent norm in the Christian and folk horizons. Furthermore, internal to the world of these religious chattel are various theological patterns or issues which black people return to continually and out of which they seek persistently to make sense. These theological motifs or themes are symbolic signifiers for how African Americans give order, explanation, and rationality to their being in a world not of their own choosing, but a world where they attempt self-initiative and self-creation, given limited access to material resources—that is, social agency amidst restricted maneuverability. These theological patterns persist as codes of communal boundaries, defining and determining friend and foe—a process not only for religious formation but also, and at certain times more decisively, for life and death survival.

The most important common theological pattern or refrain in slave religious culture is that of God, especially the Hebrew Testament Yahweh divinity. For the slaves, the holy one was a seeing and hearing God who, once having seen and heard, would bear the chattel community up on eagle wings to their Canaan. As former slave Henry Bibb wrote in his autobiography: "I never omitted to pray for deliverance. I had faith to believe that the Lord could see our wrongs and hear our cries" (Bibb 1849). The designated attributes of compassion and agape resulted from bondmen and women reaching back into biblical times and appropriating Yahweh's promises and accomplishments for their contemporary dilemma. Relatedly, this God rearranged incorrect social relations on the individual or structural level, or, for that matter, in any place or space requiring justice work.

Similarly, in folk slave religion, the ultimate divinity gains the honorable title of The Way Maker, a being so infinite in abilities that anything is possible. The Way Maker finds itself in the following praise given to God when a black folk character approaches the divine throne in heaven. The protagonist beseeches God in the following manner: "Oh Lord and Master of the rainbow. I know your power. . . . I know you can hit a straight lick with a crooked stick."[7] The Way Maker can take a crooked stick—the problems of life, the wretched conditions of the poor, the humanly impossible—and hit a straight lick, correcting all the ailments and infirmities suffered by society's little ones.

Just as slave Christianity and slave folk tales manifest nuanced differences and complementary accounts of God, so too do the offices and attributes of Jesus and the role of other intermediaries dovetail in an empowering fit.

The ultimate goal of Jesus, from their perspective as chatteled Christians, was freedom. The following famous slave spiritual indicates the importance of Jesus:

> *Steal away, steal away*
> *Steal away to Jesus,*
> *Steal away, steal away home,*
> *I don't have long to stay here.*

In this instance enslaved blacks employed a double entendre as a communication code to deceive those lurking on the margins of the chattels' own construed Christian community. Accordingly, at certain times "Steal Away" utilized Jesus to represent a secret prayer meeting of the Invisible Institution. In other cases Jesus meant preparation for passage on the underground railroad to the north and Canada. For Nat Turner, "Steal Away to Jesus" symbolized the gathering of his prophetic band of Christian witnesses as rehearsal for an assault on the institution of slavery. Regardless of the various ways that the symbol "Jesus" was encoded, whether as a free space or a meeting to plan for freedom or freedom in heaven (the land of milk and honey), the essential being and goal of Jesus was freedom.

Similarly and quite often, in folk tales the Way Maker relates to humanity through an intermediary Trickster figure. On the one hand, the

Trickster exhibits exceptional cunning, unbelievable bravery, and a special relationship to the Way Maker. On the other, this intermediary individual shares the ups and downs of the human predicament, whether in the form of human finitude, circumstances, or striving for the fulfillment of aspirations. The trickster intermediary—like Brer Rabbit or Signifying Monkey—is one who feels called or caught in circumstances which demand siding with the unfortunate in the jungle or woods; the Trickster, in other words, believes that the meek should inherit the earth and its riches. And this trickster intermediary sets out to sacrifice himself or herself to realize this ultimate goal.

In the Christian slave worldview, thought and beliefs, God's spirit— the Holy Spirit—played an empowering role of hope. As one former enslaved African American responded in an interview:

> *Many of the old negroes were ignorant, they could neither read nor write. They knew that the entrance of "the Spirit of God" made a difference in their lives but they did not know how to express it only in their limited way. (Rawick, 127)*

Here the Holy Spirit acts as didactor and discerner of movement from a rootless, meaningless existential predicament to the extended parameters of "somebodiness," where "difference" now becomes self-confidence, self-awareness, and self-transformation.

The Christian Holy Spirit, God-talk operated in a creative tension with the existence of a parallel pantheon of supernatural appearances. Some revealed themselves as the spirit of a deceased ancestor who pledged her spirit to come back from the dead if her last will and testimony were not honored by her surviving family members; others revealed themselves as spirits—small "s" and plural—who were wicked or otherwise malevolent entities failing to obtain peace in death or hell-bent on returning to torture the land of the living; still others acted as conjuring powers able to cause bodily pain or even make someone fall in love; and, some came as haints who rode their victims while the latter were asleep. For enchained African Americans, this theological theme of spirits (e.g., mythopoetic revelations of supernatural powers) could be harbingers of either evil or good will.[8]

THEORETICAL FRAMEWORK
Slave sources and the guidelines, norm, and theological themes which have been presented so far, in addition, raise queries that are best answered by developing an interpretive schema or theoretical framework. In a word, what types of bodies of knowledge and disciplinary constructs would enable one to better unveil the faith meanings and belief thought patterns of the slave

religious mythos and ethos? These questions, it seems to me, can best be approached by examining the recurring problematic and possibilities embedded in the everyday religious experiences of the chattel community.

One of the most apparent puzzles and a distinct media of faith, thought and expression is the language of the enslaved African Americans. This discourse is pregnant with rich metaphors and redefined symbols, as well as with English grammar and syntax with a difference. For example, unlettered African Americans often refer to the presence of God coming upon them as if they had been "struck wide open." Likewise, their portrayal of the conversion experience connotes the journey of traveling from the old world of evil and sin to the newness of life; consequently, they embellish—with their own cultural linguistic powers—the conversion process with the appellation "coming thru religion."[9]

Thus the sources pose the question of how to access and assess, and how to challenge and cherish the theological text of slave religious language. Given this interrogation on the part of the text to the reader, the discipline of literary criticism comes to the fore, especially as it pertains to symbols and metaphors (Paul Ricoeur) and coded and decoded written language (Umberto Eco).[10]

An analytical interrogation of language by way of codes, symbols, and metaphors affords us the opportunity to enter the world of the text by initially suspending our presuppositions and predilections, particularly since we are attempting to increase our knowledge from texts that illustrate a strange and different world from our own. By entering this new world of religious metaphors and symbols, we begin both to peel away multilayered meanings and, perhaps unexpectedly, to encounter the multivalent and multivocal contours of slave faith affirmations and thoughts. The text, rephrased, offers subterranean discourse and proffers a new world-horizon of meanings. Spirituals which contain verses about "down by the riverside," or "steal away to Jesus," or "I'll meet you across Jordan," or "follow the drinking gourd," or "I'm bound for Canaanland" embrace and connote profound symbolic and metaphorical meaning for the enslaved. "Down by the riverside" was often a symbol of places where chatteled blacks were refreshed and renewed by the Holy Spirit amidst the pain of institutional slavery. Earlier, we dissected the theological import of "Steal away to Jesus." The phrase "I'll meet you across Jordan" could mean a family reunion in heaven, a gathering place of the local secret religious worship services, or a meeting of potential slave escapees. "Following the drinking gourd" usually meant a song that a runaway slave sang as she or he pursued the big dipper, traveling late at night. And similarly, the refrain "I'm bound for Canaan land" connoted the goodbye song of enslaved blacks who were preparing to immediately depart for the north and were thus offering "fair thee wells" to other plantation members. Obviously, the Canaan signifier very often conjured up meanings of heaven.

The linguistic interpretation does not cease with our entering the world of the text and simply uncovering the multileveled nature of the symbolic and metaphorical discourse. Our participation in interpretive unveiling resumes when the intentions of the enslaved's linguistic text are appropriated by the reader who seeks some theological meaning. The result is the enhanced self-knowledge and transformation of the reader.

Investigating coded language also aids in acquiring theological meaning from the faith experiences and religious thought of bondmen and women. Assessing coding, encoding, and decoding engages the formal dimension of the enslaved's religious text and is the dynamic process of signs and codes or rules of operation and their interrelationships. Moreover, it touches upon the structure and composition of the text. There are certain structures and rules in the language employed by oppressed blacks when referring to the difference between "stealing" and "taking." In slave discourse, "stealing" references illegally removing that which belongs to another slave, whereas "taking" denotes the removal from the plantation owner of that which was needed by the slave for survival and, in certain contexts, liberation. Therefore in the day to day conversation and communication of the enslaved, signification was precise for those initiated in the encoded messages of appropriate and inappropriate signs. Often in the slave narratives bondmen and women are confronted with the question: "Did you steal from the white master's storehouse or meathouse?" The enchained black person would respond, "no." If approached, other enslaved persons would concur with the negative response, while later that night all the chatteled blacks would enjoy the meat which had been recently "taken," not "stolen," from the plantation owners' storage.

This taking-not-stealing rule of operations, regulating signs in black talk, accompanied another type of sign-meaning called "discourse of solidarity." Numerous former enslaved persons recount how it was understood that they did not tell on those who had run away. For instance, one person being interviewed narrates a story about a cave that a runaway had built in the woods during slavery. Despite the fact that all the bondmen and women knew where the fugitive was, no one turned him in to the plantation owner. As the ex-slave analyzed: "in those days, the slaves didn't tell on each other."[11] Indeed, not to tell on each other proved a vital discourse of solidarity and survival for black folk's humanity. To betray the cave of the runaway in the woods was tantamount to desecrating a place where God had revealed the inherent gift of freedom through the inevitable laws of nature, something which other blacks referenced in their interviews and autobiographies. Hence, there were definite conventions of conversation and structured ways of being, whether one was speaking to the slavemaster or among fellow blacks, which regulated the signifying meaning of the symbolic, metaphorical, and literal signs deployed in the quarters of black religious life.

Along with the discipline of literary criticism with, in this instance, its dual pronged usage of metaphors and coded language, a theoretical framework in the construction of theological methodology requires some method of refereeing the diverse manifestations of religions of the enslaved's own theology. By religions, I mean the obvious preponderance of Christian symbols, metaphors, and practices of the black community. But, as we have already gleaned, there existed a complementary, and sometimes competing, non-Christian religion operative in the bondmen's and women's worldview and style of living. This latter religious claim comprised mixtures of a multifold spirit world of good and bad haints, ghosts, conjurers, witches, and spirits. One could argue that this religious phenomenon signified a type of vodou remainder from the pre-Christian west African traditional religious practices. Therefore, alongside literary criticism we must employ comparative religious studies. Without utilizing and deploying such a discipline, one might fall into a rigid Christocentrism when looking at slave sources (e.g., the view that only with Christ would there be healthy survival and ultimate liberation); or one might not detect the positive, at least from the slaves' perspective, life-giving presence of God through the remnants of west African traditional religions on the plantations. A comparative religious approach, moreover, could aid one in fostering an interreligious dialogue.

The world of enslaved African Americans' religious sources shows the enslaved's acute sense of political power and wealth relationships on the plantation as well as in the region of the entire south. Consequently, political economy, as a third discipline in the theoretical framework, would be helpful. Black people maintained, in their perceptions of the plantation owners, a sense of unjustified and unmerited might. And this perception was overlaid with religious language and phrases such as "servants of the devil" or "Satan's kingdom" (e.g., white unearned resources), versus "the vineyard of God" or "the Lord is the creator of all things" (e.g., divine gifts to all). In a word, structures of wealth, its ownership and distribution, along with the political leadership of slaveowners comprised the realm of Satan. By implication, a move to Jesus' realm implied a reorganization of political might and economic monopolization—a free and sacred space on earth of equality and democracy. The enslaved's macro political economy instincts suggest insights from Karl Marx, especially in his claim that all societies have larger economic structures in play and there are always, despite disguises of language and political claims about democracy, a class of people who have control of wealth and systemic power (Marx, 1978).[12]

The fourth discipline or body of knowledge that could possibly facilitate a theoretical framework for approaching meaning in enslaved theological sources is what one could call studies in mechanisms of power. In contrast to the discipline of political economy, mechanisms of power (paraphrasing Michel Foucault) concern those areas in slave life that do not directly or immediately deal with macro power of wealth or power in the state apparatus under slavery.[13] Yet these micro power mechanisms are fluid sites of contestation and struggle between plantation owners and their God and the chattel and their God. Some examples include the power held over black folk by laws which attempted to prevent the enslaved from learning to read or write. Slave narratives indicate how many enchained African Americans risked life and limb to illegally acquire literacy in order to access the Bible. To read was to draw nearer to the word of the divinity, to enter that world and become one immediately with stories familiar and unfamiliar. Likewise, the ability to write offered the potential to write one's own travelling-pass and therefore become a free human being who could move from slavery— the land of Satan or Egypt, as blacks referred to it—to Canaan—as the enslaved referred to the north, Canada, and even England.

The enslaved's quarters or dwellings signified another mechanism of power, where African Americans fought to transform the ownership of slave shacks from the hands of the plantation masters to the sacred space of worship of God.[14] Numerous accounts of former chattel include stories of how late at night, in an illegal religious meeting in the servants' quarters, the enslaved would turn over an iron pot so that the noise of the religious meeting would not reach the ears of the overseer or master. As one former slave remarked regarding the innovative usage of the pot and religious practices:

> *Time has been that [whites] wouldn't let them have a meeting, but God Almighty let them have it, for they would take an old kettle and turn it up before the door with the mouth of it facing the folks, and that would hold the voices inside. All the noise would go into that kettle. They could shout and sing all they wanted to and the noise wouldn't go outside (Fisk University 1968, 19-20).*

A fifth and final discipline would be cultural identity—a body of knowledge and power representing how issues of self-portrayal and self-evaluation play out in the theological dimensions of black religious sources. (Here I underscore the more limited definition of culture as identity in contrast to my overarching usage as a total way of life.) In one interview, an ex-slave retold the following:

> *[The whites and the master] wanted me to take the name of*
> *Harper, but the [master] wanted me to stay on the place and*
> *treat me like a slave, and I wouldn't do it. My father was named*
> *Robinson, so I kept his name after I got free* (Fisk University,
> 1968, 22).[15]

This former bondman pinpoints the normative cultural struggle of the enslaved community—that is, to remove a mask imposed by agents of evil forces and, thereby, unleash the full identity which God had given the person in a pre-chattel existence, in the black person's original created state. Thus naming—the process of claiming identity—signified becoming a whole person, an unfettered life, and a fuller congruity with the divine providence. The intellectual stance of Malcolm X elaborates upon this discipline of cultural identity—how oppressed people forge a self-portrayal within their total way of life.[16]

CONCLUSION

My claim is that enslaved African American experiences—as religious culture—can serve as an intentional location where theological method can learn from cultural studies. Theological method—how one goes about studying convictions and practices about the most ultimate meaning in life—can no longer consider itself as located at a metaphysical height that assures neutrality. Cultural studies, especially social sciences, presents a bounteous opportunity to strip away, map, and reconfigure the multiple layers of theology. The academic study of theology (its confessions and witnessing) entails a deeper interrogation of the "word" becoming "material" (the "theos" and the "logos").

First of all, a constructive theological method presupposes the incarnational, embeddedness, and embodiness of divine or ultimate space and being on the human level. Put differently, ultimate questions are found in sources. This manifestation of spirituality in materiality brings us to the second point. To detect the crossing of the divine and the human, theological methodology speaks to definable and identifiable communities of faith. Third, theological sources require a set of guidelines representing the dynamic dimensions of life: the interplay between men-women, Christian-nonChristian, political-cultural, and church-non institutional church. Fourth and fifth, one must clearly state one's norm and theological themes. Sixth, and very important for the excavation of, heuristic implications for, and didactic lessons of these sources, is a coherent theoretical framework, which can rely on any body of knowledge which facilitates the resolution of problematics and opportunities proffered by the African American sources. Finally, based on one's own personal faith stance or vocational conviction, a theological methodology must leave itself open to conversation, criticism, and self-criticism. For it is in the realm of various publics (e.g., the academy, institutional religion, and broader civic geographies, spaces, times, desires, and structures) that not only the theologian finds herself or himself, but also, I would argue, so do the multitudes of communities which are struggling for a new social order and seeking clarity about ultimate meaning while earthly boundaries and distances are rapidly shrinking. In a word, contemporary constructive theology emerges out of and deepens holistic faith commitments manifested in aspects of religious reflections and cultural analyses found in James H. Cone's institutionalization of a black theology of liberation (Cone, 1970).

REFERENCES

Abrahams, Roger D., ed. 1985. *Afro-American Folktales: Stories from Black Traditions in the New World*. New York: Pantheon Books.

Agger, Ben. 1992 *Cultural Studies as Cultural Theory*. London: Falmer Press.

Arnold, Matthew. 1960 *Culture and Anarchy*. London: Cambridge University Press.

Bibb, Henry. [1849]. *Narrative of the Life and Adventures of Henry Bibb, An American slave, Written by Himself*. Reprint, Philadelphia: Historic Publications.

Blassingame, John W. 1977. *Slave Testimony: Two Centuries of Letters, Speeches, Interviews, and Autobiographies*. Baton Rouge: Louisiana State University Press.

Breitman, George, ed. 1966. *Malcolm X Speaks: Selected Speeches and Statements*. New York: Grove Press.

Cone, James H. 1969. *Black Theology and Black Power*. New York: Seabury Press.

————. 1970. *A Black Theology of Liberation*. New York: Seabury Press.

————. 1972. *The Spirituals and the Blues*. New York: Seabury Press.

————. 1975. *God of the Oppressed*. New York: Seabury Press.

————. 1984. *For My People: Black Theology and the Black Church*. Maryknoll, N.Y.: Orbis Books.

————. 1986a. *Speaking the Truth: Ecumenism, Liberation, and Black Theology*. Grand Rapids, Mich.: Eerdmans.

————. 1986. *My Soul Looks Back*. Maryknoll, N. Y.: Orbis Books.

Cone, James H. and Gayraud S. Wilmore, ed. 1993. *Black Theology: A Documentary History, Volume One: 1966-1979*. Maryknoll, N. Y.: Orbis Books.

————. ed. 1993. *Black Theology: A Documentary History, Volume Two: 1980-1992*. Maryknoll, N. Y.: Orbis Books.

Dirks, Nicholas B., et al., eds. 1994. *Culture/Power/History: A Reader in Contemporary Social Theory*. Princeton, N. J.: Princeton University Press.

During, Simon. 1993. *The Cultural Studies Reader*. New York: Routledge.

Easthope, Antony and Kate McGowan, ed. 1993. *A Critical and Cultural Theory Reader*. Toronto: University of Toronto Press.

Eco, Umberto. 1986. *Semiotics and the Philosophy of Language*. Bloomington: Indiana University Press.

Epps, Archie, ed. 1968. *The Speeches of Malcolm X at Harvard*. New York: William Morrow & Company.

Fisher, Mark Miles. 1978. *Negro Slave Songs in the United States*. Secaucus, N. J.: The Citadel Press.

Fisk University, Nashville, Social Science Institute, ed. 1968. *Unwritten History of Slavery: Autobiographical Accounts of Ex-Slaves*. Washington, D.C.: Microcard Editions.

Foucault, Michel. 1972. *The Archaeology of Knowledge*. New York: Pantheon Books.

———. 1985. *The History of Sexuality, volume 2: The Use of Pleasure*. Harmondsworth: Penguin.

———. 1986. *The History of Sexuality, volume 3: The Care of the Self*. Harmondsworth: Penguin.

———. 1995. *Discipline and Punish: The Birth of the Prison*. New York: Vintage.

Gordon, Colin, ed. 1980. *Power/Knowledge: Selected Interviews and Other Writings by Michel Foucault, 1972-1977*. New York: Pantheon Books.

Grossberg, Lawrence et al., ed. 1992. *Cultural Studies*. New York: Routledge.

Hopkins, Dwight N. 1989a. *Black Theology in the U.S.A. and South Africa: Politics, Culture, and Liberation*. Maryknoll, N.Y.: Orbis Books.

———. 1993. *Shoes That Fit Our Feet: Sources for a Constructive Black Theology*, Maryknoll, N.Y.: Orbis Books.

———. 1997a. *American Culture and Black Theology: Lessons from Slave Religious Experiences*. Minneapolis, Minn.: Fortress Press.

———. 1997b. *Introducing Black Theology*. Maryknoll, N. Y.k: Orbis Books.

Hopkins, Dwight N. and Simon Maimela, ed. 1989. *We Are One Voice: Essays on Black Theology in South Africa and the U.S.A.* Johannesburg, South Africa: Skotaville Press.

———. et al., ed. 1991. *Cut Loose Your Stammering Tongue: Black Theology in the Slave Narratives*. Maryknoll, N.Y.: Orbis Books.

———. et al., ed. forthcoming. *Liberation Theologies, Post-Modernity, and the Americas*. New York: Routledge.

Johnson, Clifton H., ed. 1969. *God Struck Me Dead: Religious Conversion Experiences and Autobiographies of Ex-Slaves*. Philadelphia: Pilgrim Press.

Lovell, John, Jr. 1986. *Black Song: The Forge and the Flame*. New York: Pargon House Publishers.

Martin, Luther, et al., eds. 1988. *Technologies of the Self: A Seminar With Michel Foucault*. Amherst: University of Massachusetts Press.

Marx, Karl. 1978. "Preface to *A Contribution to the Critique of Political Economy*." In *The Marx-Engels Reader*, ed. Robert C. Tucker. New York: WW Norton & Company.

Milner, Andrew. 1991. *Contemporary Cultural Studies*. Sydney: Allen and Unwin.

Osofsky, Gilbert, ed. 1969. *Puttin' On Ole Massa*. New York: Harper and Row.

Perry, Bruce, ed. 1989. *Malcolm X: The Last Speeches*. New York: Pathfinder Press.

Purdue, Charles L., et al., ed. 1980. *Weevils in the Wheat: Interviews with Virginia Ex-Slaves*. Bloomington: Indiana University Press.

Rawick, George, P., ed. 1972, 1977, 1979. *The Slave Narrative Collection: A Composite Autobiography*. 41 vols. Westport, Conn.: Greenwood Publishing Company.

Ricoeur, Paul. 1976. *Interpretation Theory: Discourse and the Surplus of Meaning*. Forth Worth: Texas Christian University Press.

Starling, Marion Wilson. 1988. *The Slave Narrative: Its Place in American History*. Washington, D.C.: Howard University Press.

Williams, Raymond. 1965. *The Long Revolution*. Harmondsworth: Penguin.

X, Malcolm. 1956. "We Rose From the Dead." *Moslem World and the U.S.A.* (August-September).

NOTES

1. See Williams (1965, 63): "I would then define the theory of culture as the study of relationships between elements in a whole way of life."

2. Arnold (1960) represents such a top down, anti-popular culture position.

3. See Starling: "The slave narrative records extend from 1703 to 1944. They are to be discovered in judicial records, broadsides, private printings, abolitionist newspapers and volumes, scholarly journals, church records, unpublished collections, and a few regular publications" (1988, xxvi).

4. See Will Coleman's chapter in Hopkins et al. (1991) and Hopkins (1997a forthcoming, chap 3).

5. For the complexity of the new community signified in the Invisible Institution, see Hopkins et al. (1991, intro.).

6. Regarding the engaged or non-engaged debate in cultural studies, see Angela McRobbie's "Post-Marxism and Cultural Studies: A Post-script" (Grossberg et al. 1992).

7. See "The Man Makes and the Woman Takes," in Abrahams (1985).

8. For an excellent analysis of ancestors and spirits, see Will Coleman's chapter in Hopkins et al., 1991.

9. Relative to "struck wide open" and traveling, see Johnson (1969).

10. The following aspect of the theoretical framework (e.g., linguistic analyses, hermeneutics, and semiotics) relies partially on Ricoeur and Eco. For concise statements of their major corpus, see the reference section.

11. Ex-slave Ishrael Massie (Perdue et al. 1980, 210).

12. It is in this "Preface" that Marx unveils the core of his historical materialist methodology, epistemology, and worldview.

13. Regarding Foucault's insights, I am mainly concerned with his microphysics of power, his techniques of the self, and ethics for the self.

14. For accounts of how slave owners and blacks used mechanisms of power, see Hopkins (1997b), especially chapters 2 and 3.

15. Malcolm X emphasized a two-part strategy around identity, first showing the slave mentality of African Americans and then their positive contributions to humankind.

three
APPLICATION

THE RECOVERY OF SACRED MYTH:

TONI MORRISON'S *SONG OF SOLOMON*

James Evans

> *The songs are indeed the siftings of centuries; the music is far more ancient than the words, and in it we can trace here and there signs of development. My grandfather's grandmother was seized by an evil Dutch trader two centuries ago; and coming to the valleys of the Hudson and Housatonic, black, little and lithe, she shivered and shrank in the harsh north winds, looked longingly at the hills, and often crooned a heathen melody to the child between her knees.*
>
> – W.E.B. DuBois

The religion and literature of African Americans have been—and still are—two chief means of resisting oppression and affirming self-worth. Through their religion and their literature African Americans have preserved and refined their collective identities, put into sharpest relief the distinctive sensibility which is the heritage of people of African descent, and given expression to the struggle for liberation which is the central feature of their historical experience. The common ground between the religion and the literature of African Americans is culture: that curious blend of black folk wisdom, African retentions, European influences and Christian morphology which has shaped their aesthetics, their politics and their theology.

The analysis of a given text requires an interpretive schema for understanding the relation between African-American religion and literature as types of cultural expression. An underlying assumption is that there is no radical separation between the quest for beauty (aesthetics) and the quest for ultimate truth (religion) in black experience. The European cultural tradition has tended to separate these at various points in history, placing aesthetics in judgment over religion (Matthew Arnold), or religion in judgment over aesthetics (T. S. Eliot). In African-American culture, beauty and truth, religion and aesthetics, co-exist as norms in the struggle to wrest meaning and joy from experience. The central argument of this essay is that African-American religion and literature are both cultural acts which embody the struggle for liberation and integrity among black folk. Further, it will be shown that types of literary expression can be correlated to types of religious expression. While the schema presented here is an attempt to explore the various dimensions of the movement toward a holistic notion of freedom in African-American religion and literature, only the examination of a specific literary text can put flesh and sinew on this interpretive frame.

Under conditions of oppression African-American religion and African-American literature have found several avenues of expression. W. E. B. DuBois identified three of them in his classic work, *The Souls of Black Folk*.

> *when to earth and brute is added an environment of men and ideas, then the attitude of the imprisoned group may take three main forms,—a feeling of revolt and revenge; an attempt to adjust all thought and action to the will of the greater group; or, finally, a determined effort of self realization and self development despite environing opinion. (DuBois 1961, 45)*

DuBois adds that all of these attitudes can, at various times, be traced in the history of African-Americans. These responses constitute "moments" in African-American culture and can be identified with distinct modes of expression in religion and literature. In literature these moments appear as the types of expression move from "pure" autobiography to "pure" fiction. In religion they appear as the types of expression move from a single minded rebellion against the past to a sober revalorization of origins. There is a fourth moment, however, which is not mentioned specifically by DuBois but is exemplified by *Souls* itself. This particular moment is one of cultural renewal; that is, the recovery of those indigenous religious and aesthetic resources which can make life more human.

This moment in the African-American cultural act takes the form of mnemonic discourse; its goal is cultural renewal, and its chief means is the recovery of origins. Mnemonic, when used as an adjective, means relating to, assisting, or designed to assist the memory; as a noun, it refers to a device such as a formula or rhyme, used as an aid in remembering. Mnemonic discourse comes to terms with the past and the future in the context of the present. It is a way of countering the effects of temporal and spatial dislocation. In theological terms, eschatology becomes a primary theme in religious expression, because the problem is one of discerning the role and authority of the past and the anticipated future in the present struggle for liberation. At the beginning of the twentieth century DuBois saw the outline of this moment as he surveyed the development of the slave songs. These songs were themselves a type of mnemonic discourse because they looked back in order to look ahead. This kind of discourse, whether one calls it eschatological or mnemonic, lies at the heart of African-American religion. Although it arose out of an ecstatic vision in the churches, it has functioned not as a substitute but as a catalyst for worldly freedom. In the context of oppression, mnemonic discourse says that the existence of the victims is never closed but is radically open to possibility. It says that one does not have to abolish history in favor of eschatology, or politics in favor of culture. Instead, it says that it is possible to achieve, finally, freedom of expression.

The goal of this moment is cultural renewal. It is important to note that this renewal does not occur chronologically after the political consciousness has been raised. Rather, the political consciousness is molded and shaped by the renewal of the cultural resources, and vice versa. Thus, political liberation and cultural renewal are not in conflict, but are realized only in relation to one another. The revolution of values in African-American culture and the transformation of socio-economic conditions are two sides of the same coin. The goal of cultural renewal requires a new eschatological vision which radically opens the future, and then a political imperative which compels the believer to exercise the freedom which has already been given.[1] This means that African-American religion is both cultic and cultural. When renewal therefore takes place the resiliency of the culture emerges and the sacredness of the cultus is celebrated.

The means by which this goal of renewal is accomplished is the recovery of origins. In this moment Africa, again, appears in the African-American lexicon. Africa assumes importance because the idea of it provides the grounding which is necessary for a diaspora people to preserve their identity. Yet, that identity is not limited to the existing historical paradigms which Africa may provide. Instead, Africa, as a mythical reality, empowers African-Americans to make their own future. Africa is not only a fact of the historical past; it is also the promise of the eschatological future. Nothing exemplifies this more than DuBois' choice to spend his final years in Ghana. The revalorization of Africa makes possible cultural renewal and social transformation. The idea of Africa for African-Americans is both Alpha and Omega, and their identity is both grounded and free.

The literary counterpart to this religious moment is "pure" fiction, its primary expression being the novel in which the community, rather than just the protagonist, reaches a deeper level of consciousness. This type of novel is "pure" fiction because it is funded by "a commitment to vital possibility" (Americo Castro). It suggest that wholeness and liberation are possible for African-Americans when wholeness and liberation have no existing models. It confronts the nihilistic chaos of racial oppression with the logos of ultimate worth and dignity. To paraphrase Hebrews 11:1, this type of narrative is based on faith as the substance of things hoped for and the evidence of things unseen. This literary moment takes the form of mnemonic discourse in which memory looks ahead rather than just back. Frank Kermode refers to this as "a kind of forward memory, familiar from spoonerisms and typing errors which are caused by anticipation, the mind working on an expected future" (Kermode 1967, 53). In the novel this forward memory contributes to the complication of the plot because the reader's expectation may not be confirmed, and ironic twists may create space for radically new possibilities. In the end, the reader's expectation is confirmed, but in an unexpected way. This same process occurs in African-American religious expression when a steadfast faith in the providential Lordship of God meets the harsh contradictions of present reality. The response is "The Lord may not come when you want him but he's right on time." The timeliness of God is guaranteed by God's past acts. Yet God's freedom also means that the future is open. In African-American "pure" fiction the mnemonic form of discourse looks forward and backward at the same time.

The goal of this moment is cultural renewal. In the context of the fictive act this means that the African-American novel as "pure" fiction cannot be reduced to "protest" literature. Certainly this kind of novel is, in a sense, political, but always in relation to the totality of African-American experience. Ralph Ellison described the goal of this moment as the identification of

> *those boundaries of feeling, thought and action which that particular group has found to be the limitation of the human condition. It projects this wisdom in symbols which express the group's will to survive; it embodies those values by which the group lives and dies. (Ellison 1953, 171)*

African-American wisdom is resurrected, the sapiential resources of the people are recalled, and their future is radically opened by this fictive act.

The means employed to accomplish this goal is the recovery of those literary origins which have historically been denied, repressed, or misinterpreted. African-American novelists, in this instance, acknowledge the extent to which European-American influences have affected their art. Yet the origins of that art are profoundly African. The antecedents to the contemporary African-American novel are, ultimately, not the written text but the oral text. The writer's journey back does not end with written text, but with oral expression. DuBois' examination of African-American culture led him to the "sorrow songs" of slavery, which unlocked the secret of survival, and provided an interpretive framework for that culture. In much the same vein,

Houston Baker has proposed the *blues* to be a hermeneutical schema. He defines African-American culture as "a complex, reflexive enterprise which finds its proper figuration in blues conceived as a matrix . . . The matrix is a point of ceaseless input and output, a web of intersecting, crisscrossing impulses always in productive transit" (Baker 1984, 3). The sorrow songs and the blues are forms of cultural expression which take the novelist back to the origins of his or her art. They involve the spontaneous generation of new meanings and the exercise of expressive freedom. The past is valorized in order to present a liberated world radically open to possibility.

Song of Solomon by Toni Morrison was published in 1977 and is the second novel by an African-American writer to be named as a Book of the Month Club selection (Morrison 1977).[2] There are several important features of this novel which link it to contemporary fiction by other African-American women.[3] First, it is directed toward the inner, psychic, cultural and spiritual life of the African-American community. Second, it attempts to recover the constitutive resources present within the African-American community. Third, it displays a style in which the thickness of language and the intricacy of plot reflect the complexity of African-American life. Fourth, it presents African-American women as a redemptive presence in the cultural and political lacunae of contemporary African-American life. There are, on the other hand, features of this novel which link it to the more progressive tradition among African-American male writers.[4] It presents an analysis of the multiple strata or, if you will, the Dantean depths of African-American experience. Second, it views the African-American predicament as broadly cultural in origin, and not just political or metaphysical. Finally, it suggests that music holds the key to unlocking the hidden dimensions of that predicament.

The aim of this chapter is to examine the moral vision of *Song of Solomon*. This examination will focus on the central problematic of African-American life and the possibility for redemption which the novel suggests. The central problematic is the tension and conflict between cultural grounding and cultural uprooting. This dilemma is evident in the development of the primary characters of the novel, and in its tone, which presents certain aspects of African-American life as a cultural wasteland. The possibility for redemption lies in the reclamation of the original resources of African-American culture. This can only take place through the recovery of sacred myth. The mythical recovery of those cultural resources includes, by definition, the recovery of religious and spiritual resources.

THE CULTURALLY UPROOTED AND THE CULTURALLY GROUNDED

Song of Solomon opens in the middle of Robert Smith's leap from the roof of No Mercy Hospital. This entry point into the temporal sphere of the novel demands that the reader make a distinction between beginnings and origins. The novel begins with the leap, but it originates at some point before the leap. The context of this event is the African-American community. It is a community which is named by its inhabitants in spite of extraneous controls. Therefore, Mains Avenue is Not Doctor Street, and Mercy Hospital is No Mercy Hospital (Morrison 1977, 4). Because to name a thing is to escape its tyranny, the characters in this novel are immediately established as ones whose principal dilemmas do not center directly around confrontations with white people. The central problems which the characters face are determined by the extent to which they are culturally grounded or culturally uprooted. Cultural grounding refers to the capacity of a character to draw sustenance from the indigenous environment. Cultural uprooting refers to the incapacity of a character to draw upon those resources. However, it is not the opposition but the juxtaposition of these types which furnishes the literary force of the narrative. The dialectic which results speaks to the heart of the contemporary problematic of African-Americans. This dialectic is evident in the juxtaposition of the characters of Pilate and Macon Dead, Jr., Ruth Foster and Guitar Bains.

Macon Dead, Jr. is described as leading a sterile life consisting primarily in the acquisition of property. The symbols of that acquisition are the keys which he carries with him at all times. After threatening one of his tenants with eviction,

> Macon Dead went back to the pages of his accounts book, running his fingertips over the figures and thinking with the unoccupied part of his mind about the first time he called on Ruth Foster's father. He had only two keys in his pocket then, and if he had let people like the woman who just left have their way, he wouldn't have had any keys at all. It was because of those keys that he could dare to walk over to that part of Not Doctor Street (it was still Doctor Street then) and approach the most important Negro in the city. To lift the lion's paw knocker, to entertain thoughts of marrying the doctor's daughter was possible because each key represented a house which he owned at the time. Without those keys he would have floated away at the doctor's first word. (22)

The keys are not symbolic of access to the resources of the African-American community. In fact, just the opposite is the case. For Macon Dead the keys have become disconnected surrogates. Secondarily, the keys are linguistic symbols for Macon. Rather than illuminating reality, the keys have become inert substitutes for it. Words obscure and distance reality. This is why he regards the naming process to be "monumental foolishness" (15).

In spite of his possessions and his keys, Macon struggles with this status as an outsider.

> *Under the cover of darkness, the mystique of ownership be-*
> *comes enigmatic. During the day they were reassuring to see;*
> *now they did not seem to belong to him at all—in fact he felt as*
> *though the houses were in league with one another to make him*
> *feel like the outsider, the propertyless, landless wanderer. (27)*

Macon's uprooting is clearly evident in the ritualistic Sunday automobile rides. "These rides that the family took on Sunday afternoons had become rituals and much too important for Macon to enjoy" (32). However, the slavish repetition of this performance robs it of any truly ritual efficacy:

> *He never went over twenty miles an hour, never gunned his en-*
> *gine, never stayed in first gear for a block or two to give pedes-*
> *trians a thrill. He had never blown a tire, never ran out of gas*
> *and needed twelve grinning raggle-tailed boys to help him push*
> *it up a hill or over to a curb. No rope ever held the door to its*
> *frame, and no teen-agers leaped on his running board for a lift*
> *down the street. He hailed no one and no one hailed him (32).*

The sheer vacuity of the Sunday drive meant that it could not truly be a ritual since it no longer served an integrating function. It no longer brought its participants into the presence and joy of the deeper meaning of life. In essence, it became desacralized, turning into what Eliade describes as mere repetition. "Repetition emptied of its religious content necessarily leads to a pessimistic vision of existence" (Eliade 1957, 107). Instead of animating its participants this repetition mortifies them. Thus, the Packard was called "Macon Dead's hearse" (Morrison, 132). Because of his unregenerative tendencies, Macon had to be conjured into sleeping with his wife and fathering his son (125). His uprooting is further evident in his response to the surrounding topography. Instead of seeing in the land and the landscape the possibility for cultural grounding, he sees only the possibility of more profit. His view of the shoreline area Honore (33) as a potential possession makes the shore an end rather than a beginning, and contributes to rather than alleviates his sense of alienation. This issue of possessions and cultural displacement is rooted in Macon's inability to appropriate the resources of his tradition. Macon, like his sister Pilate, is motivated by the legacy of his father, Macon Dead, Sr. The novel presents two different accounts of the events surrounding the death of Macon, Sr. and two distinctly different heritages are the result. Macon, Jr.'s heritage was the thirst for gold (171)—the quest for property and wealth without an understanding of the cultural purposes for its acquisition. Macon Jr.'s distortion of his heritage is evident in the scene in which his father's success is described.

> He had come out of nowhere, as ignorant as a hammer and broke as a convict, with nothing but free papers, a Bible, and a pretty black-haired wife, and in one year he'd leased ten acres, the next ten more. Sixteen years later he had one of the best farms in Montour County. A farm that colored their lives like a paintbrush and spoke to them like a sermon. 'You see?' the farm said to them. 'See? See what you can do? Never mind you can't tell one letter from another, never mind you born a slave, never mind you lose your name, never mind your daddy dead, never mind nothing. Here, this here, is what a man can do if he puts his mind to it and his back to it. Stop sniveling,' it said. 'Stop picking around the edges of the world. Take advantage, and if you can't take advantage, take disadvantage. We live here. On this planet, in this nation, in this country right here. Nowhere else! We got a home in the rock, don't you see! Nobody starving in my home; nobody crying in home, and if I got a home you got one too! Grab it. Grab this land! Take it, hold it, my brothers, make it, my brothers, shake it, squeeze it, turn it, twist it, beat it, kick it, kiss it, whip it, stomp it, dig it, plow it, seed it, reap it, rent it, buy it, sell it, own it, build it, multiply it and pass it on - can you hear me? Pass it on! (237)

The fruitfulness of Macon Sr.'s efforts lead to his being killed *for* his possessions, while the futility of Macon, Jr.'s efforts leads to him being "killed" *by* his possessions. Unlike Macon Sr., Macon Jr. is incapable of passing on his heritage and tradition. Although he is nominally related to his heritage because he is named after his father, he is actually separated from it. He is culturally and spiritually uprooted. It is not until Macon Dead III reaches maturity that the male side of the family is reconnected to its primordial source.

Pilate, Macon Jr.'s sister, is obsessed with life even though she was born in death. The irony surrounding Pilate is deepened by her lack of a visible sign of her connection to her ancestry. Macon Jr. recalls that after their mother died,

> *She had come struggling out of the womb without help from*
> *throbbing muscles or the pressure of swift womb water. As a re-*
> *sult, for all the years he knew her, her stomach was as smooth*
> *and sturdy as her back, at no place interrupted by a navel. It was*
> *the absence of navel that convinced people that she had not come*
> *into this world through normal channels; had never lain, floated,*
> *or grown in some warm and liquid place connected by a tissue-*
> *thin tube to a reliable source of human nourishment. (27)*

The irony of Pilate's lack of a navel is that it says more about Macon Jr.'s sense of alienation than it does about Pilate's. "He was already seventeen years old, irreparably separated from her and already pressing forward in his drive for wealth, when he learned that there was probably not another stomach like hers on earth" (28). Pilate's house is a fecund place where memory and music interact to give meaning to life (30). Her house, which she shares with her daughter Reba and Reba's daughter Hagar, is a woman's place, a repository of African-American culture. A symbol of Pilate's relation to her culture and tradition is evident in the opening scene of the novel in which she sings and "had wrapped herself up in an old quilt instead of a winter coat" (5). Macon Jr.'s house, on the other hand, is a place where there is no music (29) and thus, no cultural memory. While his daughters had been "boiled dry from years of yearning" (28), Pilate's daughter and granddaughter are saved from the deadening effects of deprivation by music. When Hagar complains about a hunger that is both physical and metaphysical, she points to a hunger which is the lot of the modern culturally alienated African- American. Pilate is able to see that in her complaint "she don't mean food" (49). In response Pilate begins to hum—to invoke an ancient muse of music which satisfied that peculiarly African-American hunger. Music is the key to the recovery of cultural vitality. An informative contrast here is provided by Richard Wright's Bigger Thomas who, in the novel *Native Son*, is confronted by the request of Mary Dalton to perform an African-American musical ritual. His response was that he couldn't sing.

For Pilate language informs reality, so she insists that people say what they mean. In relation to those around her who used words carelessly or inaccurately, "She was too direct, and to keep up with her [one] had to pay careful attention to [one's] language." Pilate, however, is not captive to language as Macon Jr. is to his keys. Rather, she is able to use language to illuminate the hidden crevices of reality. Her use of words is symbolized by the artifacts in her house. "She had dumped the peelings in a large crock, which like most everything in the house had been made for some other purpose. Now she stood before the dry sink, pumping water into a blue-and-white wash basin which she used for a saucepan" (39). On a variety of levels, then, Pilate is a cultic artist. Charles Long observes that "though the cultic art expresses the religious quality most decisively, the artistic quality of utilitarian art objects reveals a religious world. In many cases utilitarian objects carry the same designs and are shaped by the same techniques which produced the cultic art. The religious character of the cultic object is a function of its use in the ritual" (Long 1963, 29). The objects in Pilate's house are cultic because their purpose is the result of their function, and not vice versa. Pilate's role as an artist is also evident in her use of language. The purpose of a word is the result of its function. Pilate's role as artist is inseparable from her role as ritual leader. It is within the context of ritual that language and cultic objects are brought to bear upon reality. A prime example is the ceremony of boiling eggs:

> Now, the water and the egg have to meet each other on a kind of equal standing. One can't get the upper hand over the other. So the temperature has to be the same for both. I knock the chill off the water first. Just the chill. I don't let it get warm because the egg is room temperature, you see. Now then, the real secret is right here in the boiling. When the tiny bubbles come to the surface, when they as big as peas and just before they get big as marbles. Well, right then you take the pot off the fire. You don't just put the fire out; you take the pot off. They you put a small folded newspaper over the pot and do one small obligation. Like answering the door or emptying the bucket and bringing it in off the front porch. I generally go to the toilet. Not for a long stay, mind you. Just a short one. If you do all that, you got yourself a perfect soft-boiled egg. (39)

The act which Pilate describes has the ritual effect of equalizing inequalities and of demanding discipline. More importantly, however, a common culinary act is converted to an uncommon spiritual one without losing its common character. Unlike Macon Jr.'s Sunday ride, Pilate's ritual aims at the perfection of the social and cultural order. Pilate's ability to merge the common and the uncommon aspects of life is observable in her attitude toward holidays. Neither Pilate nor Reba celebrated holidays (92). In their scheme of things there are no "holy days" because there are no "unholy days." The futility of Macon Jr.'s automobile ride is precisely the fact that it occurs always and only on Sunday. For Pilate, every day holds the possibility of a theophany.

Pilate's ritualistic approach to life makes it possible for her to fathom the central fact of African-American existence, that of blackness itself.

> *You think dark is just one color, but it ain't. There're five or six kinds of black. Some silky, some wooly. Some just empty. Some like fingers. And it don't stay still. It moves and changes from one kind of black to another. Saying something is pitch black is like saying something is green. What kind of green? Green like my bottles? Green like a grasshopper? Green like a cucumber, lettuce, or green like the sky is just before it breaks loose to storm? Well, night black is the same way. May as well be a rainbow. (40)*

In this passage the multiple strata of the idea of blackness are exposed, and the grainy texture of this cultural fact is examined. A second result of the ritualistic approach to life is that it provides Pilate access to her cultural heritage. She carries her name in a brass box earring, a kind of phylactery or reminder of the past (53). Pilate's cultic association with Africa, in addition to Macon Jr.'s comparison of Pilate with the folktale of the snake indicates that she does not suffer from the African-American historical identity crisis in the way that her brother does (54-5).

PILATE'S INSIGHT INTO THE PROBLEMS OF MODERN AFRICA

American life is a result of her marginal position. She recalls that she "was cut off from people early" (141). She spent a significant portion of her life in "a colony of Negro farmers on an island off the coast of Virginia" (146). Her life among this cutoff people explains her spiritual development. This island had a hymnal but no Bible (147). There was an emphasis on rhythm rather than melody, music rather than doctrine. Pilate's life on the boundary of the socialized world is one in which she achieves a kind of balance. Her "equilibrium over-shadowed all her eccentricities" (138). There she is able to balance time and space, history and geography. "She gave up, apparently, all interest in table manners or hygiene, but acquired a deep concern for and about human relationships" (150). She is a "natural healer" and "reconciler," because in her cultic role she preserves the cultural tradition and participates in the regeneration of the African-American.

Pilate's inheritance is related to her concern for geography. At several points in the novel she is reading a geography book (93). Her concern for geography, her practice of collecting rocks from wherever she visits, indicates a different view toward the land than that of Macon Jr. The land for Pilate is the opportunity to affirm her cultural grounding. She inherits from her father a quest for spiritual renewal which gives priority to people over property. Pilate's lack of a navel points to her status as physically cut-off from her ancestry, but culturally and spiritually, she is connected to her past.

A second instance of the contrast between the culturally grounded and the culturally uprooted in *Song of Solomon* is observable in the comparison of the characters of Ruth Foster and Guitar Bains. Ruth Foster is the wife of Macon Dead, Jr. and she is a woman obsessed with death and regeneration. Her stance toward death, however, is one in which the potential for new life is always present. It is the potential for new life which she attempts to pass on to her son by breastfeeding him well past infancy:

> *It was one of her two secret indulgences—the one that involved her son—and part of the pleasure it gave her came from the room in which she did it. A damp greenness lived there, made by the evergreen that pressed against the window and filtered the light. It was just a little room that Doctor had called a study, and aside from a sewing machine that stood in the corner along with a dress form, there was only a rocker and tiny footstool. She sat in this room holding her son on her lap, staring at his closed eyelids and listening to the sound of his sucking. Staring not so much from maternal joy as from a wish to avoid seeing his legs dangling almost to the floor. (13)*

The images of greenness and her nurturing act point to Ruth's association with the regeneration of life. This regeneration, however, is dialectically related to the necessity of death. Her son sees this aspect of his mother's existence and describes her using tropes of flora and fauna.

> *Now he saw her as a frail woman content to do tiny things; to grow and cultivate small life that would not hurt her if it died: rhododendron, goldfish, dahlias, geraniums, imperial tulips. Because these little lives did die. The gold fish floated to the top of the water and when she tapped the side of the bowl with her fingernail they did not flash away in a lightning arc of terror. The rhododendron leaves grew wide and green and when their color was at its deepest and waxiest, they suddenly surrendered it and lapsed into limp yellow hearts. In a way she was*

jealous of death. (64)

The natural cycle of death and regeneration is also the focus of Ruth's second secret indulgence: lying down on her father's grave (123). This act points to a need for connection in Ruth which neither her husband nor her son understands. Her husband describes his encounter with Ruth and her father on the eve of his death:

In the bed. That's where she was when I opened the door. Laying next to him. Naked as a yard dog, kissing him. Him dead and white and puffy and skinny, and she had his fingers in her mouth. (73)

The relationship between Ruth and her father was set when he delivered her from her mother's womb (71). It established in Ruth a predilection for connection which her husband refused to honor when he ceased sexual relations with her when she was twenty years old (125). It was this refusal which led Ruth to seek Pilate's aid in arranging the conception of her son. The living memory of Macon Dead, Sr. was a source of strength to Pilate, while Ruth found a source of sustenance through the decaying remains of her father. Both had "close and supportive posthumous communication with their fathers" (139).

The dialectic between death and regeneration is alluded to in sacramental terms in the episode in which Ruth, a Methodist, attends a Catholic Mass. Ruth takes the host unaware that it is reserved for Catholics. She does not understand how an act which is so central to life for her can be selectively administered. For her, "communion is communion" (66). It is not just a religious act but a natural one devoid of ordinary socio-political and ecclesiastical distinctions. The religious significance of this act can be construed in Christian terms in that the body of Jesus Christ is seen as food, and in the eating the participant shares in his death and resurrection. However, this religious significance can also be construed in non-Christian terms. In certain primitive religions the body of an immolated divinity was changed into food. In eating and dying the participant shared in the immortality of the gods (Eliade 1957, 101). Ruth is culturally grounded, a fact which is exemplified in her refusal to surrender her maiden name Foster, and be called Ruth Dead. She is able to pass on to her son the one feature which she most admired in her father, his hands (133). Her life's aim is to restore the natural order.

Guitar is a man whose life is consumed by the racial problem. Every historical misfortune and every social evil is seen as the responsibility of white people. "Every job of work undone, every bill unpaid, every illness, every death was The Man's fault" (108). Guitar's obsession is the result of his inability to see the coherence of love and freedom in the historical order. This inability is, in turn, a consequence of his own displacement. He flounders between the North and the South, between Honore and Alabama (113-5).

This sense of dislocation colors his entire perspective, and he remarks that "I do believe my whole life's geography" (114). From his position or dis-position in the "No-Man's Land" of cultural uprooting, the entire historical order appears out of balance. He has very little confidence in the power of words or language to affect reality. This lack of confidence is evident in his attitude toward names. He observes that "slave names don't bother me; but slave status does" (161).

For Guitar, the resources of African-American culture are not sufficient to restore equity to the historical order. The only remedy for the historical violence which has distorted African-American life is historical counterviolence. Therefore, his membership in the Seven Days, a Mau-Mau-like secret society, is part of his attempt to balance the socio-political, historical order; to keep things on an even keel" (155). For every African-American who dies at the hands of white people, the Seven Days kill a white person. This is necessary to keep the "ratio the same" (156).

The weakness of the Seven Days' scheme is its capitulation to the tyranny of historicism, and the concomitant blurring of the distinction between love and hate. Guitar argues that "what I'm doing ain't about hating white people. It's about loving us. About loving you. My whole life is love" (160). However, the inner conflict which assails Guitar undermines his conviction. "It *is* about love. What else but love? Can't I love what I criticize?" (225). That inner conflict is rooted in a sense of despair about the possibility of a redemptive and sacrificial death in history. "The single, solitary death was going rapidly out of fashion, and the Days might as well prepare themselves for it" (174). Macon Dead Jr.'s sense of despair about the prospects for redemption is a result of the enigmatic circumstances surrounding his father's death, and the same is true of Guitar. His father "got sliced up in a sawmill" and the boss' estimation of the value of that perished life is summed up by the bag of candy which he gave the grieving children. "Divinity. A big sack of divinity. His wife made it special for us. It's sweet, divinity is. Sweeter than syrup. Real sweet" (61). Guitar cannot, from that point on, eat anything sweet. It reminds him of dead people, white people. Unlike Ruth, Guitar is unable to participate in the eating and dying of *divinity*. The death of his father is senseless; he appears to Guitar as a victim of the imbalance of history. In

Christian terms, Guitar's view of history precludes the possibility of a Christo-logical sacrifice and atonement, and thus he cannot participate in any form of communion. Of the Seven Days, Guitar is "the Sunday man" (162). It is his responsibility to avenge the death of any African-American which occurs on Sunday. The irony is, of course, that this vengeance is doomed to absurdity. In non-Christian religious terms, no single solitary death can appease the despot-ic gods of history. Guitar is culturally uprooted and cut off from his past by the meaningless death of his father. More importantly, however, he severs his own genealogical line when he submits to the requirement of the Seven Days that they never have children (336).

MILKMAN AND THE AFRICAN-AMERICAN CONFLICT

Macon Dead III, or Milkman, the protagonist of *Song of Solomon*, is de-scribed as the first black child born at No Mercy Hospital. He was born with a caul or veil, and as DuBois would say, he was gifted with second sight. He was given the name the Milkman, because he was discovered nurs-ing at his mother's breast by Freddie, one of his father's tenants. "A milk-man. That's what you got here, Miss Rufie. A natural milkman if ever I seen one. Look out, womens. Here he come. Huh!" (14). Freddie's cryptic prophecy points to Milkman's potential capacity for insight into women's experience. Along with this capacity, however, Milkman embodies the cen-tral dialectic of the novel, that between cultural grounding and cultural up-rooting. He is born as Robert Smith leaps from the roof of the hospital in a vain attempt at flight. Smith was one of the Seven Days in whom the pecu-liar African-American conflict had become a crisis. He is born as his Aunt Pilate sings in the street below, literally clothed with the "quilt" of African-American culture. Conceived by virtue of conjure, born in the nexus of des-peration and hope, Milkman embodies both the promise and the peril of African- American life.

The novel traces Milkman's search for his cultural heritage. The prob-lem is that he often searches for it among black males, who themselves have been the most effectively decultured. This is evident in the scene in the bar-bershop where the men perceive life in empty formal terms (58-6). African-American life is presented as a wasteland, given character and being only by what it lacks. Milkman and Guitar are read a litany of all the pleasures of life which will be denied them. This sense of cultural uprooting is observable even in the language of the passage, which is stilted and lifeless. This is not the case with the women in the novel. Though they are likewise affected by the threat of deculturation, they have seized the defensive strategies inherit-ed from the past and have made of them offensive weapons. The difference between male and female groups as custodians of culture is seen in Milkman's remark about barbershops and beauty shops:

> *Beauty shops always had curtains or shades up. Barbershops didn't. The women didn't want anybody on the street to be able to see them getting their hair done. They were ashamed. (62)*

The irony here is that the defensive connotations of the curtain are also accompanied by positive ones. If it blocks out cultural shame, it allows cultural pride to ferment.

The dialectic between cultural uprooting and cultural grounding is the context of African-American life and no character in the novel escapes its effects. Hagar is apathetic (90), Reba is needy (109-10), and Empire State is mute (111). The effect of the modern milieu upon Milkman, however, is more dramatic because it is presented as an inborn trait.

> *By the time Milkman was fourteen he had noticed that one of his legs was shorter than the other. When he stood barefoot and straight as a pole, his left foot was about half an inch off the floor. So he never stood straight; he slouched or leaned or stood with a hip thrown out, and he never told anybody about it— ever . . . It bothered him and he acquired movements and habits to disguise what to him was a burning defect . . . The deformity was mostly in his mind. Mostly, but not completely, for he did have shooting pains in that leg after several hours on a basketball court (62).*

Milkman's physical flaw is the source of his frustration because he can never achieve the "perfection" of his father, but it is also indicative of his need for redemption which leads him into the company of women: Hagar whose obsessive infatuation leads her to try to kill him (126-9), Ruth who tries to protect him (137), and Pilate who is responsible for his conception. The need for redemption is Milkman's birthright. As Pilate notes,

> *He come into the world tryin to keep from gettin killed . . . When he was at his most helpless, he made it. Ain't nothing goin to kill him but his own ignorance, and won't no woman ever kill him. What's likelier is that it'll be a woman save his life. (140)*

Milkman lives in the wasteland between commitment and resignation, between martyrdom and murder.

> *He hated the acridness in his mother's and father's relationship, the conviction of righteousness they each held on to with both hands. And his efforts to ignore it, transcend it, seemed to work only when he spent his days looking for whatever was lighthearted and without grave consequences. He avoided commitment and strong feelings, and shied away from decisions. He wanted to know as little as possible, to feel only enough to warrant the curiosity of other people—but not their all-consuming devotion. (181)*

The anomie of Milkman's life is one response to the central struggle of the novel—that between life and death, Africa and the West, order and disorder, fertility and sterility, Pilate and Macon, Jr., Ruth, his mother and Guitar, his best friend. In Milkman are seen the catastrophic results of DuBois' "double consciousness."

Part 2, or the final third of the novel deals with Milkman's search for his beginnings. It is a narrative of descent into the Dantean depths of the African-American cultural past. It is a search which he undertakes in quest of a heritage of gold, but which leads him to a resource much more valuable. There are two major geographical strata involved in Milkman's descent. The first is Dansville, Ohio, a town on the northern edge of the South. It is the gateway to his past, but is sufficiently Westernized, so that Milkman as the exemplary decultured African-American is worshipped as a hero. His clothing (229) and his demeanor distinguished him from the other townsfolk. His reception as a hero is based on his outward appearance, the extent to which he has acquired the trappings of the dominant culture. In Shalimar, Virginia, the tension within Milkman's character comes to the surface. His request for a woman results in a violent confrontation with the young men of Shalimar. His outward appearance points to his geographical alienation and stirs up in the young men of Shalimar their own sense of spiritual-cultural alienation. "They looked at his skin and saw it was as black as theirs, but they knew he had the heart of the white men who came to pick them up in the trucks when they needed anonymous, faceless laborers" (269). This violent confrontation is empty gesturing and an exercise in futility. It is Milkman's encounter with the older men of Shalimar that opens the path for his self-discovery and his redemption. It is significant that he is *reclothed* in preparation for this second test (274). In the course of the coon hunt on which he is taken his *flaw* resurfaces. "At last he surrendered to his fatigue and made the mistake of sitting down instead of slowing down, for when he got up again, the rest had given his feet an opportunity to hurt him and the pain in his short leg was so great he began to limp and hobble" (278). The coon hunt, however, is a kind of ritual in which Milkman's essential *harmartia* is exposed so that conversion and redemption may occur. He no longer felt that he "deserved" anything (279). The shallow outward facade which was his identity began to evaporate.

> *Under the moon, on the ground, alone, with not even the sound of baying dogs to remind him that he was with other people, his self—the cocoon that was 'personality'—gave way . . . Except for his broken watch, and his wallet with about two hundred dollars, all he had started out with on his journey was gone: his suitcase with the Scotch, the shirts, and the space for bags of gold; his snap-brim hat, his tie, his shirt, his three-piece suit, his socks and his shoes (280).*

All that Milkman has at his disposal for survival are his natural resources. He lacks, however, the most important one: "an ability to separate out, of all the things there were to sense, the one that life itself might depend on" (280). This discernment is a kind of literacy, the ability to speak and understand.

> *The gods, the men——none was just hollering, just signaling location or pace. The men and the dogs were talking to each other. In distinctive voices they were saying distinctive, complicated things . . . All those shrieks, those rapid tumbling barks, the long sustained yells, the tuba sounds, the drumbeat sounds, the low liquid* howm howm, *the ready whistles, the thin* eeeee's *of a cornet, the* unh uhn uhn *bass chords. It was all language. Before things were written down. (281)*

These sounds which Milkman does not understand are *musical*, a form of communication in which there is no distinction between form and content, signifier and signified. The ritual of the coon hunt immerses Milkman into his primal past, and the result of that ritual is redemptive healing.

> *he found himself exhilarated by simply walking the earth. Walking it like he belonged on it; like his legs were stalks, tree trunks, a part of his body that extended down down down*

into the rock and soil, and were comfortable there—on the earth
and on the place where he walked. And he did not limp. (284)

The limp is not indicative of mere psychological alienation, but is a
symbol of physical separation, earthly removal and exile; a physical residue
of slavery. Its presence keeps alive the longing to return to the early fecundi-
ty and generation of some primal place. The ritual is not only redemptive for
Milkman as an individual, but also for him in his relations with
women. Note the egalitarian-expressionistic language used to describe his
encounter with Sweet:

> *He soaped and rubbed her until her skin squeaked and glis-*
> *tened like onyx. She put salve on his face. He straddled her be-*
> *hind and massaged her back. She put witch hazel on his swollen*
> *neck. He made up the bed. She gave him gumbo to eat. He*
> *washed the dishes. She washed his clothes and hung them out to*
> *dry. He scoured her tub. She ironed his shirt and pants. He gave*
> *her fifty dollars. She kissed his mouth. He touched her face. She*
> *said please come back. He said I'll see you tonight. (288)*

The ritual has provided Milkman with a perspicuity which allows him
to see Ruth, Macon Jr., Hagar, and Lena as human subjects for the first time
in his life (303-5). Moreover, it provides him with a sensibility requisite for
the recovery of his past. In music, the song which Pilate sang as he was born,
the song which the children sang in the streets of Shalimar, are the innate resources of African-American culture. Pilate's ability to sing at Hagar's funeral allows her to invoke mercy and make of a senseless death a recollection of
love (323). In the music Milkman recovers the true name of his grandfather
and great-grandfather, and discovers that the latter was "one of those flying
African children" (325). He understands his own repressed dreams of flight,
and the ways in which he resembled the heavily adorned but nearly land-
locked peacock (286). As the novel concludes Guitar and Milkman, whose
day has come, are engaged in struggle. On a larger scale it is a struggle between love and freedom in history, and the outcome finally depends on
Milkman's ability to grant a dying Pilate her last request. "Sing," she
said. "Sing a little something for me" (340).

THE RECOVERY OF SACRED MYTH

The purpose of ritual is the reactualization of primordial time, in which the
participant becomes the contemporary of her gods and mythical
ancestors. The goal is the restoration of human knowledge of the

sacred. This knowledge takes the form of myth, because myth is a story about ultimate reality, about qualitative meaning in history and topography. The recovery of sacred myth in *Song of Solomon* involves the confluence of three influences or factors which constitutes the unique plight of African-Americans and, more specifically, the African-American writer.

The key to the first mythic strand is the character Circe, the midwife who delivered Pilate and her brother Macon, Jr. She is a servant in the house of the family responsible for the death of Macon, Sr. and the theft of his land. Although the artistry and craft of Morrison make any direct linkage of characters in her novel with characters bearing the same name in other works of fiction risky business, a comparison and contrast of Circe in *Song of Solomon* and *Circe* in Homer's *The Odyssey* brings to light the first mythic strand to be examined. The Homeric *Circe* awaits the arrival of Odysseus who is a wanderer and exile from his home at Ithaca. Morrison's Circe also awaited the return of Macon, Jr. "I knew one day you would come back. Well, that's not entirely true. Some days I doubted it and some days I didn't think about it at all. But you see I was right. You did come" (243). The difference here is that instead of Macon, Jr., it is his son, in whom the longing to return from exile is inborn, who comes to Circe. The house of the Homeric *Circe* is surrounded by "mountain wolves and lions" who have been rendered harmless by her magic. The house of Morrison's Circe is inhabited by the Weimaraner dogs who obey her every command (242). The similarity extends even to the sexual relationship. *Circe* invites Odysseus to sleep with her, while the sight of Circe awakens in Milkman sexual images from his childhood dreams.

> *So when he saw the woman at the top of the stairs there was no way for him to resist climbing up toward her outstretched hands, her fingers spread wide for him, her mouth gaping open for him, her eyes devouring him. In a dream you climb the stairs. She grabbed him, grabbed his shoulders and pulled him right up against her and tightened her arms around him. Her head came to his chest and the feel of that hair under his chin, the dry bony hands like steel springs rubbing his back, her floppy mouth babbling into his vest, made him dizzy, but he knew that always, always at the very instant of the pounce or the gummy embrace he would wake with a scream and an erection. Now he had only the erection. (242)*

The difference, however, is that the seduction of Odysseus by *Circe* is part of a plot the goal of which is to make him lose all memory of his native land, while Circe relates to Milkman the details of his nearly forgotten past. He learns that his grandmother, Sing, was of Indian ancestry and that Jake was his grandfather's real name (245, 250). The Homeric *Circe* is a goddess, "though her voice is like a woman's." Morrison's Circe bears a similar admixture of the human and the divine:

> *Perhaps this woman is Circe. But Circe is dead. This woman is alive. That was as far as [Milkman] got, because although the woman was talking to him, she had to be dead. Not because of the wrinkles, and the face so old it could not be alive, but because out of the toothless mouth came the strong, mellifluent voice of a twenty-year-old girl. (242)*

Rather than the mystery of incarnation which energizes Homer's *Circe*, Morrison's Circe is sustained by the dialectic of the coexistence of the "living" and the "dead." Finally, *Circe* directs Odysseus to "the Halls of Hades and Persephone the Dread" to consult with Teiresias the blind prophet. This journey into Hell is necessary if he is ever to reach Ithaca. Circe, on the other hand, directs Milkman to the cave where his grandfather's body was dumped after the murder (247).

Milkman's own greed for the legendary gold blinds him to the real significance of the cave. Although the cave is described as a place of death, he misses the signs of life in it, the "worn places on the floor where fires had once burned" (254). The cave is not a site of eternal cessation or death, but symbolic of the womb, or the beginning of new life.

The presence of the Homeric mythic strand in *Song of Solomon* is not simply the result of textual influence. Rather, it points to an important dimension of the African-American writer's task. That is, the place of *The Odyssey* as the prototype of the novel in Western culture tends to raise for the African-American novelist the dilemma of traditional literary norms and canons on one hand, and the non-traditional material which makes up African-American life and experience on the other. This struggle between competing sensibilities is what George Kent refers to in his book *Blackness and the Adventure of Western Culture*. Only by acknowledging the presence and force of western myths upon African-Americans can the African-American writer begin to deconstruct those canons which deny the humanity of black folk.

The key to the second mythic strand is Milkman's ancestor Solomon, reputed to be "one of those flying African children" (325). This is an allusion to a belief among certain slaves that they would indeed fly away back to Africa. According to this myth, presumably of Ibo origin, among the slaves brought to America were members of an African tribe who knew the secret of flight.[5] This is a powerful image in the novel and it associates Robert Smith's ill-fated attempt in the first scene with Pilate's ability to fly "without ever leaving the ground" (340) and with Milkman's inability to fly as evidenced in the image of the peacock. Moreover, flight also represents spiritual triumph and vindication. It points to a renewal which only a return to one's native topography can provide. The presence of the African mythical strand in *Song of Solomon* is indicative of an important dimension of the African-American writer's task. The African strand is the "otherness" in African-American literature which distinguishes it from typical Western literature. It is at the heart of the impulse to write about black people. One of the aspects of novels and stories by African-American women which distinguishes them from those of many African-American men is the emphasis on the return to one's roots as an end in itself. Richard Wright's fiction, like his life, reflects the tendency to equate flight with escape from one's culture and roots. Even when Wright does examine his roots, the purpose is to ultimately free himself from their debilitating effects.[6] Toni Morrison, on the other hand, is concerned with flight as return rather than escape. It is possible that the origins of this distinction lie in the differences in the historical experiences of women and men in slavery. That is, men were freer to consider escape to the North than women, who were constrained by familial and child-rearing responsibilities.[7] This theme of flight, one side of which has often remained submerged in the African-American literary tradition, is important because it points to the "otherness" inherent within that tradition, and therefore places the writer in the midst of redemptive possibilities.

The key to the third mythical strand in the novel is its title.[8] The biblical *Song of Solomon* (or Song of Songs) is a love poem. It is a cultic piece the center of which is a liturgy of reunion. This reunion has been construed as taking place between God and Israel, Christ and the Church, or, harking back to its non-Hebraic origins, between the sun god and the mother goddess. However, the work speaks in terms of the marriage of Solomon and the Shulammite maiden, who is "black but comely." This allusion in Toni Morrison's novel cannot be fully appreciated or understood without taking into account the place of the Bible in general, and the significance of the *Song of Solomon* in particular in African-American life and culture. This book of the Bible has been popularly interpreted to refer at an ultimate level to God's love for black people.

It is this theme of love which links Morrison's novel to its biblical counterpart. In both texts there is an element of pathos involved in the love which is expressed. In the biblical text that pathos is provided by the pain of separation which accompanies that love: "Upon my bed by night I sought him whom my soul loves; I sought him, but found him not; I called him, but he gave no answer" (3:1). In Morrison's narrative, this lovesickness is evident in the haunting voice of Ryna who watched as her husband Solomon flew away. Her plea "Solomon don't leave me" echoes in the gulch as an eternal testimony to her historic separation from her lover. This same lovesickness determines Hagar's infatuation with Milkman. She, like Ryna, was one of those women "who loved too hard." The love expressed in both texts, however, is ultimately triumphant. It is victorious over every obstacle and impediment, "for love is strong as death" (8:6). In Morrison's novel love is also victorious, and is evident in Solomon's love for Jake, and Pilate's love for Hagar and Milkman. The victory and redemption of love is declared by Pilate at Hagar's funeral, when she cries "And she was *loved*" (323). Love conquers death.

The biblical *Song of Solomon* originated in the cultic and ritual context of the Passover feast in which the Israelites remembered their deliverance from Egyptian bondage. In Morrison's novel the past of African-Americans is celebrated, preserved and recreated in song.

The three mythic strands in *Song of Solomon* are brought together by the strategy of commemoration. Eugene Vance describes commemoration as "any gesture, ritualized or not, whose end is to recover, in the name of a collectivity, some being or event either anterior in time or outside of time in order to fecundate, animate, or make meaningful a moment in the present. Commemoration is the conquest of whatever in society or in the self is perceived as habitual, factual, static, mechanical, corporeal, inert, worldly, vacant, and so forth" (Vance 1979, 374). This commemoration is the result of an oral performance in which the geographical opposition between Africa and the West provides an epistemological framework for all of the dialectical oppositions in the novel—life and death, order and disorder, fertility and sterility, and so on. Within the strategy of commemoration the power to remember is a conquest, and "a heroics of memory displaces a heroics of the sword" (388). The recovery of sacred myth in *Song of Solomon* is a response to the need for redemption embodied in the cultic aspects of African-American life. The purpose of the recovery of sacred myth is not to fix African-Americans in the past, but to enable them to redeem the future.

REFERENCES

Baker, Houston A., Jr. 1984. *Blues, Ideology, and African-American Literature*. Chicago: University of Chicago Press.

Bassingame, John W. 1972. *The Slave Community*. New York: Oxford University Press.

DuBois, W. E. B. 1961. *The Souls of Black Folk*. Greenwich, CT: Fawcett Publications.

Eliade, Mircea. 1957. *The Sacred And Profane*. Trans. Willard R. Trask. New York: Harper and Row.

Ellison, Ralph. 1953. *Shadow And Act*. New York: Vintage Books.

Kermode, Frank. 1967. *The Sense of An Ending*. New York: Oxford University Press.

Homer. 1966. *The Odyssey*, Baltimore, Md: Penguin Books.

Kent, George. 1982. *Blackness And The Adventure of Western Culture*. Chicago: Third World Press.

Lester, Julius. 1969. *Black Folktales*. New York: Grove Press.

Long, Charles. 1963. *Alpha: The Myths of Creation*. Chico, CA.: Scholars Press/American Academy of Religion.

Morrison, Toni. 1977. *Song of Solomon*. New York: Alfred A. Knopf.

Vance, Eugene. 1979. "Roland and The Poetics of Memory." In *Textual Strategies: Perspectives In Post-Structuralist Criticism*, ed. Josue Harari. Ithaca, N.Y.: Cornell University Press.

Wright Richard. 1940. *Native Son*. New York: Harper and Row.

————. 1945. *Black Boy*. New York: Harper and Row.

NOTES

1. This order is one way of viewing the chronology of the Civil Rights movement and the Black Power movement. The first certainly provided the vision of a new social order, and the second brought to light the political-economic dimensions of its realization.

2. All references are based on the pagination of the New American Library-Signet Book edition. The first novel by an African-American to be so named was Richard Wright's *Native Son*.

3. In this respect see Alice Walker's novels *The Color Purple* and *Meridian*, the short stories assembled by Mary Helen Washington, *Black Eyed Susans* and *Midnight Birds*, and Toni Cade Bambara's novel, *Salt Eaters*.

4. I have in mind here Ralph Ellison's *Invisible Man* and W. E. B. DuBois' *Souls of Black Folk*.

5. An African-American version of this myth, "People Who Could Fly," is found in Julius Lester, *Black Folktales*. (1969, 147-52).

6. See Wright's autobiography *Black Boy* (1945).

7. For an excellent analysis of this particular aspect of slave life see John W. Bassingame, *The Slave Community* (1972).

8. Bonnie J. Barthold suggests several ways in which this allusion clarifies some of the enigmatic aspects of the novel. See her *Black Time: Fiction of Africa, the Caribbean and the United States*. (1981, 182-4).

LIBERATION AS RISKY BUSINESS

BILL SMITH

PART ONE/THE LANGUAGE

> *And the Liberating Love of the Folk begat the Spirit
> of street courage and wisdom which begat critical risk.*

I am a queer colored man who is a Christian called to ministry in an emerging community that is marginal, coming out of invisibility, struggling with constructed forms of alienation, and confronting a devastating pandemic. I am a member of a community emerging out of the margins created by racism, sexism, and heterosexism.

In this last half of the twentieth century, queer and colored communities in America have come into critical cultural, social, and self awareness, growing economic and political power, and increasing religious and legal recognition. In the Americas these communities have also been on the front lines in coming into contact with the virus that has been named HIV. This front-line contact has resulted in the destruction of tens of millions' immune systems. In the United States queer colored men were among the pioneers in designing and leading a response to this deadly interaction. Everyday, queer colored men, working men, responded and courageously fought for their lives in the face of attack and vilification from their communities. Liberation is risky business.

These virulent attacks, especially from the African-American religious communities, contribute to the deaths of many. African-American families turned their backs on the suffering of fathers, uncles, sons, and brothers because these families' love and faith couldn't/cannot accommodate the strangeness of love's variety. African-American clergy denounced these men/us from pulpits and in the media while we were sick and dying. But we persist, and many of us are still living because of our spiritual courage in the face of a devastating plague and community rejection, and because we have constructed an alternate family and community, spiritual resources of love. Our articulation and construction of our response to the plague is a direct consequence of our resistance to oppression and struggle for personal control over the most intimate parts of our being and relations. The construction of my own identity is located in this historical context. This resistance and struggle is part of larger historical struggles for liberation of both queer and colored cultures in America. This defensive and creative posture toward the HIV plague results from the liberating spirituality coming out of the cultural context of these communities.

Our capacity to resist has been constructed out of the experiences of our lives as documented in the works of queer colored artists, poets, writers, and musicians who brought their gifts to the struggle against the effects of biologic, social, and cultural attack. Poet/performance artist Assotto Saint and film maker and cultural analyst Marlon Riggs, among many others, gave their lives in this effort. The spiritual courage and wisdom demonstrated by these men in active engagement with resisting forces was constructed out of the risk queer colored men learned to employ in their struggle to grow up and love beyond the fears of their families and communities. This process occurred within the context of history, and is part of the history of liberation and is culturally informed.

Liberation theology is the synthesis of the dialectical conversation between religious reflection, and culture analysis, or in my terms, liberating love and critical street wisdom, where the soul of the street comes into the academic conversation, where the subject and the object are engaged in dialogues of yearning and meaning. As this conversation extends deeper into the constructs of culture, into the spiritual imperative to witness to the changing appearance of truth, people who had been silent begin to speak in their own tongues in search of a common language.

As the conversation between academic religious reflection and cultural analysis is pursued in a postmodern interdisciplinary context with increasing contributions from formerly silenced populations—women, the poor, the colored, the queer, the disabled—the language of the discourse is stretched and expanded. Experiential/existential courage and wisdom and academic knowledge become increasingly familiar to each other. Strangers talk and become not so strange. Constructing common language requires the taking of risks. Making oneself vulnerable to the stranger by becoming understood and understanding expands the common language, the common talk, accessible talk, table talk. Liberation theology is the result of the risks women, the poor, and the colored took to enter into the academic conversation. Their voices articulated and used social and cultural analysis from their location, from the wisdom of their experience in their search for the constant in the temporary, in religious language, to locate the presence of God as Love in their marginalization and alienation. Womanist and feminist theologians and ethicists took the risks and located their search in the personal, rummaging around in the archaeologies of their narratives.

This contribution to the talk, my contribution to the talk, constructs memory as personal archaeology and significant memory as personal archetype/metaphor, and identifies early significant archetype as the source from which meaning and behavior are constructed. This talk, my talk, locates this personal archeology in the memories, stories and experiences in my relationships with my family and community. It is a risk to use the personal in conversation with the academy, but others have done this. It is a contribution to the historical process of liberation. There is reason to take this risk in the context of liberation, a sacred activity. It is a way to know God and as we know from Job, knowing God is risky but rewarding business.

This contribution is divided into three parts. The first part sets the theoretical framework. The second part is my rummaging in the archaeology of my bones. It is in my memories that I see my liberating love and the early development of my critical street wisdom. Part three draws upon the strength of my archaeology which allows me to live with the risk of love and learn in the midst of dying.

Queer, colored, and living with HIV is risky business. We have taken these risks for the right to love and live. Though we are here and alive, our religious communities and churches, our families and the academic social-scientific communities have denied and ignored our living, our spirituality. It is through our taking the risk of coming out of our invisibility and silence that we live. It is speaking from and of the truth of our lives that has moved us this far. Liberation is risky. It is from that foundation that this effort to contribute to the common language of liberation theology emerges. The aim is to "push the envelope" of religious discourse farther and assert another experience of liberation spirituality. This piece is an exploration of personal archaeology to locate cultural sources that inform queer colored men's spiritual journey into the courage and wisdom that enable us to risk our lives in the service of love. It is from the suffering for our liberating love that our spiritual power of courage and wisdom are constructed. As we explore the archaeology of our suffering and share the results of that religious journey we strengthen our capacity to love and live. It is part of the collective queer colored historical project to risk for love. Theology is the search for God in history. Liberating theology locates God in existential emancipation from the dominating forces of history. Liberating theology arises from culture and employs risk in the construction of liberating love. Liberating love extends and expands the spirits of wisdom and courage. It is God's presence as liberating love that gives us the strength to fight for our love in the face of a hostile church, state, and family. Our search for God must begin with reflection into the wisdom that comes from living in the streets of our communities, critical reflection that reveals the liberating love of our folk. Critical religious reflection helps us to experience the revelation of God's presence and guidance in our efforts for liberation from other people's fear, and helps find a new spiritual and cultural geography.

METHODOLOGY

Liberation is a journey into sacred space, sacred space that is built from and with real human events, our lives. I experience sacred space from within, subjectively. My theology is constructed in sacred space, in the sacred space of my personal archaeology. Examining the bones located in my personal archaeology to see how they have come to live is a religious reflection. Spiritual narrative is liberating love drawn from the African-American tradition that gave birth to "slave narrative" autobiography, catting, tale telling, and rapping. It is a self referential and self representational examining of the location of spirit within the construction of sexual identity. This examination unearths the construction of sexual identity within the interaction of the historical forces of economics, culture, social organization, and the family. It is a synthesis of the praxis of liberating love as religious reflection and critical street wisdom as cultural analysis. My personal archaeology is informed by the cultural archetypes I was raised in: Christian, colored, African-American, queer.

This journey into sacred space is also a journey into the existential Blues. Queer colored men living with HIV know the blues is a part of our existential encounter with the virus. The blues is an African-American archetypal complex of strategies for dealing with suffering. The blues is the name of the archetypal memory of African-American responses to living with and in the Cross. Our Cross is our personal location in history, where my spirit encounters the stranger. The creativity that is born from the blues is our resurrection from the sins of history. That creativity is the Christ of our salvation. Love is at the heart of that creativity. In sex we search for that love. In the search for that love, the love that liberates, we encountered a stranger—HIV. Living with HIV is an encounter in history that can lead to direct access to sacred space, to the personal archives of the sources of our spiritual strength, to the existential blues of our lives and to live we have to be informed and inspired by our lessons from the Blues.

THE HIV BLUES

And he said if you are going to be with me it means you have to realize every decision, every act is an exercise in me fighting for my life. After seven years with AIDS and with no opportunistic infections it comes down to this system, this way of my doing things and I can't afford deviations that cost me anything of what I need to be here. So being with him was a gift in learning how to live with every moment counting and me loving him, humbled by his meditation, finding ways to smoothly be a part of his life without creating a guilt that could not be erased. And I said it means we have to remove the problem before it comes and my task will be to recognize it. And he said I can't afford to struggle about it. And I said you won't have to. So here we are with me learning to live and love with AIDS now even more in my life and his T cell count drops to 24, the pollen, allergies, and me not being able to see him, and him with a developed support system and very clear about his living, his dying and me outside of that process but a part of his being nonetheless, and with nothing to do but call and find how he's doing and wait.

The Blues is an expression of the liberating love of the culture. The spirit of courage and wisdom arises out of the blues to struggle with pain critically. The Blues is critical street wisdom.

It is occurring to me that there really isn't that much time left. T-Cells somewhere between 19 and 35, Karposi's Sarcoma, and other opportunistic infections going on tell me that this is the time of decision and focus. It is the time to begin the process of designing my dying in all respects. If someone discovers a cure for AIDS and Karposi's Sarcoma then it's time for new plans.

My life's journey, my own blues, has been about liberating myself and sharing the knowledge and information I learn from this process with my friends and others. Liberation has come to mean for me exercising and developing critical consciousness and taking personal responsibility for my living, and now dying. It is a liberating love that overcomes fear. It is living in sacred space, living in conscious awareness of the spirit of courage and wisdom. I feel that now is the time to begin focusing on the dying part of that process.

Writing, talking, and conversation have been tools I use in shaping my life. It has been the shaping of being and experience into words, silent or spoken, to myself, to my friends, to my Spirit, just us folk looking at the bones, that has brought me this far in my journey. So it will be with words also that I prepare for death. Death is the last question that faces me while alive. My death is an answer to the question of my life, and not just the meaning of my life but also the result of my living.

My growing awareness of the nearness yet distance of my death creates practical questions that have to be answered. How to handle the body stuff, home or hospital, how much pain to live with, what to do with the carcass? What about the few personal belongings? What about the bills? Whom should be contacted? When and how to say good-bye?

These questions must be answered while I go about learning how to create an alternative to an immune system that will allow me to postpone my acceptance of death's invitation with little trust in what is now called the health care system. At this point I have chosen not to make these questions, however significant, the sole foci of my attention.

Somehow my journey has put me in a position to be able to respond to these questions with some measure of critical choice. My journey has had to include the exploration of my marginality, alienation and invisibility, as one who chooses to live by his spirit and his intellect. An impaired immune system and the specter of death increase and deepen the experience of marginality, alienation, and invisibility.

Folk and street wisdom tell us to use what we have to create what we need. The greater historical context is a subtext, a backbeat. It is a method of discerning truth. The discernment of truth is the primary task in the development of a hermeneutics. The search for the truth of how we are who we are in our sexuality is a personal as well as a collective task. This personal/collective process has its antecedents in colored and queer traditions and literatures, rich sources of culture.

Some human beings cannot avoid taking sexual risks, some avoid sexual risks all of the time, some avoid sexual risks most of the time, some seldom. It may be that taking sexual risks is part of our evolutionary heritage, to insure wide distribution of the gene pool through sexual bonding. In other words sexual risk may improve our chances to survive. At the same time cultural and societal mores, ethics or morality, act to limit the risk taking so as to reduce the danger to the group. Much of that limitation in the twentieth century was constructed hierarchically in the nineteenth century in America in the context of authoritarian religion. We need to critically examine and understand sexual risk in order to construct a sexual ethics and morality that relates to evolutionary and biologic realities including the realities of the sexually "queer."

Human and viral evolutionary history are tied to one another. Our encounters with HIV have often been the result of human beings stretching the limits of their sexual and ecstatic contexts because of other unmet emotional, sexual, and economic needs. Taking sexual risks with strangers increases our social and sexual geography, often with dangers that are unforeseen. Christian education in sexual ethics has always included critical guidelines in the taking of sexual risks. They have not always worked because for many the urge toward bonding, the power to love, is stronger than the fear of strangers.

Queer colored men accessed the power of love to move past the barriers of fear of sexual risk expressed by their families and communities. This liberating activity was necessary because of the pain of our lives. Destruction of and encroachment on other species' habitats, global travel, increasing multinational trade in blood products, exposure to toxic environmental contaminants, the synthesis of industrial and archaic medical treatments in unsanitized conditions in Africa, Brazil, and the Philippines create viable contexts as sources for contact with deadly micro-organisms. Sex is the bonding conduit. The risk involved with queer loving has always been dangerous and in the current historical context that risk has become deadly. Queer colored men's efforts to reduce the deadliness of that risk are essential. In order to succeed in these efforts we must critically examine the role and freeing power of sexual risk in our lives and critically reconstruct our strategies in its use as a libratory tool in our emancipation.

In the context of inter-species involvement, HIV and human, we are fast reconstructing our understanding of the immune system, and in fact reconstructing our immune systems. We are making our immune systems more responsive to critical scientific intervention. It is a slow process but a necessary one. It is part of the queer colored liberation project.

Liberation theology must begin with the subject of the process and must follow the desires and needs of the subject and guide the satisfaction of those needs and desires toward the prize, a liberating love and life. Many colored struggles for liberation have been inspired, guided, and supported by the Holy One we call God. As we become aware of our sexuality we do not and are not capable of discarding our coloredness. As our consciousness of class develops we recognize that it coexists with our sexuality and culture. This understanding does not necessarily happen in the same way for all of us, like everyone else we are unlike anyone else, but it does happen. These constructs that are reconstructed into one person acting in history are the infrastructure of potential bonds with those who might in other situations be called strangers. The suspicious interrogation of location and identity can reveal routes to understanding the other, the stranger, the alien, the queer, the virus. This is a queer colored theological/ethical quest toward that understanding.

Living with HIV is a path of terrible wisdom, as is being queer and colored, and finally that is what it is all about, living through the Blues with your spirit, looking for the constant in the temporary. I believe being who and where you are, if you persist in the work of Christian critical ethics, will yield this wonderful but terrible wisdom. Critical Christian sexual ethics must be reconstructed to include strategies that strengthen critical sexual risk as a means to discovering and enjoying liberating love, and at the same time locate and guide people through the physical and emotional dangers of sex without sacrificing queer love.

The more you point your life in the path of wisdom the more wisdom comes to visit and the longer wisdom will stay. In wisdom you will recognize love. Love makes all things possible. This queer colored wisdom comes from my encounter with the virus, an alien. My peace in this encounter comes from the wisdom I have learned in other queer encounters with strangers. This queer colored wisdom is teaching me to love, yes, love even this virus that doesn't know it is injuring me.

A common language is needed to move past the boundaries of fear that strangeness/foreigners encourage. Queer colored HIV wisdom tells me that love transforms aggression, that intimate physical loving and penetration bonds, connects, in ways that surpass conventions, confounding sense. My bonds with the virus and my healers take me deeper into the core of love, transforming and participating in the construction of healing care in their very physical and intimate penetration of me. If the virii that are in me learn the benefits of hospitality from me, hospitality that is formed in the bowels of love, this hospitality will allow mutual learning and active engaged wisdom. The boundary of this hospitality is my life. The instruments of communication are the various pharmaceutical, herbal, chemical, psychological, and physical therapies and treatments that so far keep the virii relatively contained.

We can often turn the rage of our loved ones into passionate embrace. Hospitality emerges from the recognition of the individual presence of the other and the recognition of the value of that other individual presence. If I die my virii die, like a family, you can't let the kids' innocent ignorance destroy valued relationships, because that is what we are, each one of us. Our bodies are valued relationships cooperatively organized and constructed to provide and maintain life and produce intelligence from the tiniest cell and including the organization of all the various organisms who come to live in us. The wisdom that reveals love leads you to examine difference in joyful anticipation for the Messiah and his/her/its terrible lessons in patience, hope and faith. There is no evil, only history and the themes birthed in history. Bob Dylan sang in the sixties "that whatever fight that ever I fought, the cause was there before I came."

In this process of mutually constructing common language, it is important to know your true place, your sacred space, and to see and know your limitations and boundaries. That's the job. That place is the job. Being Job is the job, which is contributing who you really are, which you know from difference, from encounters with the stranger, the other, to the mix that makes planetary consciousness, intelligence, and wisdom. History is the dialectical conversation between archetypes as ideas and events in time, looking for the constant in the temporary.

Every slave must find his/her own way to freedom, usually with some help from friends. The concretization of homophobic oppression around the site of HIV infection required queer communities to respond critically. Queer colored communities' critical response has had to include a knowledge of how we are who we are both individually and collectively, and is forcing us to demand a place at the table with the conversation constructed so that even the least can participate in table fellowship.

AIDS makes it necessary for us to make our sexuality and sexual identity a personal/individual and social/collective dialectical responsibility, a common matter. The liberation of our submerged identities from invisibility in both colored and queer communities is a necessity for our survival. The virus has made critically conscious construction of our sexuality and sexual identity a requirement for our living. Individual and collective awareness and responsibility in relation to the risks we have to take for our liberation and our living depend on our understanding of what we are bringing to the risks. A liberating Christian critical sexual ethics must be based on a responsible sex and a positive foundation that includes and encourages self esteem, mutual respect, hospitality to the stranger, responsibilty to the community, love of life, recognizing and acknowledging the value of queer colored people. We are not casualties. We are liberating pioneers and explorers of love's possibilities.

PART TWO/ **PERSONAL ARCHAEOLOGY:**
LIBERATING LOVE AS THE CRADLE OF CRITICAL LIBERATING RISK

In my personal archaeology my family has always been the cradle of liberating love. My family always called us colored. On both sides, maternal and paternal, my family came from people from Africa, Europe, and North America, and this mixture was visible. My grandfather, my mothers' father, was a shoe craftsman who owned his own business in a small middle-class suburb of Boston. My family was one of two colored families in the town and had moved there in the late 1890's. From the stories of my aunts, my mothers, their coming of age mirrored the white middle class culture in which they grew up. They were expected to remain at home until married and near home after, and were carefully chaperoned.

My first foster mother, my oldest aunt, had married an immigrant from Portugal against the advice of her father. The courtship was a traditional middle class one. She and her husband found an attractive apartment in an upper working class, mostly colored, section of Roxbury (Massachusetts). She broke the mold. Until my mother was born, this aunt was my grandfather's favorite. And she married a foreigner, married a foreigner and moved away from home. Wasn't much said. Grandfather kind of liked him but never did trust him around the women. Said foreigners have strange ways with women. There was something about my grandfather's love of his daughters that encouraged and supported them in taking risks for love.

After the First World War my family's fortunes changed. Manufactured luxury shoes replaced handcrafted ones. The revolutions in industrial production that expanded consumerism created economic hardship for my grandfather. It was during this time that my mother was born. The remaining sisters had to go to work to support the family. Like many colored people, my family saw education as the primary route of economic and social mobility. The family's economic situation meant that everybody's education had to be halted except my natural mother's, as she was just starting school.

The two remaining sisters had to take live-in domestic service jobs. Their brother, my uncle, had to give up his college education and find a full-time job. Finally during the depression, my grandparents had to sell their home. They and my natural mother moved in with one of their other daughters, who had married and had one child. Three generations, five people, lived in a small four room apartment.

My mother started courting then. My grandparents didn't like the man who was to be my father. He drove a truck, a meat packing truck, always smelled dirty, looked greasy, and didn't talk much. My mother was a trained musician, very high strung and sensitive, sheltered but also in her mid-twenties and unmarried. There were my grandparents, married close to forty-five years, my aunt, divorced with a nine year old son, my father courting my mother in a four room apartment, and then me.

These economic conditions shaped my mother's marriage, her psychological condition, and the infancies of my sister and me, as we lived in the same apartment with my aunt and my cousin.

My grandmother first, then my grandfather died shortly before my mother's marriage. These losses deeply affected my mother psychologically and emotionally. She had been trained as a concert violinist. She had been sheltered all her life. The changes in her life, happening with the rapidity that they did moved her over the edge of being able to cope. She had lost the home she had grown up in, lost her parents, married, and become pregnant, had to stop playing violin, lived in her sister's small apartment, became pregnant again, all within the space of less than four years. She began to experience deep depressions and rages that led to suicide attempts and violent attacks on family members.

They blamed the pregnancy, the second child, my sister, and my mother's psychological condition on my father. They said he couldn't control himself. Made her sick, they said, having a baby too soon after the first baby. There were arguments, lots of arguments. I spent time next door at my

mother's brother's and his wife's apartment. My aunts later told me that my
uncle and aunt never had sex. They lived with his wife's brother who made
me a stuffed scot terrier that was larger than I was. He had lots of men who
would visit him. My natural uncle spent lots of time away from the house.
Nobody was quite sure why. I was outgoing, protective of my sister, always
concerned about being hurt, very talkative and stubborn. They said I was a
good little boy and a pretty child.

The changing economic conditions that had created the crowded
quarters also facilitated my mother's stress-related suicide attempts. My father had a difficult time adjusting and finding work. His lack of income became a source of irritability to my mother and her sister with whom we were
living. The conflicts that occurred diminished his self esteem. When I was
two and my sister a year old, my natural mother was committed to the state
mental hospital because of suicide attempts coming from deep depressions.
The hospital staff diagnosed her as suicidal and homicidal. My father moved
back to his mother's home.

My mother came out of a family of five surviving children of seven
pregnancies. She was the youngest of the four girls. Two of her sisters were
married and childless, and they were much older than her. When she was
hospitalized for acute manic depression, after being found on the edge of the
roof with the two of us children, we were separated between her oldest
childless sisters. Since neither of them lived in apartments big enough to accommodate both of us, they each took responsibility for one of us. I went to
live with her oldest sister. They blamed my father for my mother's illness and
would not let him have anything to do with us for a long time.

The Depression and the Second World War had changed the neighborhood where my oldest aunt and her husband had moved. Negro migration
from the South brought a working class to Roxbury that had fewer industrial skills and different social patterns. My family's configuration was unusual
even for most colored families in Roxbury. My oldest aunt and her husband
were childless, though not by choice. She had had a number of miscarriages
when she was younger and had resigned herself to childlessness. Because of
this, as well as my aunt's deep affection for her youngest sister, my living
with them was always regarded in the way of a special gift. I always felt
wanted though I was a strange child, subject to violent seizures and with-
drawals. My family always said I was a little queer. My second mother, my
oldest aunt, is my earliest memory of liberating love in the face of family and
community fear of the stranger.

There was a problem, however. My uncle had grown up in a different
culture than my aunt. He had grown up in the Azores, an island group just
south of Portugal, south and west of Gibraltar, and west of Africa. Marriage

and sex had different meanings for him than for my aunt. My uncle had been stabbed for looking at a white woman while visiting his brother in Florida. He was reluctant to move out of the Roxbury neighborhood into areas where he would have to encounter racial difficulties, especially around being married to an American Negro woman.

The home was the province of my aunt. It was where my uncle lived but not where he spent his leisure time. Like many working class immigrant men from Mediterranean cultures, he spent much of his leisure time in the local tavern, often in the company of unattached women. In this he was not different from his twin brother, his cousins and his friends, people that we often visited as a family. The men's world was one that was very separated from the world of women and children.

He maintained control over the financial decisions. We were in a better financial condition than most of the neighborhood though some older residents had better jobs because of their participation in the armed services. My uncle had been too old to enlist. My aunt, on the other hand, had grown up in a family where her father spent all his leisure time at home and was sexually faithful to his wife. Her mother had controlled the finances. My aunt had adjusted but was very frustrated and lonely. I became her comfort. Her "little man." This closeness became the context for sexual interaction in my very early childhood through penile manipulation. As I grew older and started school, her overt sexual activity with me stopped. I was her companion for trips to see family and cousins, all Portuguese, whom I grew up believing were my natural relatives. The risks she took for love upon reflection created for me an archetype of living love.

I adored my aunt. We were inseparable. My uncle disapproved, but since he was not home at night often I was her company. She encouraged my independence and verbalness and loved to dress me up the way she thought her "little man" should look. She had been trained as a seamstress and her notion of fashion and style in boy's things always tended toward the practical and comfortable. One day in the basement of one of the apartment buildings on our street, the boys and girls were taking off their clothes. I was reluctant because my pants were different than the other boys pants. Theirs had flies, zippers, and they had belts on. My foster mom had bought these new pants that had an elastic waistband and no fly. I had to pull my pants down like a girl. Everybody noticed and they started to call me a sissy. This was the first time I felt strange, a little queer. I knew the only reason I felt uncomfortable about the pants was that the kids thought they were funny for a boy to wear. The pants made sense to me because it was easier to go to the bathroom. As I look back I can see where my way of seeing things was quite different from theirs, and mine, like my aunt's, was not appreciated but was seen as strange.

My aunt and uncle had very dear friends among the older residents of the neighborhood, but the newer residents resented them. Some of the resentment toward my uncle was cultural. He was not Negro. He spoke with an accent. Though not much was said by the adults of the neighborhood, it was always present. Since my aunt had grown up in the North and in a white middle class community, her way of being was seen as different, her speech was different. They were an older couple with a young child. They were also doing a little better financially, but not significantly.

Growing up in a working class community of color, in Roxbury, in the post-World War II era, my neighborhood childhood peers, who were more sexually aware than I, called me into the beginnings of my awareness of my otherness. In the process of raping me numerous times between the ages of six and eight, they exposed me to an awareness of my sexual difference. It was because I was other that I was raped. Until then I dimly knew that I was other but I had no way to understand it. The fact of the rapes called me to question the why of my otherness, my queerness.

I was a different kind of boy than they were and that made me a target. Their perception was that I was a "mamma's boy." a sissy, a faggot, a fairy, queer, not a real boy. This was despite other indications of neighborhood masculinity. I was athletic and physically competent but mechanically inept. I could take care of myself in most fights except those in which I was outnumbered. But I was also left-handed and a little clumsy sometimes, especially when I was trying to do things right-handedly. This clumsiness had the effect of making me seem more than a little odd. My relationship with my foster mom was the major transgression of the community norm though. Boys in my neighborhood didn't do things with their moms. My mom and I went everywhere together.

The structural conditions of working class Roxbury in the late nineteen forties and early fifties created the context for my rape and isolation and the beginnings of my critical street wisdom. My uncle and aunt had begun teaching me to read when I was three. By the time I began elementary school I could read quite well and consequently loved it. My peers, not starting with that advantage, saw that as a reason to not have much to do with me and to make fun of me. They also used my relationship with my foster mother to taunt me and made constant fun of my uncle because of his accent. Going out to play meant going out to the street. Being on the street, being made aware of my queerness in painful ways, meant I had to learn to read the signs of the street as well as the signs of books.

My ages of four through eleven were a time when the children in my neighborhood were discovering and exploring their sexuality. This activity consisted of secret rendezvous in cellars and abandoned buildings between any kind of combinations of boys and girls in varied stages of undress, exploring each others' bodies. I was excluded from these occasions until and only on the occasions of my being raped.

My relationships with the other children were occasionally friendly. There were boys I wanted to be friends with and sometimes they would play with me, but not usually. Wanting to hang out with them I took my first sexual risk which introduced me to rape. I had tagged along after them into an abandoned building on our street to see what this secret activity was. They began to pull out their "private parts" and play with each other. Almost as an after thought they began to include me, introducing me to the activity. Then all of a sudden I was the object of the activity, strangely and excitedly enjoying the physical sensations, but feeling intimidated and being forced to do what they wanted me to do.

There I was again, should I risk the humiliation again? Tired of being left out, being called a sissy, a girl, I entered the sex games. But they hadn't changed, they still saw me as a boy wanting to be a girl and treated me the way they saw me. My second sexual risk, group sex, male to male sex, drawn to it, involved in it, but not as one of the fellas, but as a sissy, humiliated me.

After that I felt very sad and isolated. The next time it happened I thought that it would be more "fair." It wasn't. After these encounters, fights between me and the other boys started to occur more frequently, often with them ganging up on me, making fun of me and my family. For them, my resistance to accepting the role they wanted me to play all the time, the one of being penetrated, made fun of, was queer, was other, something they couldn't understand or accept. If I acted like what they thought I was trying to be, a girl, why didn't I like being treated as one. I liked being a boy, liked the way my aunt treated me, as a man. I liked being close to boys and men. The only way they would be physically close, sexually intimate with each other was to make believe one of them/us was a girl.

I remember earlier though, when I was three or four years old, my aunt was caring for another boy my age. He would often sleep over in my bed. There was no other bed and we were small enough to fit. I remember how good it felt, how warm especially when he wet the bed, of course, then how cold. So we snuggled up closer. It felt good. Contradictory archetypes, rape and sadness, intimacy and warmth are memories that informed my growing street wisdom.

I began to take refuge in reading. I knew I was different. I also knew that my being raped had not made me different. I was different before the rape. I also knew my difference had something to do with the way I felt inside my body, the way I felt about boys and men and the way I acted about what had happened. My problem was, I liked the physical feeling that accompanied the male touching and entering but I did not like the feelings of being made to feel dirty and humiliated. I did not know what to do about it, especially when the feelings would not go away and were with me all the time. My shame was that I didn't know how to demand respect on the basis of what I felt was fairness, or how to get it.

The boys who raped me also enjoyed the touch and penetration of male bodies and even their own bodies. It was not that which made me different. They had been experimenting and exploring their sexuality with each other and the girls in the neighborhood before and continued to do so after our encounters. What made me other to them was that I wouldn't accept the role they felt I should. They felt that because I had such a weird family, that I was with mom so much of the time, interested in reading, especially interested in stories, that I was so different from them that the only role that was appropriate for me with them was for me to accept what they wanted to do with me. I knew in some kind of internal way that my difference was a reason for me to not let them do whatever they wanted to me even if I did want to play with their bodies as much as they did.

Though I knew my difference, my queerness had something to do with my foster mother. That wasn't all of it, I couldn't understand why I had such a hard time making the other boys treat me fairly. I was not the same boy I was before I had the experience, which at the time I didn't call rape. This new feeling made me see that experience, the shame as my fault. Maybe if I wasn't with my mom so much they wouldn't think of me like that. So there were these two sets of feelings, the feelings of rejection by my peers because of my family and my attachment to my family, and this new awareness of something strange inside of myself that made me resist the role my peers wanted me to play in their sexual games.

Both were connected in a concrete way to social conditions that created our neighborhood. Economic conditions had brought my family and my neighbors into proximity. Colored families came from the South to improve their economic conditions in the North. These families shared a sense of identity and community that my family was only on the fringes of. My family's experience in the North had contributed to my sense and awareness of the importance of my individuality. My family appreciated and loved my strange ways; in fact to them, they weren't strange at all. I was just moody like my natural mother. That my otherness, my queerness, my strangeness wanted to be a part of what the other kids were doing and wanted to be treated fairly, treated like a boy, was something that was difficult for the other kids to understand. It was also difficult for them to understand how important it was for me.

This end of innocence made me aware of what had been an unconscious sense of dread, made me aware that I felt bad when no one else was around, made me wish that I was someone else, made me wish hard that I was someone else, somewhere else. I knew that feeling of dread had something to do with my mom and me, and living in that neighborhood, but was only dimly aware of my grieving my natural mother's absence. The neighbors were aware of my seizures and the kids would goad and taunt me into one. The opportunity to be someone else, somewhere else came when I was nine. My aunt and uncle who were caring for my sister bought a house on what was then called the G.I. Bill. I spent my summer there. It was in a predominantly white, working-class, mixed ethnic neighborhood. I had a great summer. I wanted to live there. My dream came true. The family decided that it would be good for me to move there, knowing nothing of the pain and isolation I felt in my neighborhood, in order for me to go to school and for my sister and I to get to know one another better.

My second foster family, my mother's second oldest sister and her husband, were quite different than my first. She had been studying to be an artist, a painter, when she had left school to work and help support my grandfather, grandmother and mother. It was an ache in her that was not bitter, yet it informed her relation to us. My uncle came from Panamanian and southern Negro parents and had been a promising jazz/Blues musician when my mother went into the hospital and my sister came to live with them. He also was a composer, and when he wasn't working he was writing music. He worked two full-time jobs all throughout the years we were growing up. My new foster mother also worked three and four days a week as a domestic worker. It was necessary if we were to have the house.

The neighborhood was Irish, Italian, Polish, Portuguese, and Jewish, mixed ethnically and religiously. There were lots of kids. We were all poor, working-class families. My family rented out the bottom apartment to an Irish family with three kids for the first three or four years we lived there. The proximity created an intimacy between the two families. Both of our families knew that we were trying to solve the same kinds of problems and that making a living was hard. My family's love in trying to end my sadness by moving me away from the aloneness of my first neighborhood made me have to learn to read new street signs.

All my new friends were white. I seemed to know things they didn't, but they played attractive new games that allowed for more physical activity. Left-handedness was not a problem here. I was not as clumsy. I was growing into my body with more confidence. My seizures ceased. Puberty was good for me. There was more girl-boy separation. I became close to several of the boys and learned the same kind of sexual exploration was going on here as in my older neighborhood. This time though I had a choice and when I was invited, I declined. I was not going to spoil this new place with the possible repeat of what had happened in the past. I remained friends with my new playmates despite my not joining in the secret sexual games.

There we were in another cellar. The two of them and me. I ached to be a part of what they were doing but was afraid of the potential humiliation. As I interrogate the memory I can see that the context was different. The outcome might not have been the same. These boys never thought of me as a sissy. They just wanted to have fun. Missed chance, I thought later and for a long time, because I really liked both of them. It was during this time that I began to recognize differences between my family and the children of my new neighborhood. We were the only children not living with their natural mom and dad. The elementary school I had gone to in lower Roxbury had never asked the children about family information. We were too young to know about birth certificates, family income and whatever other official information they needed to collect. I was embarrassed to talk about it. Nor did I know until then that my mother was in a mental institution or even what that was. My folks then had to tell us the story of how my natural mom became ill, placing the blame on my father but trying not to. I was odder than even before, but this time the neighborhood kids didn't care about our family's unusualness. Most of the neighbors were second generation immigrants and their experience made them take difference and strangeness in stride. It was the early and mid-fifties and we were all trying to be good and fair Americans.

I had visited my natural father's home two or three times. My sister had spent more time there. While we were there we spent most of our time with our grandmother. Granny Smith was wonderful. She had six children that lived. My father was her youngest, also her darkest in complexion. This last fact had been the cause for much tragedy in the family. My father's father and the rest of the family were light enough to pass for white and they did. That is until my father was born. They used to hide him whenever their white neighbors would be in proximity. They kept to themselves. They lived in the country, on the northern outskirts of Boston's factory towns.

On two occasions, upon discovering that, in fact, the family was colored, because somehow they had seen my father, the neighbors had burned down my father's family's house, houses that my grandfather and his older sons had built with their own hands. My grandfather was an electrician and had worked on the construction of the Boston Elevated Railroad. He was a member of the A.F. of L., the American Federation of Labor, a segregated union, with no colored allowed. It was discovered he was colored. He died during construction after being pushed in front of an on-coming train. My grandmother and her oldest sons finished the third and final home. My father felt responsible. His father had always blamed him for their troubles. It was easy for him to accept the blame for my mother's illness and institutionalization. My mother's family never knew what my father and his family had been through. Colored people were not supposed to go crazy.

I loved that home and met a friend there. We would run around the woods, throw stones at the infrequent cars that passed, and sleep over at each other's house. I was careful not to go too far in touching though there was that feeling. He lived across the road. He was one of the reasons I loved going out to my Grandmother's house. The visits to Granny didn't last long. I was, they claimed, too much for her to handle.

Back at school I had met a special friend. He was Irish and Scottish. I was the only colored kid in class. We were inseparable. I was the last kid in the last row, he was in front of me skipping a seat. Although Boston schools were desegregated at the time, the teacher felt some need to keep me apart from the other children. We started talking to each and changed our seats to be closer, despite the teacher's admonitions and moving us apart. We spent nearly all our time together. We wrestled a lot, and also followed the careers of TV wrestlers. Our favorites were the ones with well proportioned bodies. My memory of my earlier encounters with sexual exploration kept me from even thinking about going farther in our physical contact than wrestling, although at times we did get close to that possibility.

Because everybody's parents in the neighborhood worked much of the time, there were few adults to supervise our activities. Those that did made sure the fights stayed within the shouting and bloody nose range, and that any damage to houses was confined to a broken window every once in a while from a baseball or stray rock. I had friends now and was insulated from the effects of the resentments and taunts of the children of the old neighborhood.

My first foster father had not only taught me how to read, he also had taught me how to work. I had occasional part-time jobs since I was five. After moving in with my new foster family, my best friend, who also had a paper route, got me one. My new foster father also found weekend work for me. From the ages ten through thirteen, on the surface I felt great. I had money. I had the freedom to move around. School was a snap. On the inside my questions about my otherness were growing more problematic.

My ability to read and remember gave me more freedom in school and was not seen as negative in this neighborhood. Because I was working I had more privileges and mobility than my sister or peers. I had always been an explorer. Because of the trouble I had in the old neighborhood, I would travel outside my neighborhood to meet new friends. This was another thing that made me odd. Very few of the kids on my street ever left our street. Even when I had moved "up the hill" it was unusual for the kids to ever venture off our street. I loved to be on my own and wandering, meeting new boys, new friends. Also, I would return to my old neighborhood to spend the weekend with my first foster mom and dad every week. Since I didn't really have any friends there anymore, I loved to walk around and meet new boys on other streets, in other neighborhoods. It was safe to do that then. I came to know many parts of Boston very well. I was starting to understand more about how things worked. I was still haunted and wanted to find out why I still felt bad whenever I was still. This feeling fed my hunger for more knowledge.

Then I discovered Playboy magazine and other "girlie" magazines. My second foster father was in the habit of bringing home stacks upon stacks of magazines: Look, Saturday Evening Post, Colliers. He planned to read them and never did. He also was a collector of everything. When he noticed I was reading them he felt justified about ignoring my aunt's pleas about collecting all these old magazines. One day in the mix of magazines I discovered Esquire, Playboy, Evergreen Review, and Nugget. I found the "Beat Generation." It was in this way I read about homosexuality for the first time.

My uncle, as a handyman, had started working for a family that had two sons in there early twenties. These magazines were among the ones they threw away. More and more of them started to appear. My uncle, as a jazz/blues musician, had a very relaxed attitude toward the magazines. My aunt, as an artist, also felt quite open about sex and nudity, so I didn't have to sneak and could talk to them if I wanted. I seldom did.

Sometime later he began including paperback books in what he brought home. Among them was the novel *Giovanni's Room*. James Baldwin (his picture on the cover told me he was a black man) had written a short novel of two men falling in love with each other, resisting it, but nonetheless falling in love. I was spellbound. Here it was, a story about what I was feeling. Life changed. I started hunting out paperback books and discovered novels about "gay women" and "sexual deviates." Although that inside sense of otherness was still there with a feeling of shame, I was beginning to feel stronger. I knew there was a name given for what I felt, an identity. I had discovered Malcolm X and the Black Muslims through my godsister when I was nine. Malcolm X's teaching and the literature I had been reading about black people had taught me how to recognize prejudice. I suspected the same in reading about homosexuality, but it was still going to take me some growing up and adulthood to separate my otherness from the rape.

During my adolescence I had several girlfriends. It was still the fifties, birth control depended on condoms and diaphragms. Birth control pills were not readily available. Sex was still much of an actual mystery for me, albeit theoretically understood. These experiences only further confused my sense of who I was. I felt intense sexual and emotional attractions to the girls I was involved with and was suppressing any feelings I had for boys. Except for one. I had met him on one of my adventures and we started hanging out together and then hanging out at each other's homes. We were getting more and more physical, something my folks noticed and then warned me about.

I had left my first foster mom the way one leaves a lover he still loves but can't handle the situation. Though hurt, she had tried to understand why I had to move. I now wanted to spend more time with her and my uncle. Also my friends "up the hill" had started to move away. The neighborhood was changing, more black and brown faces, younger children. During my time away from the old neighborhood, it had also changed. There were new boys that had moved in. I wasn't strange to them. We became buddies and hung out together. There were no sexual games but we did go to parties together, do our first alcohol drinking, and pot smoking together. We all had after school jobs. We were very close.

Once when I was visiting one of my friends, I started telling him what had happened to me when I was younger and why I had left. I thought he might understand. He lived alone with his mom who was very much like my first foster mom, and the guys in the neighborhood teased him in much the same way they teased me. As I was talking I felt very intimate. We started wrestling. We stopped. Later when we were hanging out other friends told me that he had told them what had happened and that I had made a play for him. They were cool about it and wanted me to know it was cool. It didn't seem like they would reject me but it was too dangerous to admit. I had misjudged these kind of situations before. So I denied it and called the boy with whom I wrestled a liar and chased him. I lied but I couldn't take a chance on losing my friends. We remained friends through high school and the service. Until we all got married. Then we sort of drifted apart.

My family, although being open about sex and bodies, would try to steer me from extended physical contact with other males. They frowned when I wanted to hug and sit on male relatives' laps when I was very young. Although they accepted my wrestling, they kept an eye on it. Along with my shame about my early experiences, my family's responses kept me from going very far in my sexual explorations.

I quit school at sixteen. I had not been going much before the January I quit. I started hanging out at pool rooms, corners, cardrooms. I met some new friends. They were into a heavy street scene and the underground economy, stealing cars, small time dope dealing, gambling. Through them I met two women who were sex workers. They had children. I would babysit while they were working. Both of them had sisters my age. I ended up going out with both of the sisters—not at the same time. After I broke up with one of them I really fell in love with the other. She had been abused as a young child by her mother's "tricks" and had a tough time trusting boys. We enjoyed just hanging out and laying back. She would stay with me while I babysat. She had a neat slim tomboy build, she was pretty. Although there was a lot of petting and fondling neither of us was prepared for intercourse. We would wrestle around, get pretty hot and then stop. We gradually stopped seeing each other, not for any specific reason. Later, when I was in the Marine Corps, I learned she had been killed in an alley, in a knife fight, defending her girlfriend, a sex worker whom she had been protecting.

After quitting school I joined the Marine Corps where I had to confront the question of whether I was homosexual or not. On a form at the induction center I wrestled with that question and answered no. However, soon after boot camp I met another new black Marine and developed a crush that wasn't acted on until months later and then only furtively and clumsily. Later I came across other Marines who were sexually attracted to men. My fear of discovery prevented me from seeking out any relationships with them.

My coming out as a sexual being was there in the Far East like a lot of other Marines. We visited sex workers to confirm our manliness and caught our first sexually transmitted diseases and made babies with women we would never marry and bragged about it. We were young, we were Marines. It was still risky business, but so was being in the Marine Corps. The male bonding that military training and preparation afforded opened new avenues for intimacy and male trust. Even with this intimacy and trust the desire for physical intimacy remained.

In my last year in the Marine Corps I fell absolutely in love with one of my former girlfriends and became engaged. Our relationship at first dispelled my sense of otherness. We married after my discharge from the Marine Corps. Our child was born later that year. It was a short time after that I had to acknowledge that I still had strong sexual attraction to men. It was New Years Eve. My wife was visiting her family. I was coming home from work and felt some one looking at me. I looked back. I kept on walking. He followed me. I slowed down to find out what he wanted. I learned what "cruising" was.

From that experience I began learning the difference between sex between a man and woman and between man and a man. I learned that there was a significant difference in my responses and the kind of pleasure available. I had to question why this form of pleasure was forbidden. I also realized that I didn't feel that I had done anything wrong. I knew that I had broken the rules but I began to see that the rules did not create enough space for me to understand who I was. I realized that I was going to have to create the space that would allow me to discover who I might be.

PART THREE/**ARCHETYPES IN THE CONTEXT OF THE PRESENT:**
LIBERATING RISK AND PRAXIS

In the following pages of my journal, a day in the life of constructing critical intelligence in encounters with AIDS, I draw upon the archetypes of liberating love inspired by my family's ability to risk loving strangers and the existential/experiential critical street wisdom I learned in taking carefully considered risks. The intentional employment of my personal archaeology in the present, in the context of my living and dying, helps to remind me of the concrete value of these memories. Loving strangers, my first foster mother's loving of a foreigner, my natural mother's love of my father, my foster mother's love of me, enables me to enter into the intimacy of stranger penetrating my body with strange fluids and supports me while I construct new street wisdom in observation and talk with others facing death.

> *dripping from the shower as i dry myself while i look out the window closet butch queen that i am i dreamed of all these wonderful lounging clothes and cute boys running around giving me care, meals delivered, massages rendered, you know a life befitting retiring suffering royalty, with members of my court gathered around for those last important spiritually uplifting words but lo the good old days of AIDS are over and now we're like everybody else and my dreams of being the ultimate dying diva are shattered and i have to get up like everyone else and figure what am i going to eat this morning and oh hell there's no milk, look at the clock and no i'm going to be late and it's rush hour*

*and into the shower and what am i going to wear and where is
my wallet and i would look much better if these things on my
face and torso black purple swellings against a brown skin in an
incomplete mosaic would just leave—mirror image looks back
and says they didn't look at you before you had them and they
are not going to look now, get over it, and get out the door and
running downstairs checking everything like my keys after i have
locked the door, out into sunny California and its still windy and
fog and around fifty at the middle of june—and its like going to
work this going to the doctors—like i am this fabulous model
they want take pictures of—so onto the subway and some quiet
peace crossing the bay to Berkeley—which is like going to a
Brookline mixed with Cambridge fantasy except the shops are
much tackier—i do miss east coast shopping even after nineteen
years of being on the west coast—i go to the cancer center at
Alta Bates hospital for my chemo—the staff at the center are
waiting for me—at least i do have an appointment—they have
just moved from a smaller older part of the complex into a
newly built facility post-modern comfortable airy social almost—when i first started going they had just moved in—it was
weird they had not got their routines down—so there were mix-
ups mistakes that you knew/hoped would work themselves
out—but the competency of the staff worked to ensure that pa-
tients were minimally affected—but you always have time to
spare in the waiting room—learn so much about waiting waiting
in the waiting room—we see each other—some of us pay attention to the runnings of the place—we know this place has cost a
bundle and we're going to be the ones who pay for it one way or
another—it's a staff that really is into what they're doing—less
bureaucratic than most hospitals—the clients/patients are truly a
diverse mix of people—financial status means little—we know
the gig we are all fighting to maintain however much of our life
that medical and pharmaceutical science can squeeze out for us
with whatever measure of dignity that can be sustained—sometimes its warm and friendly, talkative—all ages of people are
there—older people women, men children families little children
little little children, young women, young men—many of us
aged through encounters that accelerated actions of our immune
systems cancer kaposis sarcoma breast, testicular ovarian brain
lymphomas uterine lung cancers and more—some with oxygen
tanks, canes, some blind—pain is like breathing some times—*

sometimes pain and breath are indistinguishable—sometimes pain is the price for living—and sometimes pain is living

we wait and we learn from watching each other—we wait and we learn courage from watching each other—we know we are paying for this new facility—or our insurance companies or both and the government—its an enormous investment—this facility—it eats savings and inheritances—we invest a lot in the extension of life, both corporately and individually—this extended, sometimes painful life is very expensive—we pay expensive money for this—wisdom is constructed here—knowledge is constructed here and passed on—this is a good place—people care— i am lucky i have a good internist Roxanne Fiscella who knew one of the doctors here —he has been treating KS for ten years — he is caring and unsentimental —i learn much in being in his care —i am fortunate—i have and have had friends who suffered terribly from KS with unsympathetic doctors and ineffective bureaucracies—it's a funny crossroad—in as critical condition as someone may be, no matter how much pain we might be experiencing, some pain we will live with until we leave this life—it is one of those things you learn to live with—because at some point you can't talk about it anymore without causing more pain—we learn how to manage pain—we learn that pain is not the worst that can happen—we have lived through the worst that can happen—or so we thought—and then we learned there are an infinite number of shoes that will drop

we sit and wait patiently until an attendant ushers us into a room to give blood for the lab work and to get our vitals—we are then ushered back into the waiting room—recent issues of all kinds of magazines—we wait again—we are ushered into a room to see the doctor—there is always a wait here—in a room cold with a gurney a sink small cabinets an examining room— alone—for sometimes up to thirty minutes—the doctor comes in—examines your chart—goes over it with you— discusses options—you measure them—you make some decisions—cost and benefits—its always a trade off—this pain for that one—pain for time—intense time—you know there is only so much time—you know it is never coming back—injuring and sometimes killing one part of the body—to save another—we learn how to measure time it's a new career—this is important useful work—someone has to do it—human life is constructed out of work like this—out of knowledges that are produced by our pain—the cost of life is never cheap and we all must pay some portion of it for however much we have and might have of it—not all our learning will make us rich loving wealthy fulfilled alright—but our learning will contribute to life—depression pain fear make us make some sense out of this—we all bleed so that some one else may not experience as much pain and maybe will live longer—we don't do this out of altruism—we do it because we have few other or no better choices—it is our job

it is not only the medical and pharmaceutical knowledges that are constructed out of our time here—daughters and sons sitting with mothers and mothers and fathers of fathers and mothers— sitting with a growing terrible patience—needing their lover husband wife partner longtime companion friend baby momma poppa, brother, sister to just hold on, hold on as long as they can—silent prayer, tears, laughter, stroking, caressing—many are somebody to somebody else and that has an importance that witnessed can help someone else take another step—as painful as that may be—to the treatment room—actually a series of ten private hospital rooms—comfortable no tv's yet—we bring our books and magazines and settle in for the duration—iv's placed in our bodies in the best vein—we must be careful, the poison we are taking if it lands on the skin will burn to the bone and heals very very slowly and painfully—my skin has learned this— it must go directly into the vein—and when they are no longer serviceable—ports—permanent tanking up places in an accessible part of the bodies—we are cyborgs—as we lie down—taking up some of us for an hour some for two, some for four, some with family, some with friends, some alone, we socialize with the nurses—get to know them—they get to know us—we are in it together—just doing our job

we have to remember and realize everybody needs positive and encouraging attention to get the job done—a job we didn't particularly ask for—jesus wanted everybody to eat at the table with him—and had to describe the conditions that would support that eating—be like children practice forgiveness—continue to increase the domain of love—share and cooperate—do the

very best you can—love what gives you life love consciousness
memory and imagination with everything you've got—you've
got to remember there's room and nourishment for everybody
we have to become large enough to invite fundamentalists to the
table—and make sure there's something on the table they like to
eat— and at the same time make sure there's something we like
too—we've got to be fair—we have to share the attention—we
have to learn and teach how to give attention

SUMMARY

This paper puts personal and academic languages in conversation. For me, cultural analysis and religious reflection are deeply incarnated in personal narrative. Therefore, on the one hand I write to explain and interpret, on the other I write to share my story. By hiding the full identity of the author, especially relating to sexuality, the academy and its language too often obscure the personal journey of the author. The form of this chapter is itself a conversation between the academy and soul of the street. The purposes of Parts Two and Three are not only to give flesh to the theoretical framework, the bones (Part One); they are there so that you the reader will become part of the risky business of queer and colored humanity. I know it is a strange and unfamiliar journey for you but if we are to have conversation it is important for us to walk together and in each other's shoes. On this path at times I extend my own analysis and hermeneutic. At other times I listen and try to hear what you may be asking of me. Still other times, as you question me in the conversation, you are obligated to bring your own hermeneutic to the table.

The form of the journal does not follow academic prose styles but it is the literary form where liberating love and critical street wisdom speak through in my living and dying with the virus. Part of being free is to expose my self to you in my most intimate writing. Liberation is risky business. The courage we construct as queer colored men enables us to face the worst and move on. Religious reflection occurs in the facing of death. The language used is drop dead personal. Extending the dialogue between religious reflection and cultural analysis to include the spiritual victories of queer colored men means constructing common language that will include the stranger.

REFERENCES

My sources for this paper have been inferential rather than referential. As I mentioned above I have been influenced greatly by the use of narrative/autobiography by African-American queer authors to critically analyze their location and identity. Postmodern critical studies by gay authors have also influenced my methodology in this work.

Baldwin, James. 1956. *Giovanni's Room.* Dial Press first publisher 1956; New York: Dell Publishing.

———. 1985. *The Price of the Ticket.* New York: St. Martin's/ Marek.

Delany, Samuel R. 1993. *The Motion of Light in Water.* New York: NAL Penguin Inc.

McNeill, John J. 1995. *Freedom, Glorious Freedom: The Spiritual Journey to the Fullness of Life for Gays, Lesbians, and Everybody Else.* Boston: Beacon Press.

CULTURE AND POLITICS IN BLACK AND AFRICAN THEOLOGIES[1]

EDWARD P. ANTONIO

In this paper I do not offer an argument as such. What follows is rather a number of claims about the nature of the relationship between culture and politics as two constitutive aspects of all social formations. Taken together the claims I make provide the basis for an argument regarding some possible ways in which that relationship may be conceptualized.

I claim not only that culture is an essentially contestable idea and should therefore not be taken for granted, as it tends to be in theologies of protest, but also that every domain of cultural production is a space of struggle over hegemonic control and distribution of symbolic capital. Both the word "culture" and its signifieds represent differential or multiple sites of conflict about large questions of class position and social identities. In other words, there is no culture without politics. Cultural acts bear the inscription of political contestation. But in the same vein it must be acknowledged that the space of culture itself marks out the arena for political struggles.

I shall claim that the very act of defining "culture" is foregrounded in some field or another of cultural production which is always politically overdetermined; it is always already (by which I mean that human experience has no cultural outside) implicated in the space-time conjunctions of social and political positions which constitute the social structure. In order to demonstrate this I shall describe in some detail a famous debate between Black theology and African theology.

Defining culture is itself a cultural act which, as such, is never innocent but always entails a hegemonic claim. I use hegemony here to refer to the means by which a group of statements, a claim or a definition is endowed with the capacity—real or imagined—to dominate the symbolic and material processes of social understanding. Hegemony thus understood involves staking out a claim for discursive primacy and leadership. It is an expression of certain relations of power at the level of understanding, an idea perhaps akin to Marx's famous notion that the ruling ideas of an age are the ideas of its ruling classes. What is important here is the fact that hegemony signals how some ideas become dominant in a society and that the impact of these ideas is not purely notional since they reflect concrete social relationships. To claim, then, that defining culture is hegemonic is to recognize two important things: first, that culture by its very nature, being that region of life which shapes the form and content of human experience, is especially susceptible to hegemonization. Second, that this is because culture is the terrain of contestation for the control of human experience. Examples of this abound. When the New Political Right seeks to influence governments and societies to adopt a certain code of conduct or to have society ordered on a theocratic model it is expressing its desire to control life in terms of its beliefs and values. Or, to give another example, when western governments argue that liberal democracy is the best form of government they are putting forward an understanding of politics with far-reaching consequences for the organization not just of politics but of culture, too, as was once evidenced by the politically informed cultural differences between the then Soviet Union and western countries.

What makes culture so open to hegemonization is the way in which the symbols and meanings by which humans seek to guide their lives are always anchored in some system of discursive control so that those symbols and meanings are not left free-floating. This system of control is what gives the myths, stories and rituals of a culture their particular configuration, thus helping to differentiate it from other cultures. At one level the system appears natural, at least to the members of the culture which it embodies, for they are not only born and socialized into it but the rules by which it operates are largely implicit or eclipsed by the ideological nature of socialization itself. It is of course these hidden rules which are the substance of the system of control under discussion here. Their function is to regulate how the myths, stories, memories and ideas of a culture are defined and communicated, thus effectively establishing hegemonic claim in setting up the dominant modes of cultural self-understanding.

All this might seem abstract until it is remembered that the rules of a culture do not come into being, nor do they operate independently of the people whose culture they constitute. They are socially constructed but they also construct and shape the lives of those who produce them in the first place. The hegemony they represent is therefore a hegemony not of abstract rules or of a rarefied system but one of social relationships coded and expressed through them. Reference here to culture as socially produced should not of course blind us to the fact that members of a culture do not all participate to the same extent in shaping it. This is because access to cultural resources or to the power to manage them is not evenly distributed in the social structure. Those who own or preside over the means of cultural production (priests, educators, journalists, spirit mediums, artists, historians, etc.) have the power to define hegemonic practices within a culture.

This is true whether the space or field of cultural production within which culture is defined is art, literature or theology. To come at the issue of culture in this way is to problematize the category of "culture," to place a question mark over the notion that culture is a homogeneous totality un-problematically shared by all members of a class, race, ethnic or gender group. Stated somewhat crudely, my contention is that doing theology and defining culture are both cultural accomplishments caught up in the identities of those whose acts they are. Those identities are dispersed (in Foucault's sense) in and between different social and political *interests*. Any claim therefore to speak on behalf of the poor or to represent their culture must always be rendered transparent (i.e., made to reveal whose interests it represents and by what authority), not only because such claims often involve either assimilating the categories of the culture of the poor into the discursive universe of the elite (as when middle class Black and African theologians pretend that they really share the culture of Blacks in the ghetto) or imposing the categories of elite culture on the poor (the role played by the vanguard in the Second International vis-à-vis the working class), but also because making the voice of the poor heard through the mediation of the elite requires acts of "position-taking" which represent political intervention. Speaking on behalf of the poor consists in carving out a double political space: that of the one claiming to represent the poor and that of the poor themselves. The idea that in cultural terms Black or African theologians do not necessarily represent those on whose behalf they claim to speak will, I am certain, strike concerned parties as tendentious; but that is precisely part of what I shall suggest here.

The appropriation of forms of meaning, life-styles, and social identities and the articulation of strategies of resistance within theologies of protest were for a long time premised on the supposition of a single experience of oppression. When that was challenged by womanists and feminists the terrain of struggle was redefined to accommodate their interests. But incorporating women into political culture did not go far enough. For to redefine the terrain of struggle in order merely to accommodate the concerns of the oppressed in terms of dominant discourses is not necessarily the same thing as opening it up in order to show how different experiences of oppression articulate with or relate to each other. A theory of articulation (i.e., a theory of how different moments or aspects of the social structure are linked or related to each other) is important because on it (or its lack) depends how social formations are understood. When the Marxism of the Second International defined oppression strictly in terms of class, its understanding of the nature of social formations was very largely shaped by its conceptualization of the relationships between social groups, the means and relations of production, and above all by the ontological role of the economy in determining those relations. Similarly, when Black theology spoke about race as the object of its critique it presupposed some form of articulation between race and the topography of forces represented by the American polity or, better still, by American political culture. In other words notions like class, race, and sex are explanatory variables in the configuration of "the social." They refer to patterns of relationships, to practices and institutions which constitute social reality by the manner of their articulation. A crucial part of my argument is that this social reality is not given but results from the very nature of social struggles. The social is discursively constituted as a relative aggregate of struggles. Relative because no struggle, however revolutionary, is total or absolute. Aggregate because the social is a site of many struggles. Thus to say that race, class, and gender allow for acts of resistance or affirmation in the context of certain relationships, institutions, and practices is to characterize the historically articulated or relational nature of social formations. There are a number of ideas here to which I shall return: the idea that social reality is discursively constituted; the notion of the historicity or relativity of struggles and finally that of the aggregate character of all social positionalities.

In the debate that I describe below my concern is to highlight how the social is falsely presented as though it were made up of two disarticulated or unrelated segments: politics and culture.

The problem that will serve as a point of departure for my argument is the division of the African theological project between two competing methodologies, arising from a supposed incompatibility between the Africanist/culturalist and Black theology/Black consciousness accounts of the form African Christianity ought to take. There have been, as I shall show, two basic charges leveled at Black theology by some culturalists: one political and the other theological. Politically and historically, the point has been made that Black theology is as foreign to Africa as Western theology itself and that, as such, it cannot be accurately described as African theology. Furthermore, African theologians operating in countries where the problem of racism—at least in terms of black/white relations—has not been an urgent question have tended to see the agenda proposed by Black theology as outside their search for an indigenous theology; that is, they perceive a certain "incommensurability" between their project and that of Black theology. It is this aspect of the problem which will be one of the primary concerns of this paper.

Theologically, John Mbiti and Byang Kato have, in their different ways, attacked Black theology as divisive and as thus impeding the process of reconciliation engendered by the Gospel.[2] In a public lecture, in 1975,

Mbiti in particular argued that Black theology is based on the spirit not of joy, but of bitterness. Both these writers practice what I have called in this paper the culturalist approach. By this I mean the tendency in African theology to make paradigmatic use of the notion of culture to set the agenda for theology.

Central to the manner in which the debate has been structured is a problematical way of thinking about culture and its relationship to politics. The disagreement between Black and African theologies is basically about "theorizing" the extent to which perceptions of the relationship between culture and politics shape different conceptions of the nature and tasks of theology; it is about the conflict between conceptions of the nature of social formations and hegemonic imprints on the theological accounts of social experience which these formations bring into being. We need not suppose that either of these theologies has a fully worked out theory of the assumed objects of their discourse—"the social," "the political," "the cultural," etc.— for the argument implied in my remarks here to work. In fact, if space allowed, it would not be difficult to show that it is precisely the inability of either theology to speak in a theoretically sophisticated fashion about culture and politics which has resulted in dualistic formulation of the relationship between the two. Here I shall not pursue the problem of theory in Black and African theologies. I simply take the terms of the debate at face value and interrogate their ways of understanding the social.

The seduction of dualism to which these theologies have succumbed demands a critique of essentialism, which is, of course, always the price of such dualism. Dualism logically entails essentialism.[3] The point of my paper, then, is to draw attention to a false problem in the conception of social formations proffered by the two theologies, thereby illustrating that theological recourse to the categories of culture and politics can be ideologically dangerous if the logic of social reality is offered as fixity rather than complexity.

Perhaps an appropriate point at which to begin the discussion is with the account Black theology itself has attempted to give of the nature of African theology and the response to it by its critics. My strategy here is to approach the discussion through a set of representative figures whose writings have been instrumental in shaping the debate between the two theologies. The writings of these theologians can be divided into five main groups: those that are more or less against African theology (Buthelezi, Boesak); the African response, itself highly critical of Black theology, offered by Mbiti, Dickson and Kato; the South African response to the African critique of Black theology (Tutu); the sympathetic appropriation of Black theology by some African theologians (Magesa and Nthamburi); and finally, the Afro-

American critique of African theology (Cone). In this paper I shall leave out of consideration the writings of Cone, Magesa, Nthamburi, Tutu, and Kato. I shall discuss those of Buthelezi, Boesak, Mbiti and Dickson.

SOUTH AFRICAN BLACK THEOLOGIANS ASSESS AFRICAN THEOLOGY
MANAS BUTHELEZI

I shall start, then, by discussing a criticism which is frequently brought against the culturalist approach by other African theologians, notably those based in South Africa.

One of the foremost proponents of South African Black theology is Manas Buthelezi. Buthelezi sees the difference between Black and African theologies as a methodological one. He holds that a crucial element of what we mean by theology is method itself. It follows from this that the phrase "Black theology" indicates a particular option of theological method vis-a-vis so called "African theology" (Buthelezi 1973, 30). To be sure, both types of theology are indigenous to South Africa. The contrast between them, however, derives from two approaches which have generally been used to represent their respective structures: the first, Buthelezi refers to as the ethnographic approach, what we have called in this work the culturalist approach; the second he terms the anthropological approach. This is a distinction which belongs to the debate about method in social anthropology. But Buthelezi himself does not acknowledge this fact. Nevertheless, the general outline of his critique is similar to Mudimbe's interrogation of ethnography as part of wider epistemological practice, i.e., that of classification of peoples through race and culture.[4] Another South African Black theologian who uses the term anthropology with regard to the debate between Black and African theologies is Desmond Tutu (Tutu 1978, 368). But his use is very different from that of Buthelezi. For Tutu, anthropology appears to be the same thing as ethnography. For example, he accuses African theology of being too anthropological in its approach, and cites as evidence of this what he sees as its excessive concern with the past and its lack of a diachronic (my term) attitude towards that past revealed in such treatment.

Buthelezi, on the other hand, uses anthropology, it seems in two senses: to refer to the human being as such, that is the human subject, and to refer to the human being in a social and political context. He explains this methodological divergence in the following words: "The distinction centres on whether the point of departure in our theological method should be an ethnographic reconstruction of the African past or dialogue with the present day anthropological realities in South Africa" (Buthelezi 1973, 30-1). Buthelezi says that his aim is not to call into question the possibility of ethnographic reconstruction, but rather its validity as a starting point in theological reflection. He has two basic criticisms of this approach: its "tendency towards cultural objectivism," and "its tendency to overlook present day realities." As far as the first is concerned, Buthelezi argues that the culturalists place excessive emphasis on the African world-view, "as if it were an isolated and independent entity apart from the present anthropological reality of the African man." Moreover, "The quest for an indigenous theology seems to be understood as originating from the problem of a conflict between two world-views: the European and the African" (32). But, in Buthelezi's view, the difficulty here is that the human factor is relegated to the background. On this model, theology is conceived not in terms of its significance for humans but as a "problem of epistemological entities; of fixed impersonal data—things 'out there,'" namely, the body of categories for interpreting the universe. These categories are static entities which form something which can be located, studied and described—thanks to ethnography!" (32) We find here not only what seems to be an implicit rejection of an essentialist account of Africanity but perhaps one of the earliest critiques of the "othering" function of objectivism in anthropology as a discipline.[5]

The second problem is not unrelated to the first. Here Buthelezi's contention is basically that African theology, as distinct from Black theology, tends to romanticize the African past, again at the expense of the present. Buthelezi does not deny that the African past and world-view have a legitimate contribution to make. His point is rather that "there is a difference between psychologically living in the past in order to escape from the harsh realities of the present which one cannot face squarely at the moment, and living in the past because it can give the spiritual and physical bread for the day" (32).

It seems here that Buthelezi is distinguishing between two attitudes towards the past. One attitude refuses to connect that past with the present, and the other uses it to make sense of the present. What is common to both is that they are instrumentalist in the sense that they depend upon a politics of the past. In other words, the indigeneity of theology which the culturalist theologians are after should not be looked for simply in the old institutions and patterns of behavior, because the realization of black humanity cannot be confined to that. Rather, what is worthwhile in the African past will be activated only as Blacks experience emancipation in the present (Buthelezi 1973, 34). For Buthelezi, then, the project of reconstructing memory is subordinate to that of establishing the dignity of blacks here and now; indeed, the latter serves as a condition for the former. A man who is not yet "psychologically redeemed" is a man easily enslaved by the past. Thus if the Gospel is to be relevant to blacks it must aim to restore and rebuild their self-respect and self-confidence. In a paradoxical remark Buthelezi says, "If the Gospel means anything, it must save the black man from his own blackness," i.e., from translating the symbolism of the color of his skin into a sign of non-being (34-5).

Having thus dealt with the problem for African theology of the past, and of its dependence on the culturalist approach, Buthelezi now turns to the anthropological approach. The starting point here has already been hinted at in the foregoing remarks, namely the existential situation of blackness, for it is in this situation that blacks meet and are met by God, that they are reconstituted anew in Christ through God's forgiving love. Blackness matters because it is the all-encompassing medium of the existence which defines and shapes all of one's existential possibilities (Buthelezi 1973, 33). Perhaps he calls this approach anthropological because he is after a theology which will take seriously the problem of, and the need for, a theory of the black subject. Anthropology in this context describes a theory of the nature of the human being. The difference between a theory of this kind and ethnography (cf. Geertz [1988]) appears to lie in their historical orientation (ethnography, as understood by Buthelezi, seems to be about describing and analyzing small scale or so-called primal collectivities), and at the level of political consciousness. But Buthelezi himself does not tell us how the alleged historical character of his theological anthropology produces or leads to Black Consciousness as a form of political resistance.

ALLAN BOESAK

Buthelezi's is not the only critique of the culturalist model to emanate from South Africa. For example, in *Black Theology Black Power* (1978), Allan Boesak distinguishes between contextual and indigenous theologies by identifying the former with Black theology and characterizing the latter as descriptive of a white, western version of African theology. This indigenous theology, says Boesak, pretends to be politically neutral and ambivalent towards white racism. Hence its acceptance by white South African theologians (Boesak 1985, 117). Besides, there are two further problems connected with the term indigenization itself: one is how it was used by the advocates of apartheid to promote the fragmentation and isolation of groups along racial lines. Thus in this context, its theological utility tends towards the dangers of what Boesak calls "a homeland theology."[6] The other problem is that "Indigenization has too much of a colonial aura clinging to it and has been used too one-sidedly in the sense of response to the gospel in terms of traditional culture." It is interesting to contrast, very briefly, Boesak's reservations about indigenization with African theologians like Kwesi Dickson. For Boesak it is the negative political overtones which attach to the notion of indigenization in South Africa which make it suspect. Dickson, however, is concerned with the epistemological or conceptual limits of that notion. Thus he poses the question of alternative possibilities concerning, for example, the materialization of the possibility of a conceptually more adequate model of theological reflection than that of indigenization itself. Dickson does not address the problem of how such models can avoid legitimating a tribalistic theology (on the danger of which see Tutu [1978, 367]). In other words, does not the success of a process of indigenization in a particular culture beg the question of how the product of such a particularized process can escape being a tribal theology?

Discussing the possibility, nature, and status of an African philosophy, L. Keita makes a similar point when he says that the institutionalization of tribal or ethnic beliefs in Africa would tend towards the danger of "ontological" distinctions within the state (we could put Church in place of State here) and thus encourage tribalism and ideological fragmentation (Keita 1987, 39). The issue here is not that responding to the Gospel within the political context of apartheid is incompatible with responding to the Gospel within the structures of traditional consciousness. Boesak wants to affirm the African identity of Black theology but he wants to do this in such a way that the struggle for justice and human flourishing, which is the goal of this justice, and which is characteristic of the objectives of Black theology, is highlighted (Boesak 1985, 13-14). He sees the differences in these two modes of theological reflection in terms of the criteria for the difference between authentic and inauthentic theology. Thus he writes:

> A contextual [i.e., Black] theology must be authentic. It must not yield to uncritical accommodation, becoming a "cultural theology" or a religion of culture. An authentic contextual theology is a prophetic one; it is not merely an exhumation of the corpses of tradition as African theology was sometimes understood to be, but attempts to make critical use of those traditions from the past which can play a humanizing and revolutionizing role in contemporary society. It takes from the past what is good, thereby offering a critique of the present and opening perspectives for the future. (Boesak 1985)

The above quotation contains a two-pronged attack at two different kinds of theologies which have two different goals, but are bound together by what we might call their "conservative" use of the idea of culture. Thus Boesak's use of the phrases "cultural theology" and "religion of culture" is on the one hand an implicit reference to South African civil religion, in which the Dutch Reformed Church, for the black part of which Boesak is a minister, has played no small supportive part.[7] On the other hand, those same phrases serve as a critique of the direction in which African theology is moving. For to speak of indigenization in a context in which that notion is interpreted within the practice of a civil religion which justifies the oppression of blacks is, ultimately, to surrender the terms of African protest to an oppressive theology. By thus implicitly linking the issue of "cultural theology" to that of civil religion, Boesak enables us to put in a wider critical framework the whole idea of indigenization and thus to raise the following question. Does not African theology's (speaking now of African theology outside South Africa) "apparent"[8] separation of politics from culture, in countries where both are united and "ideologically" organized in the phenomenon of a bourgeois nationalism expressive of State interests, actual or utopic, imply an "ideological" conjunction? I mean by "ideological conjunction" the connection between African intellectuals and the State and its functionaries. In this sense there is a close parallel in what I am saying here with Gramsci's theory of the relation between hegemony and state domination. Gramsci distinguishes between, on the one hand, civil society—i.e., the realm of the private, and on the other, political society—i.e., the State. The function of both these realms is to ensure hegemonic control by the dominant group and "direct domination" through the State. According to Gramsci, "The functions in question are precisely organizational and connective. The intellectuals are the dominant group's 'deputies' exercising the subaltern functions of social hegemony and political government" (Gramsci 1971, 12). This raises the important question of whether or not this role is played by all intellectuals. It is important, however, to distinguish two things here: it is one thing to say that, because all intellectuals are by virtue of their social position privileged, they can be co-opted by or choose to offer their services as intellectuals to the State. It is another thing to say that all intellectuals are necessarily implicated in the work of the State because of their status as intellectuals. The former position allows the intellectual the freedom to choose either to be co-opted or offer her or his service to the State. Here whether or not an intellectual serves the State is a matter of ideological choice which depends on the intellectual's own sensitivity, or lack thereof, to the social reality around her or him. This position leaves room for critique of ideology in the work of intellectuals, whereas if all intellectuals are condemned to be State functionaries because of their status, critique of ideology becomes pointless. The point of my argument is not that proponents of African theology are linked to dominant groups and those of Black theology are not. What I want to claim, rather, is that the manner in which African theologians have set up their theological agenda on the basis of the paradig-

matic importance of culture rather than politics involves an implicit ideological choice which is less sensitive to African political realities and which
therefore has, consciously or otherwise, resulted in a pretended apoliticism.

THE ALLEGED APOLITICISM OF AFRICAN THEOLOGY

It is therefore interesting that the charge of apoliticism which both Boesak
and Buthelezi make against African theology has also been echoed by theologians who would not technically call themselves Black theologians and
who are based outside South Africa. One such theologian is Mercy Amba
Oduyoye. It is her conviction that African theology will be irrelevant to its
context if it fails to advert to the socio-political problems therein. And, even
more to the point, the ambiguous nature of missionary Christianity in yield-
ing to more indigenous forms is, she warns (rather like Boesak), not in itself
a guarantee against the hazard of African Christianity becoming established,
respectable and co-opted and thus reducing the symbols of the faith to
"mere talismans and hollow incantations" (Oduyoye 1986, 9). In a similar
vein, Adrian Hastings has observed that "A straight appeal to withdrawal
from this-worldly concerns is indeed a widespread phenomenon in African
Christianity as elsewhere" (Hastings 1976, 93), and that the African Church
has identified with oppressive regimes when, for example, some of its leadership has been "effectively encapsulated within the elite, the racial minori-
ty" (83-5). Interestingly, however, Hastings also attributes a certain political
consciousness—with regard, for example, to the rejection of racism—to the
phenomenon of independency among the so-called "Spirit-Churches." He
does this by arguing that racism cannot be entirely discounted as one of the
secular factors which gave rise to these Churches (24), a view which is supported by Richard Sklar when he says that messianic nationalism in Africa
sought to defend racial dignity (Sklar 1985, 12). It is against the background
of these charges of apoliticism that we must seek to understand African theology's account and critique of Black theology, and it is this that we must
now address.

THE AFRICAN RESPONSE TO SOUTH AFRICAN BLACK THEOLOGY
KWESI DICKSON

The critique of Black theology I shall consider is that of Kwesi Dickson. The
difference between Black and African theologies is explained by Dickson in
terms of the complexity of Africa's social realities. He admits that, generally,
the charge of apoliticism is valid (Dickson 1984, 131-2). There are two reasons for this. The first is linked to his own reservations about the term indigenization. Dickson attacks indigenization for its assumption, as he sees it,
that there is a core of the gospel uncontaminated by culture to which

Africans have direct access in their search for indigeneity. Here he complains against African theology's conceptualization of the theological task as "nothing more than indigenizing in the sense of replacing Western cultural incidentals with African cultural elements." Although Dickson is not explicit on the relationship between indigenization and apoliticism in African theology, the implication of his argument seems to be that too heavy a focus on culture detracts from political engagement. The result is a theology which talks about culture as though there were no such thing as a politics of the cultural.

The second reason for African theology's apparent lack of political commitment, and thus for the popularity of the culturalist approach, is the relative absence of racial conflict in many parts of Africa (Dickson 1984).[9] Dickson rejects what he sees as Buthelezi's view that the culturalist approach was instigated by Europeans. In his view, it was the fact that the early missionaries denigrated African culture and beliefs which led to the awareness among Africans that theological reflection could not properly proceed without taking African culture seriously: "Hence to say, as Buthelezi does, that the cultural emphasis in theologising in Africa is a European introduction is to ignore the long history of reactions, from the cultural standpoint, to Christian evangelism from the inception of missions in Africa" (Dickson 1984, 133).

But does the polarization between Black and African theologies mean that there is no common ground between them? This question, says Dickson, cannot be answered without posing further questions about the proper manner of characterizing the context which defines the conditions for the two forms of theological discourse presently in vogue in Africa, that is, questions about the appropriateness of defining the nature of that discourse in terms of either politics or culture. According to Dickson, the culturalist approach cannot afford to overlook socio-political problems for two closely related reasons: in the first instance, "social concern" is central to the African sense of community wherein no social or political oppression is permitted. In the second, this "social concern" is a demand imposed by the fact that black rule in modern Africa has at times been unjust and oppressive. And, consequently, engaging in theological reflection aside from socio-political concerns is apt to lead both to an inauthentic cultural approach and to disobedience to the scriptural demand to do justice for the poor (Dickson 1984, 134-6). To be sure, social and political injustice are not in themselves exhaustive of the totality of African reality, although it is in fact the intention of the culturalist model to embrace all of that reality. The point of balance between these two concerns—politics and culture—is established as a product of the task of theology itself. Thus, urges Dickson, theology judges as well as affirms, and "what it affirms ranges from the African humanity to the Christ; and there is much in the religio-cultural reality which could facilitate actualization of the twin roles of judgment and affirmation" (Dickson 1984, 136-7). In other words, African theology has within itself the resources to articulate a critical awareness of its social problematic. At the same time, however, even the diversity of African social reality cannot ultimately justify the tension between Black and African theologies because, as far as Dickson is concerned, "Africa's basic contradiction is cultural." Stated another way, there is no necessary tension between the removal of social contradictions and the acquisition of the cultural freedom rendered possible by the reaffirmation of Africanness, since social freedom itself belongs to the "wider freedom which is cultural." It is interesting to observe here that Dickson rationalizes African culture by describing it as the "wider freedom," and although he subjects politics to it he is not making the important point, which we shall ourselves make later on, that the dialectic between contextualization and liberation is ill-formulated when cast in terms of the pseudo-distinction between culture and politics. Presumably this means that the "wider freedom" should be accepted as it is, i.e., be declared rational. If so, then Dickson needs to defend his remark against the charge of conservatism.[10] Over and above this, Dickson begs the question as to whether his identification of culture with freedom does not in fact turn culture into an essentially political problem, that is to say, whether his cultural reductionism does not end up achieving the very opposite of its professed intention. If the cultural status quo is rationalized in the name of its being a wider freedom, then has not Dickson simply problematized culture politically? Who defines what this freedom is? And do the various groups in the cultural "whole" enjoy that freedom to the same extent? How is it possible in a continent riddled with corruption, social injustice and military rule to attribute freedom to culture? These questions are ignored by Dickson. He does not even bother to discuss how, given both the largely negative impact of the colonial process on African cultures and the fact that before and after colonialism African cultures themselves were not entirely innocent of repressive, if not oppressive tendencies, we can speak of culture as representing the "wider freedom." Coupled with this neglect of these important questions is the issue of the status of the critical awareness which Dickson claims for African theology. Is this critical awareness or judgment as he calls it, not blunted by the very possibility of its cultural determination?

The question to be briefly addressed now concerns the validity of Dickson's account of Black theology's critique of African theology. It can be suggested here that his account, embodied in his critique of Buthelezi, is not well-founded. He appears to think that the latter rejects the role of culture in reconstructing African theology; yet as we saw, Buthelezi's quarrel is not with the problem of culture as such but with the problem of ethnography, with the extent to which African theology has uncritically bought into its representations of Africans, and, in particular, with the issue of posing a foundationalist epistemology—albeit one formulated in the categories of ethnography—as a basic framework for delineating the character of African theology as a function of this epistemological foundationalism.

This is of course not to suggest that Buthelezi's arguments against the culturalist approach are themselves not open to criticism. It can be argued, for example, that by focusing, as he does, almost exclusively on the faults of ethnography in its rendition of African culture, he runs the risk of identifying the former with the latter—ethnography with culture. If culture and ethnography are conflated two rather unfortunate results accrue. First, culture is reduced to a set of techniques for analyzing primal collectivities. The problem here is that although one can still critique the politics of the uses of those techniques as formerly applied to African societies one cannot thereby legitimately claim to have critiqued the politics of culture for culture, is a much larger reality than a set of techniques for describing non-western societies. Furthermore, to understand culture as being identical to the operations of any discipline is to collapse human experience into nothing more than a theoretical construct, the existential implications of which then become purely academic. One of Buthelezi's criticisms of the use, by culturalist theologians, of the ethnographic approach is precisely that they objectivize African experience in terms of theoretical constructs. Yet Buthelezi's own remarks are open to the same charge.

Second, because the reduction of culture to the undesirable effects of ethnographic practice leaves one with a largely theoretical understanding of culture (i.e., culture as a methodological projection of the principles of ethnography onto a space designated as "primitive," primal, or non-western), one is left with no choice but to regard politics as the only legitimate arena for human life.

Certainly Buthelezi (and also Boesak) does not consciously intend to write off the totality of African culture in the name of the sins of old-style anthropologists who romanticized African institutions of the past. Indeed he believes, again like Boesak, that African culture has a role to play in shaping black people's experience. But this is nothing more than a gesture in the direction of tradition. There is almost nothing in Buthelezi's writings which shows us how African culture, or which aspects of it, can be usefully appropriated for black experience today. The point remains that the context within which culture can meaningfully inform contemporary black experience is circumscribed by the political boundaries of that experience. Culture on this view does not have an autonomous identity positively related to other dimensions of experience. Its identity is largely negative and subordinate to the political ontology of blackness. The trouble with Buthelezi's view of blackness is that he sometimes writes as though blackness were a socially disembodied set of existential possibilities. But what is blackness if not an ensemble of memories and cultural practices embodied in the political experience of racial oppression on the one hand, and recalled in resistance as an affirmation of African humanity on the other?

So, then, just as Dickson makes culture the controlling category for the analysis of all African experience, so too does Buthelezi make politics the focus of all such analysis. But whose politics? Buthelezi does not seem to be aware that blackness as a political category encompassess a wide range of experiences of social reality, not all of which dovetail with each other. Blackness cannot, for example, mean the same thing to black women as it does to black men. The latter often appeal to African traditions and culture (and thus in a certain sense to blackness) to justify their ill-treatment of women. Similarly, middle class black experience cannot be straightforwardly equated with the experience of the vast majority of blacks in the ghettos. The mistake of Buthelezi is, therefore, that he fails to identify different levels of blackness and the ways in which these yield different levels of both cultural and political experience for different groups of people in the social structure.

Finally, Buthelezi's strictures against the culturalist approach leave us with no idea as to how an understanding of culture not influenced by the discourse of anthropology as a discipline (i.e., by ethnography) might look, and whether it might not lead to a politically sensitive hermeneutic.

I said earlier that the debate I describe above poses a false problem. I now wish to conclude this paper by illustrating my point. I wish to suggest that the separation between culture and politics recalls a parallel problem in the history of Socialist theory, particularly in the arguments which shaped the Second International. In those arguments the variegated character of the "social" manifested itself as the tension between the "base" and the "superstructure," between the assertion of economic determinism on the one hand and the autonomy of the political or the cultural on the other. As Ernesto Laclau and Chantal Mouffe have argued, the trouble with the dominant paradigm of the Second International was that it presupposed the social as a closed space somehow determined by the necessary laws of the economy (Laclau and Mouffe 1985). The economy offered itself as a unified objective totality which explained social reality and its historical development. Politics, religion and culture expressed, by contrast, the subjective manifestations of pre-determined relations of production. In fact, the economy was both the content of the "social" and its explanatory principle. As is well known, the "superstructure" had no independent explanatory value except perhaps only in so far as it was part of the explained. It was this understanding which gave rise to the notion of Marxism as a science. Of course it was not until the work of Antonio Gramsci, who more than anyone else in Marxism was sufficiently sensitive to the reality of culture, that new and more complex ways of conceptualizing social explanation in Marxism began to emerge. Today orthodox Marxism is in crisis as its categories of analysis, especially that of class, have been confronted by the reality of New Social Movements (the feminist/womanist, peace, ecological and civil rights movements, to name but a few) which seek to render experiences of oppression, power, and resistance in ways which crisscross the whole spectrum of the "social" from culture to economics, from politics to ecology. Where before it was believed that social reality could be explained univocally, now different and even conflicting experiences of marginality impose the need for a multivocal hermeneutic of the social. All this of course has an important bearing on the theme of this book, dealing as it does with the question of the role of cultural analysis in religious reflection. It raises once more the whole problem of social explanation. In what ways is the "cultural" a basis for explaining the social, and to what extent does it articulate or link up with other explanatory elements such as the political, the economy, etc.?

As we saw above, Kwesi Dickson believes that it is the wider framework within which politics is subsumed and he does so without specifying *whose* culture constitutes that framework. He assumes, clearly despite his best intentions, not only that there is one African culture but also that what he means by culture is acceptable to those concerned with the analysis of African culture. For him culture is a master identity which informs and shapes all other activities. Indeed, culture is described as the wider freedom. On both accounts he fails to be sensitive to what I have called the need for a multivocal hermeneutic of the social, which is made possible not only by the increasing awareness in Africa as elsewhere of the cultural diversity of the continent, but also by recognition of the fact that the logic of the social is complex. The dualism between culture and politics at the heart of this debate overlooks the fact that both these aspects of the social structure depend upon the relationship (articulation) of different social forces in civil society. And of course we know that civil society is not apolitical. If it is the space in which the making of culture takes place (and there can be no doubt that it is), then it must also formally be the locus of conflicting struggles over hegemonic claims about which meanings of culture will define the space of civility and which practices will serve as the dominant ones. To put it another way, these struggles are always about opening up or blocking possibilities for establishing what counts as culture and what does not, a process marked by the exclusion of meanings that are important to those without the symbolic capital to enforce their desires. This is a process in which, even at the level of analysis, politics and culture serve as different names for different parts of the same social topography.

The emphasis on culture at the expense or politics and vice-versa, robs the social of its complexity and methodologically leads to reductionism. For example, in Dickson's thought culture is both the content of African experience and the principle of its explanation because it is ultimately the overarching structure of reality of African experience. Yet just how content and principle of explanation can be coextensive is a question Dickson never addresses. That is, his disagreement with Buthelezi whilst acknowledging the importance of the "political" in fact elides the "political" both socially and methodologically. Socially because he incorporates it into the cultural on the basis of a claim that the cultural is a wider kind of freedom, and methodologically because he has no theory of articulation which makes it possible to account for any posited relationship between content and explanation. This reductionism conceals an important aspect—the fact that culture can be understood in three different ways: as life-world, *sitzm leben* or social-location; as an object of analysis; and as a tool of analysis. Collapsing these three into each other deprives theological reflection of any way of detecting and exposing ideology. The point here is this: Dickson's claim that culture is the larger reality (compared to politics) implicates him in a political move which involves eliding the political itself. It involves a kind of negative affirmation of the political in which the latter is either nothing but an epiphenomenal expression of cultural experience or a less important part of social reality. Culture is thus given a role formally not dissimilar to that orthodox Marxism once gave to the economy.

That this is a political move can be shown in two ways. First, by pointing to its refusal to distinguish difference between content and explanation, which is evident in the ideological slippage from a description of African culture (as basically religious) into a moral/political claim that legitimizes culture as freedom. This claim masquerades as historical/anthropological explanation by insinuating the existence of an idealized pre-colonial African culture in which there was no exploitation. There is in fact nothing historical about this. It is just another moral claim made to support a previous one. Equally, there is nothing anthropological about it. No such society has yet been found anywhere, at least not in the post-Adamic world.

The second way in which Dickson's statements about culture are politically implicated involves what Bourdieu has called position and position-takings. Bourdieu defines position-takings and the space constituted by

them as "the structured set of the manifestations of the social agents involved in the field—literary or artistic works, of course, but also political
acts or pronouncements, manifestos or polemics" (Bourdieu 1993, 30). In
other words, each social agent involved in cultural production takes a position relative to the positions of other agents in the cultural field (literary,
artistic etc.). Bourdieu understands the cultural field as two related domains:
the field of forces, and the field of struggles. The latter tends either to con-
serve or to transform the former. The struggles which operate on the cultural field are determined by various strategies that are employed to improve
position-takings. Obviously this requires deployment not only of strategies
but also of power. "In other words, the field of cultural production is the site
of struggles in which what is at stake is to impose the dominant definition of
the writer" (Bourdieu 1993, 42); or again, "The fact remains that the cultural producers are able to use the power conferred on them . . . to put forward
a critical definition of the social world" (Bourdieu 1993, 44).

There can of course be no doubt that both Dickson and Buthelezi are
putting forward definitions of the social world via their positions. They both
possess symbolic capital (the cultural/political wherewithal) from which
they derive the power to do so. The question which all this raises is that of
the political relevancy of their projects. Politics here is not about party politics or ideological affiliation in a narrow sense; as Nicholas Thomas has put
it, politics in this context is about how "some intellectual projects address
the circumstances of scholars and their audiences in the world far more directly than others, in aspiring to help both parties to account for the cultural
and political predicaments that surround us" (Thomas 1994, 20). Position-
takings which advance some or other form of understanding of the social
cannot but be implicated in the question of their political relevance; they
cannot but bear the imprint of a certain politics of analysis which is either
enablingly worldly or disablingly so. They always beg the question of their
own worldliness, their own politics. Religious reflection always entails position-takings and always involves claims (sometimes explicit and sometimes
implicit) about the nature of the social. Dickson's identification of African
culture with freedom is a good example. It is one which raises an important
question which I have already hinted at: whose culture does Dickson represent? On whose behalf does he make his claim? Are we to take it that the
freedom of which he speaks is characteristic of all African cultures past and
present? If religious reflection fails, as has much of African theology, to advert to these questions it will prove rather difficult to be on guard against
sacralizing the social or any aspect of it. It will escape our attention (which
is to say we shall easily succumb to the seduction of ideology) that cultures
are not made in heaven. They are always the product of our dirty (theologi-

cally, we would say sinful) hands. It is clear from what I have said so far that Dickson cannot be speaking for the poor and marginalized of Africa, for they do not experience the realities that surround them as enabling or empowering. It is of course easy for peoples whose cultures have been denigrated, demonized and rejected to be overly zealous in defense of their narratives, histories and moral economies, thereby overlooking repression and domination in their own communities. But freedom is a task, a result of struggle and contestation rather than a gift of culture. Religious reflection will do well to remember that in its use of the latter category.

REFERENCES

Boesak, Allan. 1977. "Civil Religion and the Black Community." *Journal of Theology for Southern Africa* 19 (January).

———. 1978. *Black Theology Black Power*. Oxford: A. R. Mowbray & Co. Ltd.

Bourdieu, Pierre. 1994. *The Field of Cultural Production: Essays on Art & Literature*. New York: Columbia University Press.

Buthelezi, Manas. 1973. "An African Theology or A Black Theology?" In *Black Theology: the South African Voice*, ed. Basil Moore. London: C. Hurst and Company.

Dickson, Kwesi. 1984. *Theology in Africa*. London: Darton, Longman and Todd.

Geertz, Clifford. 1988. *Works and Lives: The Anthropologist as Author*. Stanford, Cal.: Stanford University Press.

Gramsci, Antonio. 1971. *Selections From Prison Notebooks*. Ed and trans. Quintin Hoare and Geoffrey Nowell Smith. London: Lawrence and Wishart.

Hastings, A. 1976. *African Christianity: An Essay in Interpretation*. London: Geoffrey Chapman.

Keita, L. 1987. "The Debate Continues: A Reply to Olabiyi Yai's 'Misere de la Philosophie Speculative.'" *Presence Africaine* 120 (4th Quarterly).

Laclau, Ernesto and Chantal Mouffe. 1985. *Hegemony and Socialist Strategy: Toward A Radical Democratic Politics*. London and New York: Verso.

Marx, Karl. 1975. *Early Writings*. Trans. Rodney Livingstone and Gregor Benton. London: Penguin.

Mbiti, John. 1979. "An African Views American Black Theology." In *Black Theology: A Documentary History, 1966-1979*, ed. G. S. Wilmore and J. H. Cone. Maryknoll, N. Y.: Orbis Books.

Mudimbe, V. Y. 1988. *The Invention of Africa*. Bloomington: Indiana University Press.

Oduyoye, Mercy. 1986. *Hearing and Knowing: Theological Reflection on Christianity in Africa*. New York: Orbis Books.

Rosaldo, Renalto. 1989. *The Invention of Africa*. Bloomington: Indiana University Press.

Sklar, Richard. 1985. "The Colonial Impact on African Political Thought." In *African Independence: The First Twenty Five Years*, ed Gwendolen M. Carter and Patrick O'Meara. Bloomington: Indiana University Press, and London: Hutchinson.

Thomas, N. 1994. *Colonialism's Culture: Anthropology, Travel, and Government*. Cambridge: Polity Press.

Tutu, Desmond. 1978. "Whither African Theology." In *Christianity in Independent Africa*, ed. E. Fashole-Luke, R. Gray, A. Hastings and G. Tasie. London: Rex Collins Ltd.

Villa-Vicencio, Charles. 1985. "Theology in the Service of the State: The Styn and Eloff Commissions." In *Resistance and Hope: South African Essays in Honour of Beyers Naude*, ed. Charles Villa Vicencio and John W. de Gruchy. Claremont, South Africa: David Philip Publisher.

Williams, Raymond. 1982. *Culture and Society: Coleridge to Orwell*. London: The Hogarth Press.

———. 1977. "South African Civil Religion: An Introduction." *Journal of Theology for Southern Africa* (June).

NOTES

1. Whilst it is my intention to use inclusive language at all times in this paper I shall, when discussing the writings of others, use their language so as to reflect their views accurately. I have avoided use of the traditional "sic" in order to maintain a clean text.

2. "Black Theology and African Theology," Public lecture delivered at the University of Nairobi, 27 September, 1975. Published in *Perception*. A.E.A.M. (October, 1976), 1-8.

3. I should make it clear that there is no intention here to suggest that Black and African theologies suffer from an identical dualism. The fact that these theologies are produced in different contexts means that the shape of the culture/politics dualisms which afflict them will vary depending on the contextual factors determining their respective theological trajectories. My point is therefore not to compare and contrast the different types of dualism in Black and African theologies but rather to attempt to show that whatever the nature of dualism in both theologies it has had the net result of positing a false problem in the way in which culture and politics are related.

4. See Mudimbe (1988) for a full account of his views.

5. In his book *Culture and Truth: The Remaking of Social Analysis* (1989) Renato Rosaldo calls into question the role of objectivism in anthropology in a manner very much like that of Buthelezi. Buthelezi made his remarks in the 1970s and Rosaldo's book was published in 1989.

6. The term "homeland," together with its cognates "Bantustan" and "Native Reserves," refers to the practice of white South African government during the days of apartheid of gradually depriving blacks of citizenship in mainland South Africa by creating for them nominally independent "homelands" which were established along ethnic lines.

7. For Boesak on civil religion see his "Civil Religion and the Black Community" (1977) and by C. Villa-Vicencio, "South African Civil Religion: An Introduction" (1977).

8. The term "apparent" is necessary here since our discussion is still in progress and thus we cannot yet decide the question.

9. The difficulty with the way Dickson phrases the problem is that he seems to suggest the untenable idea that the only reason for political involvement is racial conflict. Elsewhere, however, Dickson does acknowledge, as I show later in this paper, that there are many more varieties of oppression in Africa than simply oppression of Africans by whites.

10. For a critique of the idea of rationalizing the real, see Marx (1975, 63-5). There is a fascinating discussion of the relationship between politics and culture in Raymond Williams' *Culture and Society: Coleridge to Orwell* (1982).

CONCLUSION:

CHANGING CONVERSATIONS: IMPETUSES AND IMPLICATIONS

Sheila Greeve Davaney

The essays in this volume embody dramatic shifts in religious reflection, especially in Christian theology. They suggest new ways of understanding religious beliefs and practices and the relation of these religious dimensions of human life to the broader cultural and social matrix in which they are located. They call for religious and theological reflection to focus its attention no longer so exclusively on the texts and doctrines of religious institutions and powerful individuals, but on more ordinary sites of religious meaning including, especially, those of the socially and culturally marginalized. And, moreover, these essays demonstrate that such changes in direction require new conversational partners, theoretical frameworks and analytical tools and methods.

While the works found in this volume are characterized by a good deal of diversity, they also present a number of common themes and assertions. There is, foremost, the turn to the realm of culture and social formation, and with it the insistence that religious beliefs, practices and values are intricately intertwined with these broader human contexts. Several important points are embedded in this move toward culture.

First, the arena of culture to which these thinkers turn is not merely the domain of elite or high culture nor only the theater of ideas and symbolic forms. Instead, culture is broadly construed in these essays. It is taken to encompass both the discursive and non-discursive construction of meaning, and to include both the ideational and material dimensions of human existence. Moreover, these dimensions of human life are interpreted as interconnected and as generative of one another; to understand the construction of symbolic meaning in a culture or how group and individual identity is formed, or how economic power is dispersed, or how political ideology is engendered and inculcated in citizens we must first understand how all these interpenetrate, support, and also resist and conflict with one another.

Second, the holistic notion of culture operative in these essays finds particular expression in the widespread focus upon "everyday life," popular culture and, especially, the symbolic and material productions of marginalized groups. This is the case in part because the thinkers in this volume either personally belong to such groups or have self-consciously aligned themselves with non-dominant sectors of society. But it also results from a thicker notion of culture that requires exploration of multiple sites and forms of meaning formation and that assumes that these can only be adequately understood when interpreted in relation to one another. Thus while the authors in this volume often focus upon groups such as African-Americans, women or homosexuals the notions of culture operative in the essays suggest that other groups associated with the "realm of the ordinary" are also the locus of cultural production and dispersion requiring full investigation.

Other emphases are embedded, either explicitly or implicitly, in this holistic construal of culture. One is the above-mentioned call for materialist versions of culture that explicitly track material elements of culture (including everything from the distribution of political and economic resources to the organization of bodies, buildings and geography) and their relation to the symbolic and ideational forms of human culture. Another is the recognition that humans produce and construct meaning not only linguistically and textually but also in non-linguistic and even non-discursive ways. Thus while these essays often explore texts, especially texts that carry significance for non-dominant groups, they also suggest that any adequate cultural analysis must find methods and analytical tools for identifying and interpreting precisely those forms of meaning that are not expressed in a textual mode. For many of the authors in this volume, it is imperative to recognize not only that all texts are located in intricate historical traditions and cultural frameworks, but also that not all meaning is narratival or even linguistic.

Two further implications can be drawn from the analyses set forth in this volume concerning the nature of culture when it is viewed holistically. One is the constructive and syncretistic character of cultures. Cultures are creatively syncretistic in part because they are composed of varied elements that interact in dynamic, changing and not totally predictable ways. Thus internally they are varied and pluralistic, both reproducing earlier forms of meaning, practice and organization and constructing of new forms that can not be anticipated. Moreover, cultures are permeable, interacting with other cultural contexts and formations, continually reacting to and bringing together disparate elements into novel cultural productions. Both individuals and groups piece together identities, institutions, roles and symbolic universes utilizing varied, divergent and even seemingly incommensurate resources. Hence, while there is a given quality to human existence flowing from its historical nature and from its location within dense networks of meaning and materiality, there is also a dynamic reconfiguring and ongoing syncretistic reconstruction and, indeed, reinvention of cultural contexts.

Finally, this dynamic character of culture is expressed in these essays most pointedly in the uniform assertion that culture is not stable. Instead it is an arena of conflict in which individuals and groups contend for identities, roles, power and institutional location. This claim has particular relevance for the interpretation of more marginalized groups in a society, for it suggests that they are not passive recipients of the cultural productions of the elites and the powerful but are instead active and creative agents involved in ongoing struggles to shape their identities and roles. Hence, there is a pervasive attempt in this volume to identify the sites and ways in which this contestation or this negotiation takes place and to trace, with special attention, the cultural creativity of the modest, the ordinary and, especially, the politically, economically and socially marginalized.

Thus, for all the particular interests embodied in these essays when they are taken together a holistic understanding of culture emerges that stresses not only its linguistic and symbolic dimensions but its material conditions and forms. Moreover, they point to the mutable, unstable, and conflictual nature of cultural interactions and the creative, if always circumscribed, agency of all cultural participants. Finally, they direct attention to locales where identities, roles and meaning are continually constructed, inscribed and contested—the realm of day to day life.

This move to a holistic notion of culture is not the singular or unique preoccupation of the scholars represented in this volume. It mirrors shifts that are taking place in many academic disciplines, as the authors' myriad references to cultural studies, certain forms of anthropology, literary theory and political analysis demonstrate. What is particularly significant about the pieces in this volume is that these shifts are being brought to bear upon the topic of religious beliefs, practices and values. The locating of religion thoroughly within historical and cultural matrices harbingers important changes both for the study of religion and for current approaches to cultural analysis.

Within the western study of religion there has been an enormous, though certainly not exclusive, emphasis upon the analysis of religious texts, especially the "classics" of particular traditions. Moreover, when non-textual phenomena have been studied, they have frequently been interpreted as text-like realities. Historian of religion Lawrence Sullivan has noted this textual orientation and contends that this dominance of the text has had increasingly problematic repercussions and "now stifles the attempt of religious studies to confront the full range of religious experiences and expressions—even those recorded in texts" (Sullivan 1990, 46). Anthropologist of religion Talal Asad has pushed this contention even further, arguing that even when symbols, rituals, or other non-textual realities are the focus of study, the analytical method is exegetical and the object of study is seen as embodying meanings that await decoding as a text awaits hermeneutical unpacking (Asad 1993, chaps. 1,2).

Such focus upon texts has been especially prominent in theological works which consist of an exegesis of and commentary upon sacred texts or earlier theological material. The raw materials, so to speak, for theological reflection have been beliefs and ideas expressed in textual form. Moreover, these texts have been related to other texts, ideas and beliefs to other ideas and beliefs. While these have been taken to refer to extra-textual realities such as God or human existence, in fact much theology has referred to other theological reflection. Thus exegesis, hermeneutics, translation and critical appropriation of ideas have often been the hallmark of theological work.

The writers in this volume collectively propose and embody a new direction for the study of religion and, especially, for theological reflection. They consistently assert that we cannot understand religion, in all of its manifestations, apart from its cultural settings and its concrete historical lineage. This conviction carries wide-ranging implications. To begin with, it entails the recognition that religious beliefs and practices do not exist in general or as free floating realities unencumbered by society and culture. Instead, like all other cultural manifestations, they emerge out of, are shaped by and in turn influence particular strands of historical existence and concrete social contexts. Thus one can not inquire about religion without also inquiring about social realities, political power, economic systems and social formations. To isolate religion from its social and cultural matrix is to empty it of its concrete content, to endow it with an unreal life far removed from the living realities of religious movements and persons. Religious texts or belief systems are also adequately understood only when their intimate relation to social life and history is traced and examined. Beliefs and ideas are not abstractions divorced from the dynamics of concrete reality, but are implicated and involved in these dynamics at every moment. Thus, neither religious beliefs nor theological ideas can be interpreted and evaluated only in relation to other beliefs and ideas. Nor can they be viewed as purely abstract systems whose validity depends on an internal coherence and consistency unrelated to the ways in which they come into being and function within and have impact upon their historical and social locale.

The overemphasis upon texts and beliefs and the tendency to utilize textual models for interpreting non-textual religious material are challenged, at least implicitly, by a number of essays in this volume. The recognition that the linguistic is not the only means by which meaning is produced and inscribed, even though our analysis of it takes linguistic and textual form, leads these scholars to explore other sites of meaning and value, including the body, institutions, and nondiscursive formations. These, too, must become the data of religious reflection. Thus dual moves are made in these essays: the scope of inquiry is enlarged to include that which cannot be reduced to the linguistic or textual, and both these and linguistic, ideational and symbolic construals of reality and meaning are thoroughly located in social, cultural, and historical contexts. Notions of culture as syncretistic and conflictual are also brought to bear upon religious beliefs and practices by the scholars in this volume. Whether the essays are dealing with the religion of non-elites (Tanner), of Black slaves (Hopkins), or of gays (Smith), portrayals emerge of groups and individuals who do not exist neatly in self-enclosed traditions or cultural frameworks, but who repeatedly combine resources and continually transgress borders and boundaries. Religious traditions and communities are, in this volume, not static with clearly defined essences that endure from age to age but dynamic, hybrid, living realities undergoing continual change.

Religious traditions and communities are also, as is all culture, sites of conflict and negotiation. How persons and groups construe reality, how they express meaning in beliefs (or in symbols, ritual actions, religious art, morals, etc.) have to do, not only, and perhaps not even primarily, with assumptions about ultimate truth, but also with social location, the politics of class, race and gender, and an intricate interplay of social factors. Cultural struggles are played out through the mechanisms of religious beliefs and practices no less than on other cultural fronts.

An important implication of both the syncretistic and conflictual character of religion is that religious beliefs and practices must always be treated concretely. Beliefs, practices, symbols, and rituals are widely assumed in this volume to be irreducibly particular and hence pluralistic. There can be no easy presumption that, say, the utilization of a symbol in one context is the same as its presence in another; the content and function of the notions of spirit, Christ, and God vary as their articulators and their locales vary. To ask what religious beliefs and theological ideas mean always entails an inquiry into where they are found and how they function.

The location of religious beliefs and practices in concrete cultural contexts, and the further specification of culture and thereby religion as multifaceted, dynamic, syncretistic, and conflictual, push the study of religion toward enlarging its scope beyond a focus on texts, the assumed-to-be-settled past, or the ideas and institutions of the culturally dominant. While these moves have implications for all scholars of religion they carry particular repercussions for theologians as those interested in religious beliefs and symbolic frameworks of religious communities and traditions. No longer can the work of theologians be construed as the pursuit of a timeless truth or ultimate reality uncovered in revelation, reason or some ahistorical dimension of experience. Instead theology becomes a form of cultural and historical analysis, criticism and reconstruction. Its task is to delve into concrete and particular forms of beliefs and symbols, tracing their relations to other dimensions of cultural life, evaluating them not only for how they relate to the past or cohere internally but also how they put forth a functional coherence, making certain forms of life possible and inhibiting others. When theology, especially in its Christian mode, is viewed as a form of cultural analysis, criticism, and reconstruction, other repercussions follow. Historically, the primary conversation partners for Christian theologians have been philosophers and biblical scholars. This choice of conversation partners embodied the assumption that theology sought absolute truth, understood to be available through reason or in the depths of human subjectivity as it was delineated by philosophy or in revelation as it was set forth by the classic texts of the tradition. To be a competent theologian required biblical literacy and philosophical sophistication. While these may still be desirable skills they no longer appear adequate to the theological task as it is portrayed by the authors in this volume. Instead what is now required are theoretical frameworks and analytical tools for interpreting the concrete particularities of religious beliefs and practices. Thus the scholars working here have turned to social and cultural theorists, to political analysts and literary critics, with a concern to engage views of culture which reflect the complex, interactive and conflictual assumptions so widely present in their own religions.

The shifts suggested by these essays are momentous and not easily carried out. They call for disciplinary redefinition of the study of religion and especially of theology. They suggest new objects of inquiry, new methodologies and new norms of evaluation. And importantly, they require new skills and methods of training. The widespread tendency of graduate programs in theology to follow a history of ideas model in which theological ideas are related to other ideas but stripped of their historical and cultural trappings is no longer adequate. The scholars in this volume represent a vanguard calling for the reorganization of much of what passes for the study of religion and particularly of what is called theological reflection.

If these scholars are demanding a reconceptualization of religious studies, they also challenge those disciplines focussed upon culture in its myriad forms. For as often as not religion is ignored as a significant arena for investigation by the very disciplines with whom scholars of religion now seek to converse. This has been especially evident in such approaches as cultural studies that, while providing provocative entrees to the dynamics of popular culture, have been curiously silent about religion. For the scholars in this volume, if religious studies must redefine itself, attentive now to the claims of disciplines tracing the intricacies of social and cultural life, so, too, must these disciplines rethink the nature of culture so that it is taken to include the dynamics of religious communities and traditions.

Finally, it is not only that these essays implicitly contain a call for disciplinary reconceptualization. The authors also clearly believe that all academic inquiry, however construed, is also located within the matrices of social and cultural reality, reflecting and, in turn, influencing the dynamics of those locations. The most obvious manifestation of this recognition of the located and interested nature of intellectual and academic inquiry is the self-conscious stance, assumed by many of the authors, of identification with and advocacy on behalf of the groups being studied. Thus, they seek to trace the sites of religious cultural production by marginalized persons not merely as interesting and heretofore neglected loci of academic analysis, but as a means of nurturing the creative, resisting, and transformative potential uncovered there. Perhaps the most challenging expression of this advocacy stance is found in Bill Smith's essay, an essay that does not study others but is the performative embodiment of a gay Black man's religious and cultural identity. If theology becomes a form of cultural criticism in this volume, it also presents itself as a mode of normative discourse self-consciously attempting not only to trace cultural life but to shape it into new and more liberating forms.

These essays embody new ventures for religious reflection. They explore new materials, open up new conversations and contend for a new trajectory in religious studies and most especially in theological reflection. They also leave an unfinished agenda and many questions. What notions of culture and religion are most adequate today? Which disciplinary approaches and methodological options are the most fruitful for scholars interested in religion? How shall the relations of texts to contexts be displayed? If we must attend more carefully to the non-textual and even the non-discursive how should this be done? Although all scholarship may be interested, is there a difference between normative discourse which seeks to reconstruct religious beliefs and practices and those who only want to study these things? What would graduate programs look like if the approaches advocated in these essays were taken seriously? These are enormous questions the resolution of which will shape the direction of the disciplines encompassed in the study of religion. The importance of these essays lies not only in their individual contribution but in the fact that together they raise such significant concerns for how we understand our work; and while they do not answer all the questions they raise, they point to a direction for future reflection, a direction that we should not ignore.

The editors would like to acknowledge, with gratitude, Gene Crytzer, Sheila Davaney's secretary, and Lisa Hart-Rains, Davaney's student assistant for their work on this volume. Hart-Raines read the essays checking for editorial concerns and Crytzer edited and formatted all the essays into a uniform presentation. His editorial and computer expertise contributed significantly to bringing this volume to fruition.

REFERENCES

Asad, Talal. 1993. *Genealogies of Religion: Discipline and Reasons of Power Christianity and Islam*. Baltimore and London: The John Hopkins University Press.

Sullivan, Lawrence E. 1990. "'Seeking an End to the Primary Text' or 'Putting an End to the Text as Primary.'" In *Beyond the Classics? Essays in Religious Studies and Liberal Education*, ed. Frank E. Reynolds and Sheryl L. Burkhalter. Atlanta, Ga: Scholars Press.

CONTRIBUTORS

Edward P. Antonio teaches theology at the University of Zimbabwe. He is the author of a forthcoming volume on African and Black theologies.

Karen Baker-Fletcher teaches theology at Claremont School of Theology. She is the author of *A Singing Something: Womanist Reflection on Anna Julia Cooper*.

David Batstone teaches theology at the University of San Francisco. He has authored *From Conquest to Struggle: Jesus of Nazareth in Latin America*, and he is editor of *New Visions for the Americas: Religious Engagement and Social Transformation*.

Sheila Greeve Davaney, of Iliff School of Theology, is editor of *Theology at the End of Modernity* and author of *Divine Power: A Study of Karl Barth and Charles Hartshorne*.

James H. Evans, Jr. is President of Colgate Rochester Divinity School. He is the author of *We Have Been Believers: An African American Systematic Theology* and *Black Theology: A Critical Assessment and Annotated Bibliography*.

Mary McClintock Fulkerson teaches theology at the Divinity School of Duke University. She is author of *Changing the Subject: Women's Discourses and Feminist Theology*.

Dwight N. Hopkins teaches theology at the Divinity School of the University of Chicago. He is author of *Shoes That Fit Our Feet: Sources for a Constructive Black Theology* and *Black Theology USA and South Africa: Politics, Culture, and Liberation*.

Mark McClain Taylor teaches theology at Princeton Theological Seminary. He is the author of *Remembering Esperanza: A Cultural-Political Theology for North American Praxis*.

James A. Noel teaches religious history at San Francisco Theological Seminary. He is the author of articles on American religious history, the history of the study of religion, African-American religious history, and the Black aesthetic.

Bill Smith was a scholar activist in the San Francisco Bay area. He has written several articles on liberation theology and AIDS from a gay perspective. He died in March 1996.

Kathryn Tanner teaches theology at the Divinity School of the University of Chicago. She is author of *The Politics of God: Christian Theologies and Social Justice* and *God and Creation in Christian Theology: Tyranny or Empowerment?*.